The Sutton Hoo Story

View westward over the mounds
and the River Deben to Woodbridge,
before the start of the 1983
campaign. (C.HOPPITT)

THE
SUTTON HOO
STORY

■ ■ ■ ◆ ■ ■ ■

Encounters with early England

MARTIN CARVER

—

THE BOYDELL PRESS

First published 2017
Reprinted 2019, 2021
The Boydell Press, Woodbridge

ISBN 978 1 78327 204 4

The Boydell Press is an imprint of Boydell & Brewer Ltd
PO Box 9, Woodbridge, Suffolk IP12 3DF, UK
and of Boydell & Brewer Inc.
668 Mt Hope Avenue, Rochester, NY 14620-2731, USA
website: www.boydellandbrewer.com

A catalogue record for this book is available
from the British Library

Book designed by Simon Loxley

Printed by Gomer Press

CONTENTS

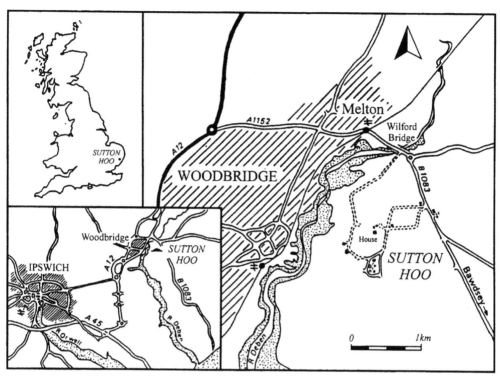

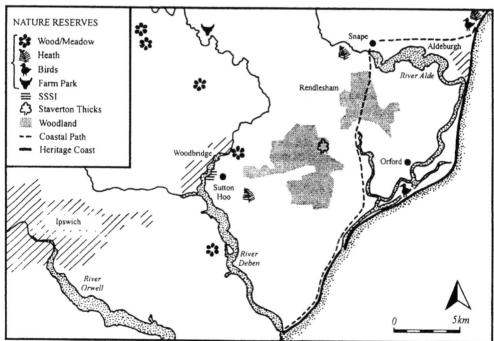

Maps showing the location of Sutton Hoo.

PREFACE

The traveller to Sutton Hoo must make two kinds of journey: one in reality and one in the imagination. The destination of the real journey is a small group of grassy mounds lying beside the River Deben in south-east England. The imaginative journey visits a world of warrior-kings, large open boats, jewelled weapons, judicial killing and the politics of independence. To both kinds of journey, this book is offered as a guide.

To find the place today, those heading for the site in a car should take the A12 to Lowestoft, bypass Woodbridge, turn off to Melton and drive straight down to Wilford Bridge, the first fordable crossing point of the tidal Deben. Beyond the bridge, the visitor turns right along the B1083 towards Bawdsey, Shottisham, Staverton Thicks and Rendlesham Forest. Here are the flat lands of the Sandlings, interlaced by thin lines of pine trees and the occasional patch of heath. At the top of the hill is the turning to the National Trust Visitor Centre at Sutton Hoo. The entrance road heads back to the scarp overlooking the River Deben, with views of Woodbridge and Melton beyond; and there, tucked into the lee of a plantation of conifers, are the humps and bumps that cover so much English history. Coming by train offers sufficient leisure to read up a bit of that history on the way, and the train journey from Ipswich to Woodbridge is especially picturesque. It runs by marsh and sedge and water's edge, and generates the same kind of excited anticipation as childhood holidays spent in the remote countryside.

The ancient approach to Sutton Hoo, used from before Anglo-Saxon times far back into prehistory, is up the river. The estuaries of Suffolk are a short journey across the North Sea from Denmark or the mouth of the Rhine, and constituted a front door for travellers and merchants. Three river-mouths lie adjacent; the most southerly leads along the Orwell to Ipswich, one of England's earliest known ports. The northerly leads up the Alde to Aldeburgh. And the one in the centre leads upstream to Woodbridge and Melton on the west bank and Sutton Hoo and Rendlesham on the east. To get into the Deben from the sea it is necessary to negotiate some shifting sandbanks, and the river subsequently runs roughly north-west, with numerous creeks and mudflats busy with waders on either side. One can imagine the instructions that a local resident of eighth-century Suffolk might have given to a relative visiting from Jutland:

> There are six main reaches from the sea, until the river narrows enough to be fordable; just before the ford is a wide stretch of open water, and above it on the terrace to the east you will see a number of burial mounds. The pagan kings of East Anglia were buried there. Beach your boat on the mud flats, but pull it well up because the tides still run high at this point. Then walk along the path you will find climbing the scarp; our farm lies beyond on the heath. It has a hall and seven outbuildings. We have cattle in the meadows and 1000 head of sheep on the heath ...

The Sutton Hoo site has attracted looters and antiquaries since the sixteenth century and in the 1930s, the 1960s and the 1980s experienced three campaigns of archaeological investigation that provide a history in miniature of the science of archaeology itself. Employing the techniques of the nineteenth-century barrow digger, the first archaeologists revealed the ship-burial in Mound 1 and the treasure that made the site famous; they had to hastily complete their work as war overtook Europe in 1939. The second campaign, in the 1960s, mobilised the resources of the British Museum, completed the excavation of the Mound 1 ship-burial and began the broader exploration of the site. The third, mounted from a university in the 1980s, took as its target the European context of the cemetery and the origins of the kingdom that created it.

There are many Sutton Hoo stories to tell, but they can be marshalled into two: what happened here, and how we know. Chapters 1-3 tell the story of how Sutton Hoo was discovered and explored, taking the three great campaigns in turn. Chapters 4-6 attempt a summary evocation of the life and times of this little piece of England over some 5,000 years and turn them into a narrative. And in Chapter 7 I discuss current perceptions of what it all means, inspired by Sutton Hoo's broad community of critical friends.

The primary records of the discoveries up to 2016 have been placed on open access in the public domain through the Archaeology Data Service at York (the Sutton Hoo Online Archive, or SHOLA). The full analysis of what we knew up to that point was published in 2005 by the British Museum in a 500-page research report entitled *Sutton Hoo: A seventh-century princely burial ground and its context*, which is referred to throughout this book using the shorthand *CSH*. Between 1998 and 2014 the report was escorted, like a corvette shadowing a battleship, by a summary account called *Sutton Hoo: Burial Ground of Kings?* This latter book, also published by the British Museum, sold

30,000 copies but fell victim to a new British Museum publication policy in 2016. With enlightened generosity, the Museum released all the rights on the book to its author, and I approached Richard Barber of Boydell Press to see whether they would be interested in a new edition.

Boydell Press has a long history of supporting, promoting and publishing Sutton Hoo. They issued *The Age of Sutton Hoo*, the proceedings of the 1989 anniversary conference, and the annual *Bulletins*, and hosted the Duke of Edinburgh's visit to the site in 1987. Sutton Hoo has a dynamic, changing and ever increasing audience, so we decided not to simply reissue *Burial Ground of Kings?* but to prepare a new version that took account of ideas and research published since 2005. The National Trust Visitor Centre was opened in 2002 and its millionth visitor arrived in 2012, so plenty of new views about Sutton Hoo have been generated in the last decade. I am particularly grateful to Angus Wainwright, Helen Geake, Sam Newton and Lindsay Lee of the Sutton Hoo Society (on behalf of the site guides) for telling me about topics that the public would like to know more about, were puzzled by, did not believe or disagreed with. I can't pretend to have responded satisfactorily to all the questions raised, but it was an invigorating exercise. The Sutton Hoo constituency contains people of all ages from many countries; they are united in their fascination for the discoveries and the admiration of the artistry, but divided about what it means. And why not? None of us was there, and we are informed only by threads and patches wrested from the ground. We will see different things, but once focused and tested by science we should find much to share in the visions of early England that are generated by an encounter with this remarkable site.

ACKNOWLEDGEMENTS

The participants of the most recent campaign are itemised in the research report, which lists the landowners, the members of the Sutton Hoo Research Trust, the Sutton Hoo Research Committee, the numerous sponsors, the 38 collaborating academic institutions, the site supervisors, specialist scientists and contributing British Museum staff (*CSH*, xxvii-xxxxi). In the online archive are also listed the 402 volunteers, including students from 16 universities, who took part (SHOLA 1/5.1). The Sutton Hoo story has been immeasurably enriched by specialist scholars who contributed to the research report. Readers who are familiar with early editions of *Sutton Hoo: Burial Ground of Kings?* will quickly see how much was learnt in 2005 and has been since. I particularly want to salute the researches of Angela Evans (seventh-century assemblages), Madeleine Hummler (the prehistoric site), John Newman (the Deben Valley Survey), Frances Lee (human remains), Julie Bond (cremated animals), Penelope Walton Rogers (textiles) and Chris Fern, who co-authored the chapter on burial rites and brought the Tranmer House cemetery to publication for *East Anglian Archaeology*.

Among all those participants in the project, I would like to acknowledge the long-term members of the research team: Andy Copp, Cath Royle, Jenny Glazebrook, Nigel MacBeth and Madeleine Hummler, who managed the excavation and prepared the online archive (SHOLA) and whose contributions to the recording, understanding and publication of the site can never be exaggerated; to record my warm thanks to Christopher Brooke, Sir David Attenborough and Sir David Wilson, who corralled the three principal sponsors united in the Sutton Hoo Research Trust (Society of Antiquaries of London, BBC, British Museum); to remember with gratitude and affection the late Peter Berry, who looked after the site, Philip Rahtz, my archaeological companion in arms, and the Nobel laureate Seamus Heaney, who opened the visitor centre for us; to salute Mac Miles and his successors as chairs of the Sutton Hoo Society; to thank the Duke of Edinburgh for agreeing to be its patron and for paying us a visit; and to thank Robert Simper, Rosemary Hoppitt, Lindsay Lee and all the Society's guides for their service to the excavation, the research and the site, and for the pleasure they have brought to innumerable members of the public for more than three decades.

I also want to record my appreciation to English Heritage (as was) and the present site owners, the National Trust for England and Wales, especially Angus Wainwright, Lynette Titford and the late Martin Atkinson, for the way they have cherished and promoted the site; and, lastly, Richard Barber of Boydell & Brewer and Susan Walby, Head of Business Planning Digital & Publishing Division British Museum Press, who have made this book possible. My warm thanks to Jo Tozer and Madeleine Hummler for advice on the text.

We are grateful to the British Museum for permission to reproduce images from their publications *Sutton Hoo: Burial Ground of Kings?*, *Sutton Hoo: A seventh-century princely burial ground and its context* and *The Sutton Hoo Ship Burial*, all now out of print. Our warm thanks also for the provision of other images as credited: Victor Ambrus, Oxford University Institute of Archaeology, Suffolk County Council, Chris Fern, Cliff Hoppitt, Russell Carver, John Bateman, Edward Morgan, Brian Marden-Jones, John Newman, and team members Jenny Glazebrook, Annette Roe, Nigel MacBeth, Justin Garner-Lahire and Madeleine Hummler. 'Sutton Hoo Archive' refers to original records in the British Museum or in possession of the author.

Martin Carver
Ellerton, East Riding of Yorkshire, 1 February 2017

View of the *Sir Paul and Lady Ruddock Gallery of Sutton Hoo and Europe, AD 300–1100*, at the British Museum. (COURTESY OF SUE BRUNNING AND THE BRITISH MUSEUM)

THE
SUTTON HOO
STORY

1 | MRS PRETTY DIGS UP A SHIP
Excavations at Sutton Hoo, 1938-39

A large white Edwardian mansion with a wood-panelled interior stood in a garden punctuated with rhododendrons and pine trees on a promontory overlooking the River Deben. This was Sutton Hoo House, built in 1910 and purchased in 1926 by Colonel Frank Pretty, retired commanding officer of the 4th Battalion of the Suffolk Regiment. Buying the house with him was his newly married wife, Edith May Pretty, née Dempster, member of a distinguished engineering family whose business achievements included the building of gasometers in the Manchester area (**Figs 1.1, 1.2**). Sutton Hoo, then an estate of 400 acres, was a tangle of sandy heath and woodland, home to a multitude of rabbits. The Prettys could enjoy fine views from the large bay windows of the house to the west over the River Deben to Woodbridge, Melton and the railway line that connects them. From the windows on the south side, across the windy heath, a small group of scarred burial mounds could be seen, riddled with rabbit holes and lying up against the spinney known as Top Hat Wood.

Edith Pretty was an adventurous traveller and one of the first women magistrates, as well as the owner of an exceptionally beautiful piece of England. But fate had two shocks to deliver. In 1930, at the age of 47, Edith Pretty found herself pregnant, and in due course was delivered of a son, Robert. Four years later her husband died, and she and her young son were left alone in the 15-bedroom house. In what must have seemed long days over the next few years Mrs Pretty suffered from ill health and withdrew from many of her public commitments. She sought consolation in the counsel of a spiritualist medium, making regular trips to London for guidance from her mentor. Whether she hoped to make contact with her husband cannot be said, but, like many another before her, she may have found some relief and reason, during the perplexity of bereavement, in the feeling that the world of the dead was an accessible and sympathetic one.[1]

1.1: (above) Sutton Hoo (now Tranmer) House seen from the mounds in 1985. (NIGEL MACBETH)

1.2: (right) Colonel and Mrs Pretty ready to go hunting. A photograph taken in the 1920s.
(BY COURTESY OF RUSSELL CARVER)

It is not unlikely that these circumstances had some influence on her decision to begin an investigation of the burial mounds visible from the large south-facing bay window. The impetus, according to some accounts, was provided by friends and relatives, among them a nephew, a dowser, who insisted that gold was to be found; while others spoke of shadowy figures around the mounds after dusk and a vision of a man on a white horse. But, whatever her sensitivity to the attentions of solicitous phantoms, Mrs Pretty was no stranger to scientific archaeology. Even as a child she was well-travelled, and had seen the pyramids in Egypt. When her family were the tenants at Vale Royal in Cheshire her father had been given permission to excavate and expose the plan of the Cistercian monastery that adjoined their house. She would have been aware of the responsibilities of excavating burial mounds and had already refused to allow enthusiastic amateurs to try their hand on hers. Her keen eye and an educated curiosity would have encouraged her to investigate them herself, just as surely as any interest in the other world. Moreover, she required no permission from elsewhere, and in this she was following a 400-year-old precedent: the prerogative of post-Reformation landowners to investigate and upturn, with shovel, spade, pit and trench, the mounds that had survived on their land.

In her need for an archaeologist, Mrs Pretty contacted Ipswich Museum, whose curator, Guy Maynard, recommended in turn a local man who had acquired the reputation of having something of a nose for an antiquity. So we meet Basil Brown, a self-taught archaeologist and amateur astronomer, whose knowledge of the past was broad, varied and eclectic (**Fig. 1.3**).[2] He had visited and investigated monuments in East Anglia over many years. Not being himself a landowner, some of his fieldwork called for ingenuity, bicycling around the lanes and using binoculars (when access was not permitted) to study exposed sections of sand and crag. He had taught himself to excavate, too, and had the confidence of one who knew the soil and seemed to know instinctively what had happened to it. He was the first to reveal the character of the Sutton Hoo cemetery, and his sensitive definition of the Mound 1 ship amounted to excavation of genius. But, in spite of Brown's undoubted talent, it would not do to romanticise his abilities. A contemporary archaeological colleague, Richard Dumbreck, described him in these terms:

> ... a character; his pointed features gave him the, not inappropriate,
> appearance of a ferret and were invariably topped with a rather
> disreputable trilby hat, while a somewhat moist and bubbling pipe
> protruded dead ahead from his mouth. He had ... gravitated to
> archaeology without any real training thanks to a quite remarkable flair

1.3: Basil Brown at about the time of the 1938/39 excavations. (SUTTON HOO ARCHIVE)

for smelling out antiquities ... His method was to locate a feature and then pursue wherever it led, in doing so becoming just like a terrier after a rat. He would trowel furiously, scraping the spoil between his legs, and at intervals he would stand back to view progress and tread in what he had just loosened ... The sad thing is that with training he might have been a brilliant archaeologist ...[3]

But there was no doubting his absolute dedication: his assistant John Jacobs remembered later how Brown had gone out in a rainstorm in the middle of the night to tend the Sutton Hoo excavation: 'I think he would have slept there if he'd had his bed.'[4]

Alerted by Maynard, Basil Brown armed himself with 'appropriate literature on the Bronze Age, Iron Age, Roman and Anglo-Saxon periods, and

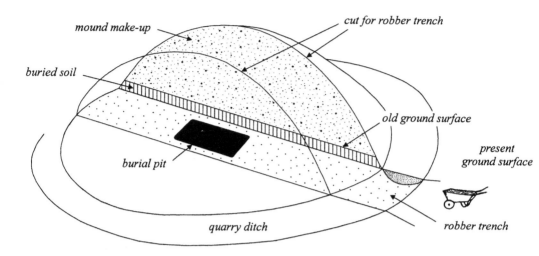

mound make-up

cut for robber trench

buried soil

old ground surface

present ground surface

burial pit

quarry ditch

robber trench

1.4: How early excavators dug burial mounds: the trench method.

some suitable excavation reports'. Mrs Pretty gave him 30 shillings a week, accommodation in an upper room of the chauffeur's cottage and the help of two labourers from the Sutton Hoo estate, Bert Fuller and Tom Sawyer. She instructed him to put all the excavated soil by the side of any trenches made in the mounds ready for refilling, so that they could be returned eventually to their original appearance.

The work began at Mrs Pretty's instigation on the largest of the burial mounds, that known to us as Mound 1. On 20 June 1938 Mrs Pretty produced a long probing iron of her own design and invited Basil Brown to drive it into the mound until he hit something solid. This he did. An excavation followed, to a depth of 1.8m, whereupon the 'something solid' was determined to be a stone of no particular significance. At Basil Brown's suggestion, the next day the team left Mound 1 for the time being and proceeded to try their hands on a smaller mound, the adjacent Mound 3. Here Brown was better able to demonstrate his technique of chamber-finding, a method as effective as it was traditional.[5] Burial mounds are, in general, made of earth and stones heaped over the ground surface. The burial itself is put into a hole (the 'chamber'), which is backfilled with the subsoil that came out of it. In places where the ground surface and the subsoil are a different colour, as on sandy sites, the backfilled burial chamber is easily distinguished. An excavator, knowing this, simply has to drive a trench horizontally through the mound at about the level of the old ground surface; the backfilled chamber will soon appear as a square or rectangle of different-coloured soil at the bottom of the excavation trench. Even when the trench is mucky with the continual coming and going of the excavators the pit containing the burial should still show up (**Fig. 1.4**). If, however, it has already been visited by a previous expedition, the contrast between the old ground surface and the refilled burial pit is often much less clear, and the pit, in consequence, harder to find. Excavators refer to an unrecorded trench cut by an earlier expedition as a 'robber trench' on the assumption that its primary purpose was to bear away the grave goods.

Spoil from the excavation trench can be piled up beside it, as in Mrs Pretty's injunction; or it can be removed down the trench and tipped in a fan beyond it. If the mound is too tall and the make-up too soft, the sides of the excavator's trench will collapse; a safer procedure, therefore, is to cut back the edges to form terraces along their length, and to barrow the spoil out along the trench. The trench in this case serves as the main thoroughfare for the excavators and the inspecting antiquaries.

Finding the level of the old ground surface can be assisted by digging a pilot trench in the side of the mound, and Brown began in this way, digging a pilot trench on the east side of Mound 3 (**Fig.1.5**). Then, using the traditional technique, he found the buried soil and the supposed burial pit a mere 60cm down, but its edge was so ragged that he introduced a second trench at right angles to the first to determine the form of the pit more clearly. By 25 June he had done so, 'at least to my own satisfaction', and was ready to empty it. The pit descended to a total depth of 2.7m from the top of the mound, occasioning trouble with landslides. Brown realised that he was not the first to enter the mound, although not, perhaps, that the pit he was engaged in defining was dug by earlier excavators. It was about 12m across and had been backfilled with turf, black earth and broken clay pieces. At the bottom of the pit was a rectangular piece of decayed wood, 1.67m long by 56cm wide. It could have been a coffin, but more nearly resembled a tray with rounded corners, and carried on it little heaps of cremated bone which proved to derive from a human and a horse. The scraps of finds that remained included some sherds of pottery, a lump of corroded iron, later found to be an axe-head, part of a small decorated limestone plaque, fragments of bone inlay from a casket and the lid of an ewer of Mediterranean origin. Brown thought the 'tray' might have been part of a boat; Maynard thought it was the bottom of a domestic chest or trough. It broke up when an attempt was made to lift it (**Fig.1.6**).

The visitors, official and unofficial, arriving on Tuesday 28 June were even less sure of what had been found. The formidable J. Reid Moir, bespoke tailor of Ipswich turned palaeontologist, and at that time Chairman of the Ipswich Museum Committee, demanded a new trench. Mr Spencer, museum assistant, told an indignant Brown he did not understand the soils in that part of the country. Vincent B. Redstone FSA, local historian of Woodbridge, pronounced that the pit was a dew-pond, and required another hole to be dug 1.8m into

1.5:: Aerial photograph of the mounds, with mound numbers.
(C.HOPPITT/AUTHOR)

1.6: (below) Plan of 'Tumulus A' (Mound 3) by Basil Brown.
(SUTTON HOO ARCHIVE)

the subsoil; upon which Fuller and Sawyer were nearly buried, and Mr Redstone was left to dig a third hole himself. A month later Basil Brown was recollecting in tranquillity this hail of advice with the wry comment, 'with a little diplomacy I got out of bother and the pit survived and finds followed on the Thursday'. On Saturday 2 July the excavation was nominally finished, but as late as 19 July Brown was cutting another trench to the central pit to suit Mr Reid Moir, which 'proved the eastern limit of the grave to everyone's satisfaction'.[6]

This first excavation was hardly auspicious, but 6 July found Brown clearing bracken from Mound 2. He dug a test pit on the south side, throwing back into it a defunct metal bucket.[7] He laid out his trench on a compass bearing approximately east-west, following the orientation of the wooden 'tray' just found under Mound 3. Almost immediately he discovered some pieces of iron and, in an act of recognition that was to be fundamental for the exploration of Sutton Hoo, decided that one of them was the remnant of a 'ship rivet' (**Fig.1.7**). These resembled bolts a few inches long, originally with a domed head on one end and a squarish plate on the other, and were used to secure the strakes of early medieval ships.[8] More rivets were to come, and by 14 July the edge of a burial pit was clear to Brown, although Maynard had noted a previous 'robber' pit. Mound 2 was big and the sides of Brown's excavation collapsed no fewer than three times (20, 22 and 28 July). In between the cutting back and carting away of collapsed mound, Brown looked for and found a boat to go with his rivets: the base of the burial pit was 'boat-shaped without any question' and some of the rivets were still *in situ* (**Fig.1.8**). The scraps of finds included a beautiful piece of blue glass, a gilt bronze disc, iron knives and the tip of a sword blade.

Undaunted by his encounter with another robbed burial, on 30 July Brown cleared the bracken from Mound 4, dug a test pit on the east side and drove a trench westwards into the mound. This mound too had been robbed, and the grave pit was very shallow. Nevertheless the cremated bones of humans and animals were found, with fragments of bronze and textile. Brown was able to

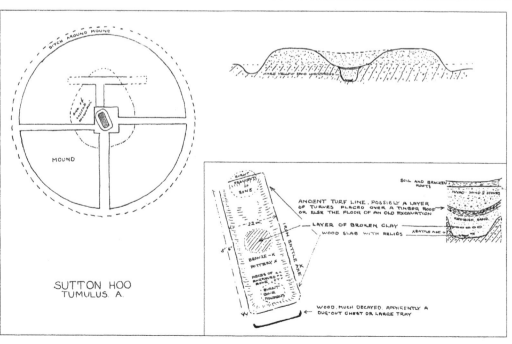

SUTTON HOO
TUMULUS. A.

1.7: (right) A ship-rivet from the 1939 excavation. Courtesy of Peter Burman. Photograph by John Bateman.

1.8: (opposite) The 'boat' found by Basil Brown in Mound 2. The sticks mark the sites of rivets.
(SUTTON HOO ARCHIVE)

make the important interpretation that the burial rite consisted of cremated bone wrapped in cloth and placed in a bronze bowl (**Fig. 1.9**).

So ended the 1938 season; three mounds had been trenched, and each had turned out to have been the subject of previous explorations. The fragments of objects that had been found suggested something of the former riches of the graves and gave an indication of their date: the imports from Mound 3 were early medieval, while the ornament on the disc from Mound 2 was Anglo-Saxon. Probably all the mounds were Anglo-Saxon, and one at least had contained a boat. In his diary and notebook Brown never seems to express much surprise, but he could be forgiven if he had; he may have expected the Sutton Hoo mounds to be of Bronze Age date, like so many others in the vicinity (as on Martlesham Heath), if not Viking, as Maynard had expected. Being Anglo-Saxon certainly made them special, but their condition was hardly encouraging. The trenches through the three mounds were backfilled, and incorporated into the backfill of Mound 2 was a pair of steel roller-skates, no doubt belonging to young Master Robert Pretty, then aged eight.[9]

A second season was already under discussion in the autumn of 1938; if Edith Pretty's expectations had not been fulfilled, her appetite was whetted and her instinct persistent. When work restarted on 8 May 1939 there was no hesitation. Basil Brown was accompanied by Mrs Pretty to the mounds and a brief conversation ensued. 'I asked which one she would like opened,' wrote Brown in his diary, 'and she pointed to 1 (Mound 1), the largest barrow of the group, and said "What about this?" and I replied that it would be quite alright for me.' The helpers this year were to be John Jacobs, the gardener at Little Sutton Hoo, and William Spooner, Mrs Pretty's gamekeeper, although Jacobs

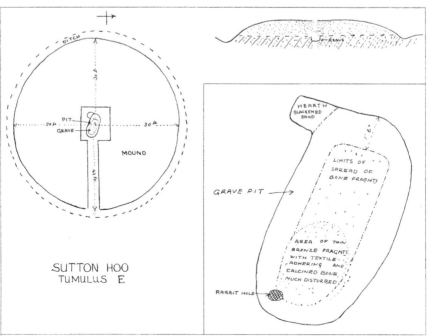

1.9: Plan of 'Tumulus E' (Mound 4) by Basil Brown. (SUTTON HOO ARCHIVE)

was busy in the garden until the following day. Brown made a survey, and then his trench, 1.2m wide and laid out east-west, was driven into the mound from the east.

One can imagine the scene, Brown with his battered trilby and his 'moist and bubbling' pipe, Jacobs and Spooner with spades and shovels ready to cut the turf and load a wooden wheelbarrow of a kind more normally used to transport weeds and dead-heads from the flowerbeds. Perhaps the job was viewed as little more than a nice rest from the routine of gardening. But a change of mood was not long in coming. At about midday on Thursday 11 May Jacobs called out, 'Here's a bit of iron', and held up a ship rivet. Brown immediately stopped the clearing operation. Carefully exploring the area with a small trowel, he uncovered five more rivets in position on what turned out to be the wooden prow or stern of a ship. It was then that inspiration took the helm. Brown reasoned that the rivets he had just found should represent the line of a vanished wooden hull. If so, he would have to dig up and over the rivets and descend on them from above, leaving each one in position. He would then be *inside* the ship and, by locating the plate of each rivet, he would be able to define the inside of the hull. Instead of trying to follow the vanished surface of the buried soil, Brown's trench now dipped down into the hollow of a buried ship. By 19 May he had learnt how to define the rivets in position: a pink patch in the yellow sand gave warning of the presence of a rivet, and a light brushing with a pastry brush would reveal the red knob of corroded iron, surrounded by crusty sand. Rivet after rivet was revealed in this way at intervals of 15-23cm, until - so confident was Brown of predicting their positions - he could afford to leave a protective coat of sand over the rivets, while tracing the inner surface of the hull (**Fig. 1.10**).

As the lines of the vessel fell away deep into the ground so did Brown's trench, always cutting into the face of the mound, until the inevitable occurred. On 30 May the trench collapsed, but Brown, veteran of so many collapsed trenches, was free within a few minutes. Within the tonnage of fallen earth were sherds of sixteenth-century pottery, which had obviously been introduced into the mound at a later date, probably by grave-robbers. Maynard, on a visit, observed the shadow of a previous trench in the face of Brown's cutting. Brown himself described the intrusion as a pit with a 'Treasure seekers' hearth' at the bottom. He left a standing sample of its fill of black sand and red ash in the form of a tall column that Jacobs christened 'the lighthouse'.

As Brown phlegmatically cleared up the mess and cut back his giant trench in an effort to make it safer, the archaeological world was beginning to stir. Searching for parallels for his buried ship, Maynard had made discreet inquiries of the museum on the Isle of Man, which held records of the Viking ship-buri-

1.10: The rivets of the ship revealed, with Basil Brown. (SUTTON HOO ARCHIVE)

als that had been excavated there. But archaeological inquiries cannot be kept discreet for long, and the rumour that a Viking ship had been found in Suffolk soon made its way to the coffee room of the Department of Archaeology at Downing Street, Cambridge, then the nodal point of archaeological gossip.

On 6 June, alerted by the rumour, if sceptical of it, Charles W. Phillips, Fellow of Selwyn College, Cambridge, paid a routine visit to Guy Maynard, ostensibly to collect papers relating to the newly formed Prehistoric Society. 'I found him somewhat distracted,' said Phillips, 'but judicious questioning soon revealed the cause.' In the company of Maynard, Phillips met Mrs Pretty at her house and together with Maynard the party made its way to the burial mounds. Phillips records:

> I was not prepared for the astonishing sight which met me when I came round to the actual work. There I saw a very wide trench cut right down into the substance of the large oval mound on its longer axis to reveal clearly the gunwale outline of much of a large boat which was interred below the level of the old ground surface. At a quick estimate it could hardly be much less than one hundred feet long. The work had been done with care and as yet there had been little attempt to remove any of the sand which filled the vessel. I could not wonder that Maynard had been daunted by this apparition.[10]

Phillips advised Mrs Pretty to exercise caution with her excavation and made telephone calls on her behalf to the British Museum and the (Government) Office of Works. As a result of these discussions a site meeting was hastily convened, and on 9 June Christopher Hawkes (for the British Museum), R.S. Simms (for the Office of Works) and Guy Maynard (for Ipswich Museum) met Charles Phillips and Mrs Pretty and her team of excavators.[11] It was decided that to excavate further would require a more experienced team and first-rate equipment, but the summer of 1939 was an awkward time to assemble them. War, if not yet certain, was threatening. The British Museum and the Ministry had other things on their minds than a research excavation. The first of these organisations was engaged in packing its treasures into cases for storage in the London Underground in anticipation of the *Blitzkrieg*, while the second was preoccupied by matters of greater moment than an archaeological dig, namely the building of air-strips and the sandbagging of the dockyards. But, if the times were inauspicious, there was no going back on the Sutton Hoo discovery. News of the find had already leaked out and at the first relaxation of scientific interest others, less scientific in motive but no less energetic in execution, would soon be on the scene. There was nothing for it but to try to gather the necessary resources with all speed. Brown was instructed to stop excavating and the meeting dispersed.

Never greatly in awe of authority, Basil Brown took little notice of the injunction that had theoretically been put upon him, and he continued to excavate without a pause for nearly four weeks. It is probably as well that he did so, since it meant that someone was always on site and could repel any attempts at trespass and pillage. His work remained careful and intelligent, and he now had an independent source of advice on ship-burials - Mr and Mrs Megaw of the Isle of Man Museum, who had visited the site on 8 June. Predicting where the burial would lie, Brown desisted from following the rivet pattern to the lower strakes amidships, leaving a dark rectangle - the collapsed burial chamber - in position. By 3 July he had successfully excavated most of the Sutton Hoo Mound 1 ship and was clearing a clay deposit amidships 'exactly above the place where I expect the chief lies'. He had also had a little poke at a cauldron, part of which lay exposed on the surface, noting the hollow sound given out by the adjacent skin of wood, through which he pushed his finger. He covered up the chamber area with hessian and continued to define the ship, consulting a large volume (in Norwegian) about the Oseberg ship-burial excavated in 1904.

The British Museum and the Office of Works had, in the interim, arrived at their decision: to place the responsibility for the completion of the excavation on to the shoulders of Charles Phillips. At the end of June, Office of Works officers contacted Phillips at Little Woodbury in Wiltshire, where he was helping Gerhard Bersu to reveal that classic Iron Age settlement, and requested him to undertake the completion of the Sutton Hoo excavation. Once he had been asked 'to take it on', Phillips accepted stoically the exacting and novel task that lay before him: 'I didn't see how anyone was going to take it on. But since no one knew anything about it anyhow, and as long as you were a reasonable and sensible person, it seemed to me we might as well have a bash; so a bash we had.'[12]

The team was to consist of friends or colleagues summoned from their holidays or awaiting call-up, and the total resources amounted to £250 in expenses, with the additional provision, from the depot at Framlingham Castle, of 12 scaffold poles and a tarpaulin - for which, remarked Phillips dryly, 'little use could be found'. A shepherd's hut on wheels and the interior of cars would offer the only shelter. Fir cones from Top Hat Wood would provide the fuel for camp-fires for making tea. On 8 July, nursing an injured thumb, Phillips arrived and assumed control. His attitude was a bit bellicose, observed Brown, but the handover between Brown and Phillips seems to have been respectfully done. Phillips was to take responsibility from now on, both for making decisions and for keeping the records, and Brown was to be designated his assistant. On 11 July Ipswich Museum was invited not to interfere: following a heated discussion, Phillips made it clear to Maynard, in no uncertain terms, who was now in command. However, much diplomacy was still required, as Phillips later wrote, 'to steer the course of this excavation through all these assorted and often intangible obstacles'. For then, as now, many people and institutions felt they had a stake in so mighty a find. On 13 July the excavation began of what transpired to be the most richly furnished burial chamber ever discovered in British soil.

Charles Phillips was a large man and he decided that as far as possible

1.11: Mrs Petty with friends watching the excavation in progress in 1939. (SUTTON HOO ARCHIVE)

the deposit in the burial chamber should be spared his weight. He therefore mainly stayed out, and the work of excavation and recording was done by the friends and colleagues he had recruited (**Fig. 1.11**). Stuart Piggott (later Professor of Archaeology at Edinburgh) and his wife Peggy (later Curator of Devizes Museum) answered the call on their holiday and arrived on 19 July. The Piggotts were to be the principal excavators of the centre and west of the chamber, and Stuart was the maker of the plans. O.G.S. Crawford, founder of the periodical *Antiquity* and chief archaeologist at the Ordnance Survey, arrived on 24 July. He was to be the creator of an invaluable photographic record. With him came W.F. ('Peter') Grimes, his assistant at the Ordnance Survey, later Director of the Institute of Archaeology at London, who was to be the excavator of the eastern half of the chamber. Another who came to assist at a crucial time was John Brailsford, while John Ward-Perkins (Director of the British School at Rome), Grahame Clark (the future Disney Professor of Archaeology at Cambridge) and his wife were there on important days. 'Under the condi-

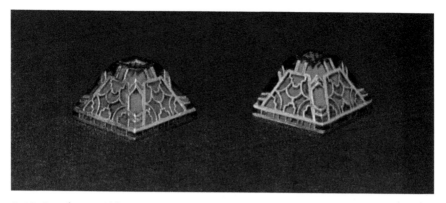

1.12: Sword pyramid from Mound 1. (BRITISH MUSEUM)

tions of the time,' commented Phillips, 'it would have been difficult to have gathered a more valuable group of workers, witnesses and general advisers.'

The excavators worked individually and in a somewhat ad hoc manner, at the east end, at the west end and in the centre, lifting off the layers of compressed decayed wood or blackened sand and revealing, defining and freeing each object. On 21 July the first piece of jewellery was encountered, a little gold and garnet pyramid, a find that greatly raised the temperature and expectations of the team (**Fig.1.12**). 'We were working quietly away in our usual morning routine,' remembered Peggy Guido, 'when quite suddenly as I was trowelling and brushing, one of the lovely garnet and gold ornaments was revealed. Of course from that moment on we were immensely excited.' The responsibility weighed heavily on Charles Phillips. When acquainted with the find he said 'My godfathers!' and for the rest of the day was heard to murmur 'oh dear, oh dear'.[13] This brilliant object, a pyramid-shaped strap-mount, was merely a humble precursor. The following day brought a veritable feast of golden objects: gold plaques in the form of patterned birds and animals from a purse-frame, which it could be seen had contained a handful of gold coins; buckles with garnet inlay that had connected the baldric of the buried man's parade-dress; and a great hollow buckle of solid gold, its surface alive with the raised forms of interlaced animals (**Fig.1.13**).

That night in the Bull Hotel at Woodbridge, which served as the excavators' base, Piggott remembered being asked the inevitable question: "'Well, old boy, found any gold today?" "Oh yes," I said, "my pockets are absolutely full," and as I spoke I was holding the box containing the great gold belt buckle in my rather sweaty hand in the pocket of my coat; and "Oh" they said "that's splendid, you must have a drink." "Yes" I said, "I need one".[14] Met at Woodbridge railway station, T.D. Kendrick, the Keeper of British and Medieval Antiquities at the British Museum and *éminence grise* of Anglo-Saxon art, had to steady

1.13: Gold buckle. (BRITISH MUSEUM)

himself when Phillips showed him, in the station waiting room, one of the simpler buckles as a glimpse of what was in store: 'When he saw the buckle, he was both astonished and elated, astonished because of its beauty and perfection, and elated because I was able to tell him that it was part of a much larger collection of pieces in the same style.'[15] All were agreed that the dazzling polychrome jewellery, and thus the burial itself, should belong to the early seventh century AD.

Over the next two days Piggott excavated at the west end of the chamber, bringing to light a whetstone and a tangle of metal pieces, which were later to resolve themselves into the sceptre, the standard, the shield and the Coptic bowl (**Fig.1.14**). Then the excavation of the eastern half began. A great silver dish, which at first was thought to be a shield, was found and on its surface were uncovered splinters of burnt bone. The next day (25 July) the dish was lifted and Grimes began to disentangle the pile of objects beneath (**Fig.1.15**). At the west end, meanwhile, work continued with brush and knife: the gold and garnet shoulder-clasps had been found, and then the sword. On 27 July an iron 'lamp-stand' (the standard) was lifted on a plank, and a purple mass of metal at the west end lifted *en bloc*. This purple heap was placed on the grass in the sun beside the excavation trench, and a few minutes later the excavators were surprised to hear a sudden click: the heap had sprung apart to reveal a nest of ten silver bowls, many in pristine condition. A scatter of iron sherds that proved to be the remains of a helmet was recovered on 28 July, and the west end was then declared completed. On 29 July the pile under the great silver dish was finished, with the lifting of a mailcoat and an

1.14: (above)
In the chamber:
Stuart Piggott draws
a plan of the burial
deposit with the aid
of a planning frame;
W.F. Grimes takes a
break. A photograph
taken by O.G.S.
Crawford, editor of
Antiquity.
(OXFORD UNIVERSITY
INSTITUTE OF
ARCHAEOLOGY)

1.15: W.F. Grimes excavating the iron 'standard'.
(OXFORD UNIVERSITY INSTITUTE OF ARCHAEOLOGY)

axe-hammer which lay at the bottom. Then the three cauldrons at the east end were lifted. Little now remained, and on 30 July the team took a day off and then dispersed. Grimes and Crawford departed and the Piggotts resumed their painting holiday.

It had been one of those magical excavations that few are given to experience: when every day brings a new discovery, and each find discovered reveals the glimmer of the next. Moments of disciplined restraint and stiff upper lip, while photography and drawing are undertaken, are followed by gasps of excitement and jubilant chatter, taking stock and racking the imagination for every eventuality before the tense commitment of raising the object from the ground. Given the conditions of the day, the operation had been carried out with intuitive efficiency thanks to the considerable native talents of the participants. Luck also blessed the enterprise, and it is unlikely that much was missed. South-east Suffolk has summer weather of a maritime variety: bright sunshine, interspersed with fresh breezes and wet squalls. Phillips reported that the firmness of the sand was remarkable and only the heaviest rain ran in and cut channels in the exposed sand. The strata were more vulnerable to a combination of hot sun and strong winds, causing the ship rivets to drop out. Fortunately, as Phillips recalled, there was very little rain or strong wind in the whole of this otherwise menacing summer.

The chamber and its treasures could be seen as anomalies, marking the smooth yellow and buff sand that filled the ship. Organic materials, including most of the timbers, had been generally eaten up over the centuries by decomposition in the fiercely acidic sand. A black line signalled a plank, end- or side-on; but where planks had been densely deposited broad side up they had devolved into corky mats, sometimes stiff enough to be pressed. Textiles survived as pads, like the unburnt newspaper in a bonfire. Red stains marked the presence of buried iron, and purple signalled silver. Nothing prepared them for the gold; a couple of sweeps with brush or trowel and the yellow metal gleamed back as fresh as if it had just been dropped.

The little team had mainly been equipped by Mrs Pretty, the landowner. The ideal tool for approaching the level of the hull or burial chamber proved to be 'a stout coal-shovel at the end of a long ash handle'. This was used to lower the surface in horizontal slices and throw the spoil well away from the excavation. When objects were encountered, the excavators changed to 'small fine brushes of the pastry type, and penknives' and the loose earth was removed by dustpan and brush. Mrs Pretty's bellows were brought into service to blow dry sand from the objects as they appeared. Jugs and basins from her bedrooms and an empty Chianti bottle provided water for washing. The objects were put into confectionery bags obtained from the shops in Woodbridge, or

1.16: The standard, the Anastasius dish and other finds boxed up ready to go.
(OXFORD UNIVERSITY INSTITUTE OF ARCHAEOLOGY)

packed in moss from Top Hat Wood and placed in tobacco tins, the ubiquitous receptacle of the pipe-smoking era. Complex objects or groups of objects
were rolled on to a plank or strapped up and removed *en bloc* (**Fig.1.16**).

Interviewed 25 years later, W.F. Grimes recalled the working conditions in
the chamber:

> There wasn't time to get any special tools made ... The two pieces of
> equipment that were used were a curved packer's needle which was very
> sharp when it started out, and an ordinary glue brush. I have no doubt
> that we did in fact stand on quite a number of the objects a number of
> times ... (but) you could have danced on that jewellery if it was in the
> sand and you would not hurt it ... not that we did! The amount of gold
> leaf that was blowing about (from the shield) was frightful. We couldn't do
> anything about it. That's one of the difficulties in excavating in the open
> air, in the wind.[16]

Such disarming statements increase, rather than diminish, confidence that
this was a controlled excavation of measurable success.

In an exhilarating 17 days Phillips's team had emptied the burial chamber of 263 objects of gold, garnet, silver, bronze, enamel, iron, wood, bone,

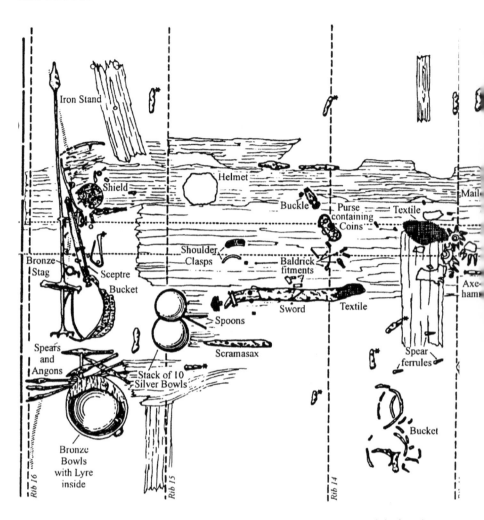

1.17: Composite plan of the Mound 1 chamber, showing the wood traces and the location of the objects. These include the coffin clamps (starred). Based on *SHSB*, I, Figs 111,112 and plans by Charles Phillips.

textiles, feathers and fur (**Fig. 1.17**). There was even a ladybird and the crushed remains of a flowering plant. Every Dark Age object that had been imagined, and a few that had not, seemed to be represented in this burial. But there was one obvious absence. The excavators found no trace of a body, which gave rise to an initial theory that there had never been one; in this reading, the monument was a memorial, a cenotaph, to someone who had died at sea or whose corpse was not available, for whatever other reason, for burial. But among the more experienced excavators (such as Piggott) the absence of the body occasioned no surprise: 'owing to the acid nature of the sand no visible trace of the skeleton remained - a condition which is however familiar to

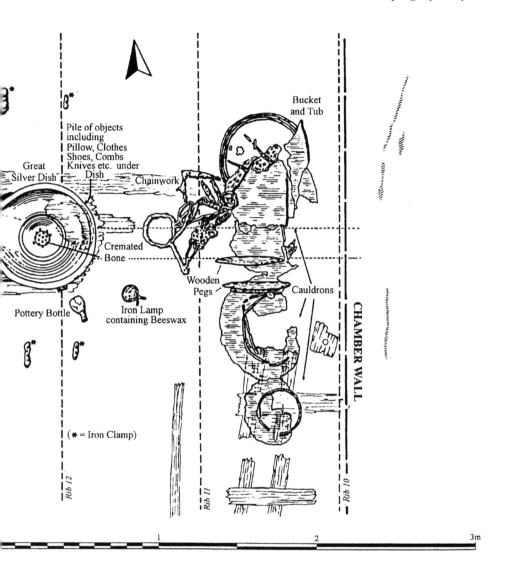

excavators in such soils', an opinion that Piggott gave at the inquest held on the discovery, and one that proved influential with the coroner.[17] The excavation was like a lucky dip; first at one end of the chamber, then at another, then in its centre, objects would emerge out of the black and yellow backcloth of collapsed decayed timber and sand. Now that we know what we know, we can think of a thousand things to look for and a thousand records to make. But in archaeology it was ever thus; the bold pioneers of one generation make space for the scientific deliberation of the next.

The site was now public knowledge: a premature press release by Ipswich Museum had stimulated a torrent of unwelcome attention. Two journalists crossed the Deben in a rowing boat and came up through the woods; others in aeroplanes flew low over the site and the press pestered Phillips in his lodgings, but intrusion on the ground was discouraged by a force of two policemen, paid for by Mrs Pretty, who were on guard 24 hours a day. The official (and accurate) press release attracted little attention; but this was 1939, and the international situation was providing the media with more urgent matters. On 31 July the finds were sent off to the British Museum for safe keeping and Phillips and Brown made their way through the trodden rectangle of the chamber checking for surviving finds. One more coin from the purse turned up, and some more fragments of the helmet and the mailcoat.

The chamber was empty; now the study of the ship could begin (**Fig. 1.18**). On 8 August a team from the Science Museum, which included Lt Commander Hutchinson and A.S. Crossley, arrived to carry out a full survey of the ship, which stretched for 27m along the great east-west cut through the mound. The lines of the hull were marked by the rows of iron rivets spaced 15cm apart, and the lines of the frame by the strips of grey-black powder and crusty sand left by the ribs, which crossed the ship at 90cm intervals. This was the dusty ghost of a wooden clinker-built ship, an impression marked upon a great sweep of sand. Commander Hutchinson, who undertook the recording of the ship, must have had a frustrating task, and few of his records have survived; but enough information was recorded to allow a somewhat schematic plan of the ship to be drawn up at the Science Museum in September 1939. Hutchinson was accompanied in his work by Mercie Lack and Barbara Wagstaff, two photographers who were present on site from 8 to 25 August and who between them took 447 photographs, 45 colour transparencies and an 8mm cine-film.

So what was to happen to the finds? On the afternoon of 14 August the North Suffolk coroner, L.H. Vulliamy (deputising for the East Suffolk coroner), convened a Treasure Trove Inquest at Sutton Parish Hall where the gold and silver objects, brought back from the British Museum, were put on display. Its purpose was to establish the ownership of the finds under an English law, ancient but still in force, that related to buried treasure. If it could be shown that those who buried a treasure intended to retrieve it, then that treasure belonged to the Crown. But if not, then the treasure belonged to the landowner. The rationale of this law remains obscure, but at its base may lie a belief that anyone burying precious metal in a hoard is probably avoiding tax, whereas anyone burying it in a grave intends it to accompany the dead to the next world. At some time, probably in the sixteenth century, when many assets of the Roman Catholic church were privatised, landowners became eligible to reap the harvest of such superstitious practices, and thus claim ownership of grave goods found on their land.

With little difficulty, the authority and good sense of Stuart Piggott and Charles Phillips persuaded the coroner that the Sutton Hoo discovery, for all its strangeness and lack of a body, was indeed the burial of a person, an important person, who had died in the seventh century AD, 1,300 years previously, when England had scarcely begun. It had been a public burial, performed in the presence, indeed with the necessary assistance, of a large number of people. It was obvious that if anyone had meant to retrieve the treasure they could easily have done so. Although the attribution of motives to people long dead is well beyond the reach of modern witnesses, let alone the law, there were few doubts in this case and the jury found that the treasure was buried without intention to defraud the Revenue and now belonged to the landowner, Mrs Edith Pretty. The Crown, as Phillips ironically noted, had thus failed to establish its claim to the regalia of one of King George VI's remote predecessors.

The local discussions that followed this verdict of a Suffolk jury are not well recorded. Charles Phillips mentions family pressure to keep the jewellery, but Mrs Pretty's own position is less certain. Her spiritualist counsellor soon came to stay with her, and Phillips took a stroll with him that evening on the heath, volunteering his opinion that a presentation of all the finds to the nation 'would be a splendid gesture'. Though she was no doubt assailed by advice on all sides, the decision in the end was Mrs Pretty's alone. In a short space of time the accredited owner of the 'million pound grave' announced that she was to give its contents to the British Museum, thus making the most generous donation to the Museum ever made in the lifetime of a donor. Mrs Pretty was offered the accolade of Dame of the British Empire, which she declined.

Among the visitors who were lucky enough to see the ship at the time of its excavation was the great Anglo-Saxon scholar Hector Munro Chadwick, of Clare College, Cambridge, who had been tracked to his Herefordshire hideaway and told of the discovery. Driven by his wife at his preferred speed of 20 miles per hour, he made his way to Sutton Hoo, arriving on 18 August. Chadwick's knowledge was and arguably remains unrivalled, and he is said to have immediately identified the ship-burial as that of Raedwald, who was king of East Anglia from about AD 599 to his death in about 625. This identification, together with his reasons for believing it, were soon published by Chadwick and repeatedly endorsed by other scholars for 50 years. Raedwald was mentioned in the genealogy of a family called the Wuffingas, whose name had survived in a British Library manuscript. According to the Venerable Bede's *History of the English Church and People*, written at Jarrow before 731, Raedwald held sway over all the provinces south of the River Humber. He had flirted

1.18: Excavation of the ship in 1939, after the chamber had been emptied.
(SUTTON HOO ARCHIVE)

briefly with Christianity before returning to his pagan loyalties, though he placed in his 'temple' altars to both Christian and pagan deities.[18]

As Piggott remarked at the inquest, the question of who was buried in the ship was 'a matter more for the historian than for the archaeologist to decide'. There was no archaeological indication, in the form of an inscription or even a body, as to whose burial this was intended to be. But Raedwald became and is still the favourite candidate for both the subject of the Sutton Hoo ship-burial and its explanation. The burial was rich - the richest ever seen, in fact - so it was logical to ascribe it to a king. It was found in East Anglia, so it would be a king of East Anglia. It was dated to the early seventh century by the finds, so it

should be a king of East Anglia who died in the early seventh century. As the largest mound at Sutton Hoo, the burial would be appropriate to the one East Anglian king who was credited with lordship over a large part of England. It contained metalwork with Christian insignia, such as the silver spoons and the silver bowls, and metalwork with pagan symbols, such as the gold and garnet jewellery with its interlaced, biting beasts - apparel and regalia that glistened with secular power and religious accommodation. It suited Raedwald very well.

The excavators of Sutton Hoo had entered a world that seemed to be the reality on which the poetry of the Dark Ages was founded. The most famous

Anglo-Saxon poem of them all, the epic *Beowulf*, ends with a description of the burial of the hero in a 'broad high tumulus, plainly visible to distant seamen', following his fatal encounter with a dragon 50 feet long, itself the guardian of the treasure in a barrow. The poem had begun 3,000 lines earlier with the description of the funeral of the Danish king Scyld, buried in a funeral ship that was loaded up and pushed out to sea:

> Rime-crusted and ready to sail, a royal vessel with curved prow lay in harbour. They set down their dear king amidships, close by the mast. A mass of treasure was brought there from distant parts. No ship, they say, was ever so well equipped with swords, corselets, weapons, and armour. On the king's breast rested a heap of jewels which were to go with him far out into the keeping of the sea ... High overhead they set his golden standard. Then surrendering him to the sea, they sadly allowed it to bear him off. And no one, whether a counsellor in the hall or a soldier in the field, can truly say who received that cargo.[19]

Although *Beowulf* does not describe the burial of a ship in a trench on land, there are numerous echoes of the ritual worlds inhabited by both the *Beowulf* poet and the Sutton Hoo burial party. Beowulf was a Geat (from Sweden) and his adventures took place in Denmark. East Anglia too, and the early English and their kings, had now joined the dark and beautiful world of early Germanic myth. It was an ironic moment to do so. The England of 1939 was about to enter a bitter struggle against the latest pan-Germanic adventure, and the site of Sutton Hoo was itself being prepared for war.

On the site the team had thinned to a small group whose task was to complete the recording of the boat: Phillips, Brown, Hutchinson, Lack and Wagstaff. They reached a satisfactory point on 25 August, after removing a few carefully levelled and located ship rivets and gunwale spikes, and the work was then brought to a halt. It was quite impossible for this small team to refill the huge excavation trench with the mountain of earth that had been extracted from it. On 3 September Britain declared war on Germany, and Sutton Hoo estate workers covered the scar of the ship-burial with bracken.

2 | THE BRITISH MUSEUM'S TREASURE
Research and excavation 1940-82

Saving Mound 1 ♦ Ancient artists and modern restorers ♦ Date of the ship-burial ♦ Allied researches ♦ Return to Sutton Hoo ♦ Publishing the ship-burial ♦ And then what? ♦ The new campaign

SAVING MOUND 1

The excavators of the ship-burial departed in the autumn of 1939, leaving the great trench open, apart from its blanket of bracken to discourage the inquisitive, and the site could return to its former tranquillity. But it did not stay tranquil for long. The threat of German invasion persisted throughout the rest of that year and the next. East Anglia is an old maritime frontier, featuring the Saxon shore forts, such as Burgh Castle, and the Napoleonic fortresses, such as Languard, witnesses to earlier threats of invasion. But this time the invasion, if it came, would come by air as well as sea, and draglines were soon busy creating a grid of deep ditches all over the flat heath of Sutton Walks to inhibit the landing of enemy gliders. These ditches came right up to the Sutton Hoo burial mounds, where they can still be seen: long slots, with humps of soil at regular intervals on each side, all now grassed over (**Fig.2.1**). As well as forming part of the anti-glider barrier, the Sutton Hoo site made another contribution to the war effort: in 1942 it was requisitioned as a training ground. Infantry used the mounds as backgrounds for target practice with the .303 rifle, the 88 grenade and the 2-inch mortar. They also practised 'platoon in the attack' and 'platoon in the defence', the defenders digging two-man slit-trenches on the flanks of Mounds 1, 2, 6 and 7, and the attackers presumably emerging from Top Hat Wood to be greeted by a hail of blank ammunition. Then the Bren-gun carriers arrived, and, frustrated by the flat lands around them, aimed for the mounds. These provided useful training for drivers, none more than Mound 1, which now took the form of two lobes at either side of a great cleavage at the bottom of which lay the ship-impression concealed by dead bracken: a challenge to the driver of a tracked vehicle and fine terrain on which to practise attacking over trenches or land carved up by high explosives.[1]

Fortunately for Sutton Hoo, these manoeuvres soon came to the attention

2.1: Sutton Hoo at war. The mechanical excavator is digging an anti-glider ditch in anticipation of invasion. These are still visible today. (ARTIST'S IMPRESSION BY VICTOR AMBRUS)

of Ted Wright, discoverer of the Ferriby Bronze Age boats on Humberside and later a Trustee of the National Maritime Museum, who was now in uniform and able to put a stop to them. The site slept again, under the whine of the valiant Spitfires and the chug of farm machinery trying to keep the country fed. In 1942 Edith Pretty died, the family subsequently moved away and Sutton Hoo House was sold. But, in defence of the site against any less scrupulous successor, the Pretty family retained, by deed of covenant in perpetuity, the right to excavate there and to dispose of any finds that came to light.

In fulfilment of Edith Pretty's bequest, the finds from the ship-burial now belonged to the British Museum; they spent the war in a disused arm of the London Underground, where they sought protection, like so many London citizens, from the bombs of the Third Reich. At the end of the war in 1945 the boxes were retrieved and returned to the British Museum, where they were gingerly reopened. The man charged with bringing the ship-burial to publication was not Brown, Phillips, Piggott or Grimes, but an assistant keeper in the British Museum's Department of British and Medieval Antiquities, Rupert Bruce-Mitford. He was confirmed in his appointment in 1940 while in uniform at army camp. 'You will also be responsible for Sutton Hoo,' wrote T.D. Kendrick, Keeper of British and Medieval Antiquities, in his letter; 'Brace yourself for this task.'[2] The task in question became Bruce-Mitford's life's work: the form of most of the objects now displayed and published is owed to him and the team he later gathered about him. This team had to work out the attributes of a unique assemblage, rapidly retrieved and sparsely recorded; to bring order to material in widely different states of preservation; and to interpret an extraordinary range of artefacts some of which had a shape or structure never seen before.

ANCIENT ARTISTS AND MODERN RESTORERS

The finds had been recovered as fragments, into which they had broken when the timber burial chamber collapsed under the weight of the mound, and the way in which the pieces fitted together was by no means obvious. The story of the stag indicates the nature of the problems facing the British Museum team, and the persistence and ingenuity required to solve them. The little bronze stag had been found at the west end of the chamber, together with an iron ring and bronze pedestal, which fitted together into a single assembly: a bronze stag on an iron ring supported by a bronze pedestal that had clearly become detached from something else. An early suggestion from Charles Phillips was that the stag should have stood on the crest of the helmet, a suitably totemic position, like the boar that stood on the crest of the Anglo-Saxon helmet from Benty Grange in Derbyshire. But the assembly of stag, ring and pedestal would have amounted to an extravagant and unstable helmet crest, and in any case had not been found near to the helmet, but next to the end of the iron 'lamp-stand'. This was a long piece of iron with a cradle or grid on the shaft and a small flat cruciform plate at the top. The grid and the plate had terminals in the form of stylised heads of bulls. At the base was a point with two scrolls, suitable to place in a leather frog for carrying on parade (see Chapter 5). The object was interpreted by Bruce-Mitford as a standard, equating to the 'tufa' mentioned by Bede as being carried before Edwin, king of Northumbria, on his progress in 'city, town and countryside'.[3] The stag would set off the summit of the standard nicely, and for 25 years it was restored in this position. But during analysis in 1970 one of the team realised that there was no convincing means of attaching the bronze pedestal (bearing its ring and stag) to the top of the standard. So, what had it become detached from, if it did not belong to the standard? The next candidate was the large whetstone that had lain just to the north of the stag. The whetstone had a knob at each end, featuring human faces in relief, and was associated with bronze fittings. This composite object was ingeniously interpreted by Bruce-Mitford as a sceptre, its base an upturned saucer of bronze which provided a seating on the royal knee; at its head could have stood the stag, a British work of art signifying perhaps a domination of all Britain (Figs 2.2a, 2.2b).[4] In an effort to provide an unambiguous confirmation of the latest hypothesis, the bronze composition of the pedestal was determined in terms of the properties of the metals that made up the alloy: copper, tin, lead, zinc and other metals. The 'fingerprints' of the composition were taken from the stag, the pedestal, the standard and the bronze fittings associated with the whetstone. This exercise confirmed that the alloy of the stag had no association with the standard, but shared with the bronze fittings on the sceptre an unusually high admixture of gold. Furthermore, the upper knob of the whetstone was stained with iron rust, most easily explained as corrosion weeping down the upright stone from an iron object - probably the iron ring that carried the stag and that could have been mounted on its end. Thus, this nimble little animal, the chosen logo of Sutton Hoo, posed briefly on the helmet, tried the standard and finally alighted on the sceptre.

The dead man had clearly been buried in parade dress and, piece by piece, his accoutrements were reassembled: the splendid baldric with its gold and garnet connectors, the purse, the sword, the spears and the shield carrying its dragon and falcon symbols. The helmet, which had corroded into a brittle iron shell, had been shattered into a hundred or more fragments of curved iron, among which could be seen elements of a crest inlaid with silver wire and panels with figural scenes. Reconstruction was first achieved by the conservator Herbert Maryon, who recomposed the pieces as a helmet of a rather 'coal-scuttle' style. It was a form that did not satisfy Bruce-Mitford, leaving parts of the face and neck quite unprotected.[5] In 1970 the conserved helmet was dismantled and reassembled (Figs 2.3a, 2.3b). The new reconstruction followed rigorous principles, using only joins that could be demonstrated and omitting altogether the fragments whose position was equivocal. The basic structure was of iron, but decorative panels of bronze were secured to sites on the face-mask and cheekpieces by riveted bronze strips. The bronze was tinned and would have had a silvery appearance, imitated in the replica that was made by the Tower Armouries.[6] In a startling symbolic composition, a snake body provided the protective crest across the top of the warrior's head. Its beady garnet eyes and gaping mouth meet the beak of a fierce bird, whose wings make the eyebrows, whose body forms the nose and whose tail forms the moustache of the implacable human armoured face. Two little boars-heads looked sideways at the tip of each eyebrow-wing. The serpent had a head at each end, so keeping a look out behind the warrior, like a rear gunner.[7] This was protection, physical and psychological, of a high order, a

2.2a: The 'sceptre' as replicated through the researches of the British Museum team. (BRITISH MUSEUM)

2.2b: The stag. (BRITISH MUSEUM)

helmet of a kind imagined by the *Beowulf* poet, such that 'no sword, however sharp and tough, might cripple the wearer when he joined battle with his enemies'.[8] This form of the helmet has become the Sutton Hoo icon and is now used the world over to signify things mysterious, menacing or pagan. It would be hard to say if its aspect, with its heavy metal dome and dark sagging eyes, has borrowed or created the image of the modern helmeted biker in dark glasses.

The Mound 1 hero was accompanied by a number of still more unusual objects evocative of the life of the warrior leader in his hall. A handful of gnarled and twisted fragments of maple wood found in one of the hanging bowls was deduced, from the holes seen in one piece, to have been part of a stringed instrument with peg holes. Initially reconstructed as a six-stringed harp, its form was subsequently recomposed by analogy with that played by King

2.3a: The helmet in course of restoration (left), and as seen today. (BRITISH MUSEUM)

David in the eighth-century Anglo-Saxon *Vespasian Psalter*; a replica of this instrument (**Fig.2.4**) was played at a concert by one of Bruce-Mitford's daughters. Microscopic examination of the wood pieces had revealed fragments of hair, which indicated that the lyre had been kept in a beaver-skin bag.[9] Drinking horns were remodelled from the metal fragments decorating the mouths, and it was realised that they were based on the horns of the aurochs, a large species of wild cattle now extinct. The forms of the crushed cauldrons were reconstructed; the greatest had hung from a chain 3.45m long, suggestively cited as indicating the height of the roof-tree in Raedwald's hall. From the pads that had survived, textiles in a dozen different fabrics were discerned: from blankets, cloaks and hangings to tunics and linen; and in the careful examination of every minute fragment, traces of otter fur were found and deduced to be from an otter-fur cap, perhaps worn under the heavy iron helmet.[10]

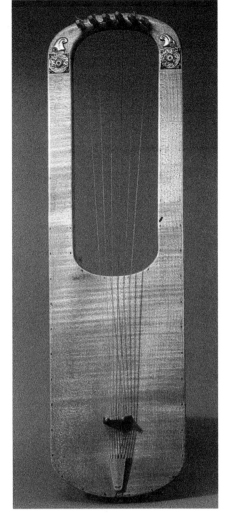

2.4: The lyre as reconstructed.
(BRITISH MUSEUM)

The analysis was to be one of the most thorough ever undertaken of a burial deposit. Every scientific technique then available was deployed, and a few new ones developed. By the time publication was completed in 1983, 96 individuals had played a part, large or small, in the work. As a result of these researches, the 263 finds were reassigned to 59 objects, or sets of objects, that had originally been placed in the chamber (see *Archaeological Records*, pp. 219-23). Progress had also been made on the question of the missing body of the buried person. At the Pathology Museum at Guy's Hospital, Bruce-Mitford inspected the evidence from a celebrated murder case, the heels of Mrs Durand-Deacon, which were all that survived from John George Haigh's tank of acid. Bruce-Mitford went on to infer a similar process, if much more pro-

tracted, in the acid bath provided by the hull of the Sutton Hoo ship, and showed that in a central area, where the great gold buckle and the baldric lay, the finds carried corrosion products that were slightly phosphate-enriched. The most likely explanation of this was that there had been a body that had lain in rainwater collected in the hull and burial chamber, acidified by its passage through the acid sand of the mound, so that over the years the body had been rendered invisible by decay. It could now be strongly argued, with scientific corroboration, that a body had lain or sat in the west half of the chamber, and the cenotaph theory was laid to rest.

While the objects were being conserved, reconstructed in the round and identified or interpreted, attempts were made to discern the background of the burial and to decide with greater certainty its date and who had been buried there. Bruce-Mitford initiated studies of the context of the jewellery, the ship, the region in which Sutton Hoo lay and the ship-burials that were broadly contemporary, especially those in the boat-grave cemeteries at Vendel and Valsgärde in Sweden.[11] The art of the gold and garnet jewellery had perhaps the greatest potential for dating and for making cultural links with the earlier and later art of England (**Figs 2.5a, 2.5b, 2.6**). Although resembling Kentish and Frankish work, the polychrome jewellery was assigned to

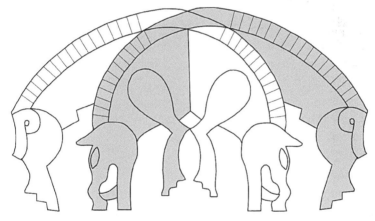

2.5: (Opposite and top) Shoulder clasp (a) and detail (b). (BRITISH MUSEUM)

2.6: Drawing of the end of a shoulder clasp showing the pattern of two boars. (FAS-HERITAGE)

a local East Anglian workshop by virtue of a type of little mushroom-shaped garnet that seemed to be confined to the Sutton Hoo assemblage. Bruce-Mitford related the interlacing or ribbon animals, known to Germanic art historians as 'style II', to their lively cousins depicted in the early Christian gospel books, showing how the work of the Sutton Hoo jewellers should be seen as the missing link between the pagan and Christian worlds in the conversion period of the seventh century AD. In prime place among these gospel books (for which the Sutton Hoo artists could now be seen as the trailblazers) was the *Lindisfarne Gospels*, made about AD 698, and Bruce-Mitford turned aside to help bring out the magnificent facsimile and commentary. Now two great British monuments of native art stood clearly at either end of the seventh century, giving the country two stepping stones across the darkest period of its early history.[12]

The perception of the richness and symbolic character of the Mound 1 assemblage had, if anything, increased rather than lessened during the years in which the objects were conserved, identified and studied. The wealth was unrivalled in a British grave; the sceptre and standard, and indeed the ornamental military accoutrements, were unparalleled in any. It was natural to conclude that the Sutton Hoo ship-burial was unique and at the top of the social order; and, in pagan Anglo-Saxon England, that meant it was the burial of a king. These assumptions have been justly challenged, but in general the interpretation has proved fairly robust. Now, the question of 'which king?' had again to be addressed, and, in spite of Chadwick's confident assertion that it was Raedwald, this was a difficult thing to prove. The historical context of the burial and the identity of the person commemorated depended principally on the date. Three main methods of dating were available: the evidence of history (the documentary record), the evidence of art history (the style of the art) and the evidence of archaeology (scientific dating and behavioural parallels). In theory, these were independent of each other; in practice, the history was then seen as providing the most senior opinion, to which the other disciplines had to defer to win acceptance.

DATE OF THE SHIP-BURIAL

The approximate date, from the widely recognised character of the objects and their ornament, was not in doubt, being somewhere in the middle centuries of the first millennium AD and almost certainly between 550 and 650. At this time, Anglo-Saxon and Latin writers describe Britain as having a number of kings and kingdoms, the peoples on the east coast creating kingdoms surviving in the memory as Kent, Essex, Lindsey and East Anglia. Sutton Hoo itself is not mentioned in early documents, but the neighbouring village of Rendlesham, to its north, was described by Bede as lying 'within the Province of the East Angles'; while Felixstowe, on the other side of the Deben, is likely to have been named after a certain Felix, cited by Bede as bishop of the East Angles. So, although we do not know exactly where East Anglia was at that time, it seems highly probable that it existed as a territory and that Sutton Hoo was located within it. If kings were buried there, they would be kings of East Anglia.

The kings of East Anglia are listed in a British Library manuscript; no dates are given there but we know some of them from Bede, who mentions one or two in his *Ecclesiastical History*.[13] If a member of East Anglia's ruling dynasty was buried in the Sutton Hoo ship-burial, it could have been Wehha (the first to rule over the East Angles), Wuffa (d.578), Tyttla (d.599), Raegenhere (in the succession, but who apparently did not rule, d.616/17), Eni (likewise), Raedwald (d.624/5), Eorpwald (d.627/8), Sigeberht (d.636/7) or Ecgric (d.636/7). It was less likely to have been Anna, who came to the throne in 636/7, or his brothers Aethelhere and Aethelwald or their successors, who were known to have been Christian, and who ruled as Christians. Raedwald was singled out by Bede as having won pre-eminence for his people and having 'held sway over all the provinces south of the Humber'.[14] Other aspects of Raedwald's career had attracted Bede's attention. Along with every politician in seventh-century England, the king was absorbed by the major question of the day: whether or not to convert to Christianity. Eventually he took the plunge on a visit to Christian Kent, but on his return to the East Anglian province 'his wife and certain perverse advisors' insisted that he retract it. When, in an attempt at diplomatic compromise, Raedwald set up altars to Christ and to pagan gods in the same local temple, the problem was by no means solved and no doubt attracted the contempt of both sides. The temple itself seems to have survived until the end of the seventh century, since Ealdwulf, a later king of East Anglia whom Bede had met, remembered seeing it when he was a boy.

Raedwald's queen, whose name we do not know, was clearly a forceful woman, and she had a high moral character. Whether or not she approved of Christianity, she was a champion of loyalty and trust. When Edwin of Northumbria was on the run from his enemy, the ferocious Aethelfrith, Raedwald's court was one of the places in which he sought refuge. Raedwald was offered a large sum to despatch him, and was much tempted to do so. But, in contrast to Lady Macbeth, Raedwald's queen dissuaded him, saying that 'it was unworthy of a great king to sell his friend in the hour of need for gold, and worse still to sacrifice his royal honour'.[15] Raedwald agreed and Edwin lived on to become the king and champion of a Christian Northumbria. Raedwald was thus special among the East Anglian kings and remained the most popular candidate for the person commemorated in the Mound 1 ship-burial. He died in about 624 or 625, and this is consequently the date generally assigned to the burial. The argument from history has been dominant, and it is probably fair to say that the dates obtained from other disciplines have been influenced in some measure by the advantages of conformity with the story of Raedwald. His unnamed wife, meanwhile, had not only proved herself the more politically astute of the two, but in the way of things probably survived to bury her husband. It is not fantastical to suppose that it was she who was the composer of this great and complex memorial.

2.7: Gold coin from the purse. It was probably issued by the Frankish king Theodebert II at Clermont-Ferrand between about AD 595 and 612. The obverse shows a figure wearing a diadem, echoing the image of a Roman emperor. The reverse shows a cross, the symbol of Christian triumph. The word 'victory' precedes the name of the king on the reverse and the moneyer (Riathi) on the obverse (*SHSB* I, 609).

The art style made a date in the late sixth to seventh century likely; but exactly when in that period? The great silver dish carried a stamp of Anastasius I, who was emperor of Byzantium from 491 to 518, so the burial was at least later than AD 491. Radiocarbon dates were taken from two carboniferous sources: a piece of timber found lying on the bottom of the ship gave a date of AD 656 ± 45, while wax from the iron lamp dated to AD 523 ± 45.

The prime responsibility for a tighter dating was placed on the coins in the purse (**Fig. 2.7**). In other archaeological periods, such as the Roman, coins are the excavators' friend, dateable often to within a few years and sufficiently numerous to provide at least some primary find spots from which to argue a date *after* which a burial was made or a building erected. But in the early medieval period coins are rare, their images derivative and their inscriptions ambiguous. The coins in the purse were Merovingian *tremisses*, minted in France, but they carry no dates. The coins do carry mint names, as well as portraits, but the names of the issuers were often blundered, or copied to lend them a spurious authority. The date assigned to the Sutton Hoo group by French experts was at first AD 650-60, and this was the dating that was accepted for the first 25 years after the ship-burial's discovery. But in 1960 the terminal date of the coin parcel was revised by the French numismatist Lafau-

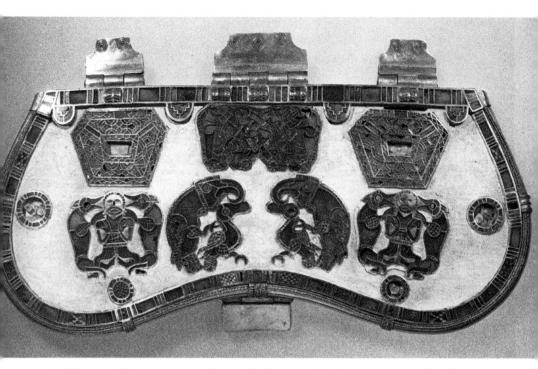

2.8: The purse lid as reconstructed in 1945. The frame and the plaques are made of gold inlaid with garnets. The plaques show two pairs of fighting horses, two birds of prey and two vignettes of a man between two beasts. These images occur in other European princely burials, but their symbolic meaning is uncertain (*SHSB* II, Plate 13a).

rie to around AD 625. Thus Raedwald, who died c.625, could now be endorsed by the coins as candidate number 1. In his own independent confirmation of this date, John Kent of the British Museum carried out an analysis of the specific gravity of the Sutton Hoo coins, proposing that the gold content of the Merovingian coinage was reduced through time, as the metal was progressively recycled. By comparing the specific gravity of gold coins from dated hoards, a sequence was deduced which ended with the Sutton Hoo parcel in the early decades of the seventh century. The character of the assemblage remained curious: were the coins currency or hoarded bullion? Could the burial have been much later than the date of the coins' manufacture? The historian Philip Grierson advanced the imaginative hypothesis that the 37 coins, three blanks and two ingots found in the purse (**Fig. 2.8**), or associated with it, represented the payment of 40 oarsmen, a pilot and a steersman, by analogy with the Roman payment of an obol to Charon who brought souls to their rest in Hades.[16] If this was its context, the date of the coin parcel could be close to the date of their deposition in the burial; no obstacle was offered to the identification of the buried man as Raedwald.

ALLIED RESEARCHES

The next task was to place Sutton Hoo in the wider context of its district, its kingdom and that kingdom's neighbours. Near the site were two famous places, Rendlesham and Snape, which engaged Bruce-Mitford's attention. Rendlesham is mentioned in Bede's *Ecclesiastical History* as the site of a palace where, in the seventh century, the East Anglian king Aethelwald stood as godfather at the baptism of Swidhelm, king of Essex.[17] Bruce-Mitford searched the archives and then looked over the site itself, concluding that there was an early Saxon cemetery there, and, somewhere as yet unlocated, a palace and an early church waiting to be found. Also nearby was Snape, the site where a ship-burial had been found in the mid-nineteenth century. It was once a cluster of nine or ten mounds on Snape Common, but most had been dug into in campaigns of 1827 and 1862. Little notice of the first of these campaigns had survived in the archives, apart from rumours of gold aplenty; but from the second campaign the record of a ship-burial - the first identified in Britain and one of the first to be correctly interpreted in Europe - has survived. The ship was at least 14m long and marked in the sand by rows of rivets spaced at 14cm intervals. It had already been robbed, but the grave goods that had survived to be reported included two iron spearheads, a glass claw-beaker and a gold finger-ring, together with a 'mass of human hair'. Bruce-Mitford reinterpreted the human hair as belonging rather to the fabric of a shaggy pile cloak, like examples from Sutton Hoo and Broomfield, and tracked down the ring, which is now in the British Museum. Snape, which had also produced cremation burials in pots, was clearly a key site for the understanding of Sutton Hoo: complementary, but different.[18]

Bruce-Mitford's researches also took him to the Mälaren district of Sweden, cradle of the Svear, a people whose kingdom gave Sweden (Sverige) its name. In this region there were two well-known cemeteries, Vendel and Valsgärde, which contained ship-burials of similar date to Sutton Hoo. Bruce-Mitford helped the Swedish archaeologist Sune Lindquist to excavate one of the ship-burials at Valsgärde, and the Swedish links with Sutton Hoo became ever more important in his mind. The Swedish allusions in *Beowulf*, the similarity of the Sutton Hoo helmet and shield with examples found in Sweden and, above all, the rite of ship-burial persuaded him of a strong seventh-century connection.

The Sutton Hoo ship-burial also became a player in a wider field, since in addition to the cultural artefacts it shared with its immediate neighbours it could be seen to have drawn objects from all over the world known to the Anglo-Saxons (Chapter 7, p.197). The 37 coins came from 37 different mints in the heartland of Merovingian France; the silverware came from the eastern

Mediterranean, in the hinterland of the residual Roman empire at Byzantium. There were textiles whose origin could be traced to Italy and the Middle East, possibly Syria, and a 'Coptic' bowl that had possibly made its way from Egypt. Here were precious objects that had arrived directly or indirectly across the seas and along the rivers or half-remembered Roman routes, from hall to hall and giver to giver in the diplomatic gestures of a dozen emerging nations of the new post-Roman Europe. The Sutton Hoo burial was becoming established as a closely dated landmark in early medieval history.

RETURN TO SUTTON HOO

There were still some problems, however, that Bruce-Mitford wanted to see solved before committing his studies to print. The ship needed a more accurate plan, since the Science Museum's was rather schematic and Hutchinson's notes had apparently been lost during the war (**Fig.2.9**). The chamber had been planned, but was uncertainly related to the ship, the ship trench and the mound, each of which had only vague dimensions. The comparable burials in Sweden had produced horses, sometimes outside the ship, but at Mound 1 there had been no digging beyond the confines of the hull. Could horses have been killed and buried here as part of the funeral ceremony? Certain pieces were missing from the conserved artefacts: could they still be found? In short, the excavation of the Sutton Hoo ship-burial was not complete and should now be finished. A published report would need a plan of the other

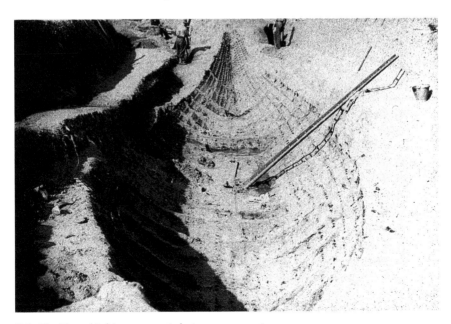

2.9: The Mound 1 ship as excavated. (BRITISH MUSEUM)

mounds, still smothered in bracken; and, while they were about it, it would be useful to know whether the putative Mound 5, placed tentatively in the gap between Mound 2 and Mound 6, actually existed. This would help with the interpretation of the development of the cemetery as a series of rows of burial mounds. At the same time it would be interesting to investigate the character of a 'Bronze Age hill-top village' beneath Mounds 1, 2 and 3, traces of which had been noted by Basil Brown in his diary.

Accordingly, after much debate and deliberation, in 1965 the British Museum mounted a return visit to Sutton Hoo on a truly impressive scale. The ship-burial site, never backfilled, was to be totally excavated, Rupert Bruce-Mitford taking charge of the completion of the ship trench, and Paul Ashbee, who had considerable expertise in the excavation and interpretation of prehistoric burial mounds, would take the remains of Mound 1 apart and establish its structure. The bioarchaeologist Geoffrey Dimbleby would exam-ine the buried soil and reconstruct the vegetation sequence. Meanwhile, a team from the British Museum's new Department of Prehistoric and Roma-no-British Antiquities would excavate between the visible mounds to investi-gate the prehistoric settlement and test for the existence of Mound 5.

All this and more was achieved. For the first time the site was largely cleared of its bracken and a contour survey made. The prehistorians found evidence of Neolithic and Bronze Age occupation, noting also a strong show-ing of Beaker material (c. 2000 BC) beneath Mound 1. Mound 5 was shown to exist, and to have had a robbed burial chamber (which was left unexcavated). Six early medieval burials were found outside and between the mounds. Three of these were inhumations arranged around Mound 5, while further to the west there was a skull buried in a pit, with two unfurnished crema-tions nearby. The skull, which was accompanied by a few scraps of metal, was radiocarbon-dated to the mid-eighth century AD.

The lobes of Mound 1 were distinguished from the spoil heaps of Charles Phillips and Basil Brown and excavated in a grid of square-cut pits - a system pioneered by Sir Mortimer Wheeler. Ashbee deduced that Mound 1 had been constructed from dumps of sand and turf scraped up from the surrounding surface. No quarry ditch or quarry pits were found. Inside the Mound 1 ship trench the mangled remains of the ship were treated with surgical intensity. A great shelter was erected over the trench, beneath which the detritus of the bracken infill and the sand kicked up by rabbits and military manoeuvres was gently cleaned away (Fig.2.10). Then appeared the rivets, still *in situ* but subjected to distortions of axis and alignment as though the great ship had twisted in a bed of agony. It had, after all, been run over by Bren-gun carri-ers. A detailed plan was made, and in spite of the obvious displacements the

2.10: The shelter erected over the remains of the Mound 1 ship during the completion of excavations in 1965-71. (G. KEILLER)

ultimate record was made: a 1:1 cast in plaster of Paris of the inside of the hull. This was transformed into a fibreglass positive and the prow section of this sad, sloughed ship-skin was later to appear in a corner of the National Maritime Museum. Diligent sieving of the ship trench spoil brought 19 scraps of solder, Stockholm tar[19] or unidentified residues, while reworking of the 1,939 spoil heaps produced 34 pieces including two small brooches, two buckles and minute fragments of tine from the bronze stag. Under the ship was a long timber stain, probably from an oar. But there were no traces of horses.

The survey of the site itself produced evidence for a total of 17 mounds, of which two (16 and 17) were questionable.[20] Bruce-Mitford proposed that the cemetery had developed along an axis running from Mound 2 to Mound 3, although there was a curious gap between Mounds 3, 1 and 7. The summits of most of the mounds were marked by a little depression aligned east-west. Bruce-Mitford called these 'ship-dents', comparing them to the depressions over the intact ship-graves at Valsgärde (Chapter 7, p.172). The Sutton Hoo 'ship-dents' were presumably seen as areas of collapse caused by the subsidence of the deck of a buried ship. The expectation was therefore that other ship-burials remained to be discovered.[21]

PUBLISHING THE SHIP-BURIAL

In an enormous work of 2,441 pages, with hundreds of illustrations, *The Sutton Hoo Ship-burial* was published over the next decade. It appeared in three volumes. Volume 1 (1975) dealt with the ship-burial and its excavation and re-excavation, and included all the other information of whatever type and character relating to the site, the structure of the grave and the mound that Bruce-Mitford and his team had amassed. It concluded that the ship-burial was the memorial of Raedwald, king of East Anglia, as Chadwick had long before surmised. Volume 2 (1978) concerned itself with the regalia, objects mainly assigned to Raedwald's kingly and warrior roles. And volume 3, issued in two parts in 1983, described the remaining finds.

Over the 30-year gestation of the publication there had been some criticism of Bruce-Mitford and his British Museum team for a procedure perceived in some quarters as ponderous and secretive; now they had produced a book that was monumentally generous, in which every aspect and analysis then conceivable of every find was reported and illustrated.[22] By the time it had all appeared there were few people whose mode of existence would allow them the time and the space to absorb the whole of such a work. The three volumes provided a quarry of information and ideas, rather than a text-book for the student or a briefing document for the busy researcher. The less engaged reader had to rely on Bruce-Mitford's immensely successful *Handbook* to the Sutton Hoo ship-burial, which already contained enough on the finds to engender a lively debate in a student seminar, supplemented by Charles Green's *Sutton Hoo: The Excavation of a Royal Ship Burial*, which was an early attempt to tell the story of the excavation and put its findings into context in East Anglia and Europe. These were later to be joined by an original account of the Sutton Hoo ship-burial by Angela Evans, a member of the British Museum's Sutton Hoo team. The objects themselves were now on display, and were soon to have a gallery of their own in the British Museum's Early Medieval room.

The public would seem to have been served at all levels. The Sutton Hoo ship-burial had sailed majestically into the annals of museum literature, and the material for any reconsideration of the evidence or any reinterpretation of the finds or burial rite was available in the public domain worldwide. The British Museum had done its duty handsomely and only the small-minded could now cavil.[23]

AND THEN WHAT?

Perhaps surprisingly, it was from Bruce-Mitford himself that the initiative came to question and amend the 'definitive version', and from the late 1970s he was pressing for a return to Sutton Hoo and for more digging there. In a later television programme he recalled what had been achieved and suggested what should come next. Standing before the cameras on the grass of Sutton Hoo, with the mounds behind him, he said he now felt confident about the date of the coins as lying between AD615 and 635 and confident that there had been a body in Mound 1. Moreover, there could be no doubt in his mind that it was the body of Raedwald; the ambiguous religious symbolism of the burial 'suited Raedwald to a T'. Now we needed to know whether Sutton Hoo was *the* burial ground of the dynasty. Were Raedwald's predecessors buried here? Could we find the grave of Raedwald's wife? Were there more ships? When did cremation stop and inhumation start? Why did burial continue there into the Christian period (as suggested by an eighth-century radiocarbon date on the skull in the 'skull-pit')? And what was the social and economic basis that lay behind this phenomenal peak of wealth and ostentation? Addressing us engagingly through the camera's lens he announced, 'The answers, my friends, are not blowing in the wind. The answers are lying in the ground. In fact, I'm standing on them.'[24]

Familiarity with Sutton Hoo's world had thus served only to make him all the more curious about it, and his curiosity was shared by those for whom archaeology's task was to supply the gaps to narrative history. This was a clientele that had little interest in the relative dimensions of rivets or indeed in the graves of the common people; the early kings of England were the movers and shakers of their day, and hidden in their spears and cauldrons were signs of their times. Few doubted the general interpretation of Mound 1 as the burial of a king of East Anglia, although there was still room for a side show of scholiastic disquisition about which king it was. Most scholars then were unconcerned to question the actual notion of kingship at all, royalty being accepted as having a permanent and welcome place in the hearts of the British people. But who could resist speculation on who was buried in the other mounds, and whether they were of the pagan or Christian persuasion? For these historians, then, the urge to see more kings was a persistent one, which demanded gratification.

Mrs Pretty's heir, Robert, owner through deed of covenant of the finds and the right to excavate, had given permission to renew the excavations in 1965. He was ready to do so again, and in partnership with Rupert Bruce-Mitford encouraged support for a new and even larger campaign under the joint direction of Bruce-Mitford and Philip Rahtz, the new Professor of Archaeology at York. In 1978 a small steering committee was formed, backed by the Society of Antiquaries of London and chaired by Rosemary Cramp, the charismatic head of archaeology at Durham University and excavator of Monkwearmouth and Jarrow, Bede's monastery. But not everyone was enthusiastic. Bruce-Mitford had retired from the British Museum and his former colleagues were expressing reservations about another campaign. The Sutton Hoo adventure deserved a rest and readers needed time to absorb the tomes with which they had been presented. Archaeology's aims had changed so much during the 1960s and 1970s that a 'royal burial' was hardly on the agenda. There was a risk that a return to Sutton Hoo would be construed as a poorly disguised treasure hunt.

These cautious views were countered by those of the steering committee: Bruce-Mitford was the greatest living expert on Sutton Hoo, and would probably occupy the position of ultimate authority to his death and beyond it. It would be foolish to fail to profit by his knowledge and experience, and that of the current team engaged in the unique and comprehensive study. However, such reasoning could be flexible: if the British Museum were reticent about a new campaign, maybe another partner could be found for the venture. In an astute political manoeuvre the steering committee managed to secure the collaboration of the Ashmolean Museum in Oxford, and Robert Pretty put his signature to a letter of agreement endowing them with all the finds that were expected to be recovered.

In this atmosphere, reminiscent of cold war diplomacy, a seminar was held in Oxford on the occasion of a conference entitled 'Anglo-Saxon Cemeteries, 1979'. The conference featured the majority of the country's practising early medieval archaeologists and a good few from abroad. The seminar was designed to test the will of the delegates for and against a new campaign at Sutton Hoo. But the case for further excavation was weakly presented, rarely exceeding, in its force of argument, an exhortation to the audience to entertain a proper regard for natural curiosity. The relevance of a new campaign to the current world of the conference participants was at best obscure. The excitement of the Sutton Hoo ship-burial belonged in most cases to their adolescence; modern students were wrestling with more exciting theoretical concepts such as the detection of social change, while fieldworkers were taking a few hours off from the manic seven-day week of the rescue excavator. The challenges of the day lay in testing new ideas or snatching new sites from the destructive machinery of road-builders and urban developers, not in reheating yesterday's archaeological discoveries, in which little was promised except more of the same.

It is an astonishing reflection of the tenacity and *sang-froid* of the archaeological establishment of the day that this reception offered no obstacle to their proceeding. This was perhaps not unconnected with the first chill wind that was immediately felt in the nooks and crannies of every state-supported activity following Margaret Thatcher's election as prime minister in the same year. The switch to project-funding signalled the end of the state archaeological service that had been created (*de facto*) by underwriting core organisations in county councils and universities. In student seminar rooms, too, the doctrine of self-dedication to the quest of piecing together the past was being questioned. At the conference itself Ian Hodder pointed out that the analytical approach to Anglo-Saxon or any other cemeteries might be flawed. There would be examples at least where graves did not reflect a real, but a wished-for, society. The evidence of material culture, like that of documents, was no longer the revelation of a simple truth. The intellectual citadel of archaeology had been captured from the natural scientists by those for whom the gift of archaeology was not reality, but text.[25]

The loss of confidence experienced by theorists and rescuers in the face of contemporary politics was probably the decisive factor that allowed an apparently anachronistic project like digging more of Sutton Hoo to persevere. Rosemary Cramp withdrew, but the steering committee forged ahead. The provocative flirtation with the Ashmolean proved effective. The British Museum was soon back in negotiation with the Society of Antiquaries and, succumbing to the sensitive diplomacy of the latter's President, Professor Christopher Brooke, had acceded to a treaty to fund a new campaign for five years. Those on the inside who had doubted that this was a good use of the Antiquaries' research money were persuaded that the country needed an archaeological 'flagship' to recover a more glamorous place in the appreciation of the public.[26]

THE NEW CAMPAIGN

If there was a more intellectual agenda for the new project to address it was not proclaimed. Indeed, rather than issue a prescription, the Sutton Hoo Committee simply announced its intentions to resume excavations in the *London Gazette*. Interested parties were invited to submit applications for the

directorship, accompanied by their suggestions for a programme of exploration. Polemic in favour of the project switched to a 'rescue' theme: the site was
in jeopardy from treasure-hunters and rabbits and must be saved by being
dug. Right on cue, on 14 February 1982, Mound 11 was found to have had a
large hole dug through the top of it, presumably by treasure-hunters. It was a
peculiar mound to choose, nearly flat and under a tree; even more strangely,
the robbers had got to the level of the buried soil and then stopped, as though
making a gesture rather than indulging in a serious pillaging operation.

Few archaeological projects can have been initiated with greater publicity
and more hostility than the Sutton Hoo research campaign of 1983. 'We *know*
how the Anglo-Saxons buried their kings in the seventh century,' wrote the
editor of *Rescue News*, lamenting the expenditure of resources better applied
to sites being lost to the bulldozer. Ostensibly for similar reasons, professional
field units were also opposed, most particularly those resident in East Anglia.
The Scole Committee, representing the latter, promised that they would formally object to Scheduled Monument Consent being given for excavations
at Sutton Hoo. Even the editor of *Treasure Hunting Monthly* condemned the
proposed project as selfish and elitist. There were clearly people to mollify
before any digging could start. And yet this was a liberating opportunity: the
chance to escape, for a moment, from the reactive, fire-brigade mentality of
the rescue scene and develop methods and protocols of use to all; above all to
address a research question with adequate means and few constraints beyond
one's own imagination and skills. How could anyone fail to respond to such
a challenge? It was a measure of the paralysis being experienced during
archaeology's great metamorphosis (or perhaps of the ethical ambiguity of
the Sutton Hoo project) that only 17 people applied for the job. On 30 October 1982 six were interviewed by the Sutton Hoo Committee, their designs
for a new campaign were assessed, and one was chosen. It was in this way
that the future of Sutton Hoo came to be placed in the hands of the author of
this book.

The successful design suggested that a new research programme at Sutton
Hoo could serve the community in three ways: it could bring new understanding to the question of how England began and the character of the society that began it; it could develop new ways of doing field archaeology; and it
could restore to the nation a monument which at the time lay in a neglected,
bedraggled and vulnerable condition.

In research, the early medieval agenda had already broadened beyond the
historical or social equations that had driven the study of Sutton Hoo up to
that point. The presence of kings was not sufficient or even necessary to the
inquiry. Scholars in Sweden had been reluctant to attribute their mounds at

Vendel and Valsgärde to kings, or even to assume that kingship was inevitable. The burial mounds could be the investments of the families of successful merchants. It was clear that at some time kingdoms had formed in the lands around the North Sea. But when, and why? The existence of early states was being proposed and tested in other periods, both Classical and prehistoric. If Sutton Hoo was just the burial ground of kings, then there was little point in investigating it further, since the argument would be a circular one: kings are buried like this because these are kings. But if the cemetery could be shown to reflect the politics, social organisation and ideology of its day then it would be worth interrogating it on these matters. In the new project the questions would be framed in a new way, seeking explanation, rather than discovery from the ground. We would ask not 'what more can be found there?' but 'why that?' 'why there?' and 'why then?'

The science of fieldwork was evolving rapidly, too. There was a certain contrast between rescue and research methods, and neither was following satisfactory procedures. Rescue projects had money but not enough time, and were liable to produce too much indigestible data; research projects had too little money and often ideas that were too big to be tested in small areas opened in short summer seasons. Both were infected with the notion that only large-scale excavation made sense. So excavations should be as large and thorough as possible, termed 'total excavation', a strategy justified when applied in the rescue theatre as 'preservation by record'. But these concepts were being challenged by a more scientific procedure dominated by the idea of 'evaluation'. Here the site is thoroughly examined by nondestructive methods and the underground strata are predicted before any destructive digging is done. The predicted character of the buried site, termed a 'deposit model', is matched to the questions being posed by researchers and the result is a 'strategy', a programme in which the *smallest* possible area is dug that will answer the questions put. The rest of the site is conserved for the future. These ideas had already been tested in some urban rescue work; Sutton Hoo offered an ideal opportunity to see if they could work on a rural site.[27]

The protection of Sutton Hoo for the future was an obvious concomitant of these ideas, and the physical condition of the site in 1983 was catastrophic. Part of it had been scheduled, and the notice announcing that it was 'an offence to damage it' had fallen over and was half buried in the bracken, which was growing nearly six feet high. Rabbits burrowed and multiplied in the barrows, and the scars of their old warrens were colonised by brambles. Clearly, the one thing that must not happen at Sutton Hoo was nothing. A 'burial ground of kings' deserved a better fate.

In an attempt to win over the persistent opposition to the project, these new approaches were presented to a public meeting held at University College London on 15 April 1983 and chaired by Charles Thomas, then President of the Council for British Archaeology. To obtain a representative professional and avocational sample, all 1,000 members of the Society for Medieval Archaeology were invited - and many came. 'Massive opposition' had been promised by *Guardian* journalist Ann Maitland, who claimed that it was widely believed that archaeologists themselves had vandalised Mound 11 in order to justify the new campaign. But, in the event, the opposition was measured and reasonable and largely confined to the archaeological profession itself. The presentation of the programme for the project by its director opened with a slide of the dragon from the Mound 1 shield and the words: 'There is a dragon which stalks the land, spreading discord ... ' (**Fig.2.11**). It was followed by an outline of the actual research design and its justification, stressing the concept of evaluation as a prerequisite to excavation. Leading East Anglian archaeologist Peter Wade-Martins expressed reservations that were widely held: why now? why this site? Have the results of the previous campaign, only just published, been properly absorbed? Surely the archaeology being forced on us through imminent destruction should have priority over a new, some would say unnecessary, project? Others objected that the proposed budget (£100,000 per year) was far too small to do the job properly, and others challenged the proposed use of students, which they thought would mean low standards.

These fears were understandable and answers were offered. Many of the objectors were no doubt calling to mind certain old-fashioned, badly resourced university excavations, which now contrasted a little unfavourably with the standards being set by professional field units. But the new Sutton Hoo project was itself to be done by a modern field unit. The first three years of the programme would be dedicated to an evaluation that would predict what was left of the site and what it could tell us. At that point, and before destructive digging began on any scale, a full *project design* would be prepared, circulated and published in support of an application for Scheduled Monument Consent. Meanwhile the site was being damaged by treasure-hunters and rabbits, and, furthermore, was a complete mess, overgrown by bracken and receiving no care or maintenance. If we continued to ignore it, it would no longer be there to argue about. The money that underwrote the project was not available for 'rescue' purposes; in fact it was only available for research. But the rescue movement could still benefit by using the project as a laboratory for new techniques. It was hoped that a summer season by the Deben would offer 'rescuers' a stimulating break from their stressful labours elsewhere. It was agreed that the budget was not big enough, and more money would have to be raised. That was the point of choosing a site like Sutton Hoo,

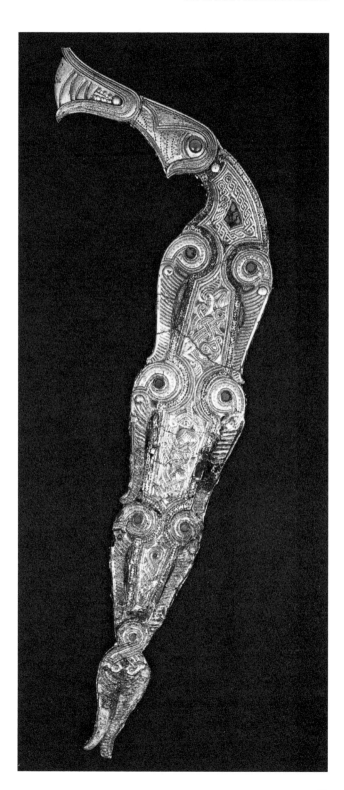

2.11: The dragon from the shield. It is an aerial creature with four pairs of wings, but also has feet with big toes (*SHSB* II, Plate 3; 63-5).

2.12: Charles Phillips on his last visit to Sutton Hoo in conversation with the author.
(EDWARD MORGAN)

which had the power to stimulate new kinds of financial support for archaeology. Using students was not necessarily a prescription for low standards. Students would be trained in formal 'field schools', not used as cheap labour. Units must not operate restrictive practices under the guise of 'professionalism': there had to be a way for a new generation to get into archaeology, just as we had all done. Why should students be introduced to field archaeology only on under-resourced, unprofessional field projects? By welcoming students, the Sutton Hoo project would help to teach a new generation of academics to dig. But the most important objective of the project was to generate useful research for both the early medieval and the prehistoric periods. The rationale for British archaeology could not remain just 'rescue'; it must be, or become, research-driven, and thus build up the stock of community support and ensure its own survival.

These arguments were largely effective. Winding up the meeting, Martin Biddle, the celebrated excavator of Winchester City, announced: 'This has been a turning point in British archaeology. For the first time a project has been presented to the archaeological fraternity before it has happened.' The mood was now more positive and generally supportive, if occasionally sceptical. Later in the year *Treasure Hunting Monthly* also revised its position, suggesting that the publicised approach was sensible, and invited its readers not to obstruct it. However, if the cautious approach was to the liking of the broader archaeological community, this would have to be translated into much patience on the part of the sponsors. The BBC had signed a contract with the Sutton Hoo Committee, paying a facility fee for exclusive coverage. Would they stoically endure three years of scientific fiddling before any new mounds were opened? Luckily their appointed producer, Ray Sutcliffe, liked the scientific approach, and the committee was unwavering in its support. Shortly afterwards the committee reformed as the Sutton Hoo Research Trust with the same membership: Sir David Wilson, Sir David Attenborough and Leslie Webster for the British Museum, and Philip Rahtz, Barry Cunliffe, Michael Robbins and Christopher Brooke for the Society of Antiquaries, with Stanley West representing Suffolk County Council. Together they steered Sutton Hoo away from the heroic age of amazing discoveries and startling finds and embarked on a scientific expedition with a new emphasis and a new vocabulary. 'Evaluation', 'research agenda', 'ethical stance', 'remote mapping', 'project design', 'horizon mapping', 'recovery levels', 'excavation strategy', 'intervention', 'analytical destiny', 'management plan': these were the catchphrases of the new campaign, and broadly represented the programme it was to follow.

The early discoverers, conservators and researchers of Sutton Hoo were giants; and we new researchers saw further because we stood on their shoulders. What we saw, however, led us off in a new direction (**Fig.2.12**).

3 | A NEW CAMPAIGN
Research and excavation 1983-2016

A context for the context ♦ *The Kingdom of East Anglia survey* ♦ *What to dig?*
The evaluation programme 1983-86 ♦ *Design* ♦ *Excavation 1986-92* ♦
The 'sandmen' ♦ *Digging mounds* ♦ *A wrecked ship: Mound 2 dissected* ♦ *Cremations*
under mounds ♦ *Horse and bed: Mounds 17 and 14* ♦ *Interpreting the discoveries* ♦
New owners, new future

The new Sutton Hoo expedition was organised in three parts: one devised for the site itself, 'the excavation programme' (including evaluation and strategy); one for the region in which it lay, the 'kingdom of East Anglia survey'; and the third, a programme of 'comparative studies' - formal and informal dialogues with scholars engaged in similar expeditions. The aim was to describe seventh-century society and determine how it changed, discover what a kingdom was, when and why the people of East Anglia had created one and how they interacted with others across the sea. For East Anglia was only one of a dozen 'kingdoms' that were beginning to make themselves visible around the North Sea coast in the fifth to eighth centuries AD (**Fig.3.1**).

A CONTEXT FOR THE CONTEXT

The comparative studies, which did much to broaden and deepen the research agenda for the project, were formalised at a series of meetings, beginning with one at Spoleto in Italy in 1983. In this conference, memorable among other things for a small but palpable earthquake, ideas were aired about what a site like Sutton Hoo could mean and how we could know more about it. Current research suggested that burial mounds, or at least big burial mounds, were something new for the Anglo-Saxons in the seventh century, and should have a special meaning for that time. They might have served, as had been suggested for Iron Age barrows in central Europe, as a way of marking the ownership of land. The barrow stood on a hill and 'documented' what the buried ancestor had owned, perhaps by virtue of what could be seen from its summit. Barrows had political meanings, too, and in seventh-century England the erection of a burial mound might have signalled the adoption of a specific political alignment. Barrow building had begun in Kent in the sixth century, in the form of large cemeteries containing numerous small barrows; at the end of the sixth century the practice appears to have migrated

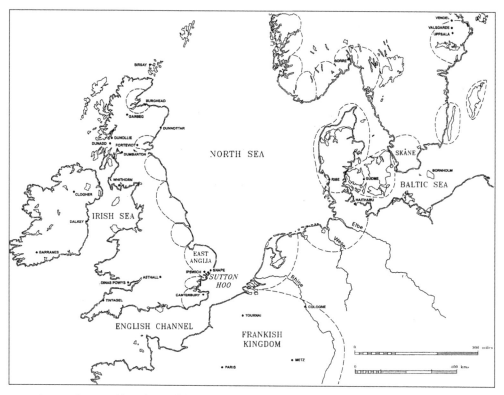

3.1: Early coastal kingdoms of the North Sea (author).

elsewhere, into Anglo-Saxon areas outside Kent. Surely it could be no coin-cidence that Augustine had arrived in the late sixth century, and that Kent had become a Christian ally of France by then? The barrows of Sutton Hoo and elsewhere could thus be read as demonstrative protests against the creep of Christianity, monuments of anti-Christian defiance. They may even have included the memorials of disaffected Kentish aristocrats, unwilling to bend the knee to Rome. The burying of Christian objects in the Sutton Hoo graves need have no pro-Christian significance. Examples from Nubia showed that the burial mounds erected there at the end of another empire (the Meroitic) had included emblems from half a dozen different religions: a scarab, a love charm in Greek, three lead curses and a gold cross. Whether or not they were the burials of kings, the Sutton Hoo mounds should be political signals, in this case of pagan defiance from a people threatened by Christian encroachment.[1]

The meaning of early medieval burial mounds was pursued in a seminar at Cambridge on 13-15 September 1984 entitled 'Princely Burials'. Such burials, the delegates agreed, must have had some connection with social organisa-tion; the community that made them should have been highly stratified, with an aristocracy on top. What did it mean, then, if a community adopted burial

3.2: The great burial mounds at Gamla Uppsala, Sweden (author).

mounds when it had not previously had them? Wolfgang Böhme showed how the building of burial mounds had begun in the lower Rhine in the fifth century and moved eastwards, reaching the upper Rhine by the eighth. This could mean that communities along the Rhine were becoming socially stratified one after another, building barrows as and when they acquired an aristocracy.[2] But there was at least one other possibility: perhaps the communities always had an aristocracy, but there had come a moment when it became politically expedient to celebrate it. Only then would an investment in such an elaborate thing as a furnished burial mound be worth the trouble. What would provoke such an investment? A political threat was one obvious answer, and the coming of Christianity may have been the threat in question. Burial mounds could thus mean either an aristocracy in the process of formation or one under threat. The Sutton Hoo mounds may have fallen into one or both of these categories.

For some, all these forays into interpretation were fanciful; perhaps Sutton Hoo was simply a traditional burial ground and had a long history of use stretching back deep into prehistory. In the countryside life moves slowly, and nothing could be understood except by what went before. The significance of Sutton Hoo's prehistory was addressed at a meeting held at Oxford in 1985. No one doubted that a prehistoric settlement existed before the Anglo-Saxon burial mounds, but there were mixed views on how seriously it should be taken. When Brian Hope-Taylor had excavated the first British early medieval palace at Yeavering in Northumbria, a site all the more evocative because it had been known to Bede, he had shown that great timber halls had stood on a site that was already ancient before the Anglian kings of Northumbria developed it. From this he created a vision of a long-lived folk centre, the scene of ceremonies and gatherings, a special place never forgotten and always significant through the centuries.[3] Could Sutton Hoo have functioned in a similar way? Few thought continuous use to be likely. In a modification of the continuity idea, Richard Bradley showed how the people of the early Middle Ages could recognise the 'vocabulary' of the landscape, choosing for new development an old site that had either never lost its meaning or could be readily reinvested with the properties of a tradition.[4] Others felt that 'continuity' was a 'con'; the Anglo-Saxons saw little and understood less of their prehistoric predecessors. Others, again, felt that the case was open, and that the prehistoric site at least required its own research programme. The suspected 'Beaker period' settlement was a rarity not to be ignored; the whole prehistoric sequence should be sampled as economically as possible, and the question of its connection with the Anglo-Saxon cemetery should be left on the table. It would in any case be wrong to give the impression to sponsors that the prehistoric period did not matter; the prehistoric features occurred at the same level, cut into the same natural subsoil, as the early medieval graves. It would not be possible to dig one without digging the other.

An opportunity to place the proposed Sutton Hoo research in the wider British context occurred again at Oxford in 1986, at a conference entitled 'The Origins of Anglo-Saxon Kingdoms'. Here the battle lines became clearer between those for whom the Anglo-Saxons had always had kings and those for whom kingship was an innovation of the late sixth century. A king, according to the latter theory, was someone who could claim jurisdiction over a territory and tax it. The onset of taxation was marked by the arrival of wealthy farmsteads with evidence for storing grain or processing animals on a large scale. The imposition of tax was also marked on this theory by an absence of grave goods from the majority of graves: the subservient classes among the English no longer needed to indicate their membership of a supernatural tribe by dressing and equipping their dead, but gave the same resources in tax to a new and real authority: the king and the kingdom. On this reasoning, kingship was an innovation of the late sixth century.[5] The fuller exploration of Sutton Hoo should test these hypotheses. Had these burials a unique, a royal role in East Anglia, or were they just the memorials of one landowning family among many?

These formal meetings – 'focus groups', we should probably call them now – were extremely helpful for drawing up the research agenda for the Sutton

Hoo project. Travels and conversations in Denmark, Norway and Sweden also added immeasurably to the strength of the project design, by showing both the problems that had been encountered in Scandinavia and the way in which many of them had been overcome. We in Britain were latecomers to the archaeological science of determining social organisation and territorial control in the early Middle Ages. The Mälaren, around Lake Mälar in the Stockholm region of Sweden, had long been studied in this way, and for south-west Norway Bjorn Myrhe had produced a fine analysis in 1986 demonstrating the existence of a chain of coastal kingdoms in the fifth to sixth centuries.[6]

Much of this educational travel was undertaken through the kindness of the BBC, with whom I was putting together a series of films. We went to Gamla Uppsala, the huge mounds in the Uppland area of Sweden, traditional burial place of the Inglinga dynasty and scene in the ninth century of the mass sacrificial hanging of men, horses and dogs that had been observed and reported by the missionary Adam of Bremen (Fig.3.2). Further up the River Fyris was Valsgärde, the cemetery of ship-graves where Bruce-Mitford had earlier lent a hand, now being slowly brought to publication, with its ships, helmets, dog-leashes and horse-harness; further north still was the famous ship-burial site of Vendel, which in Scandinavia gives its name to the period around the seventh-eighth centuries. Beyond Vendel, the forest stretches away to the Arctic Circle. These Swedish ship-burial cemeteries, which date from the seventh century to the tenth, are the sites that most resemble that at Sutton Hoo.

We later recorded footage at Jelling in Denmark, the central place of the early Danish kingdom. Here King Gorm had first been buried in a giant burial mound and then dug up and reinterred in a church on the same spot by his son, Harold Bluetooth, who, as it says in runes on the great Jelling stone, 'had conquered all Denmark and Norway and made the Danes Christians'. We visited the Viking ship-burial at Ladby, conserved *in situ* in an underground shelter by the Carlsberg Foundation. And in Norway we visited Borre, where a new project had been launched to study a cemetery of Viking and pre-Viking mounds grouped beside the Oslo fjord. There could be no doubt of the huge importance of the burial mound in Scandinavia as a symbol of rank, territorial control and political conviction. How far did England adopt this message of the mounds? Were the people of East Anglia influenced or even aware of Scandinavian ideas? It was important to know if the communities living around the North Sea in the seventh century were in contact with each other, forming a network in which to contest the political options and express their choice in monuments.[7]

Another meeting at Oxford, in 1988, explored the possibility that the mariners of the fifth to seventh centuries enjoyed a regular traffic across the

3.3: *Edda*, a replica of the Viking ship found in the mound at Oseberg in Norway, under sail in Heroy fjord in 1988. Shortly after this picture was taken *Edda* capsized and sank.
(B. MARDEN-JONES)

North Sea. If 'blue water crossings' - that is, direct voyages between Denmark, Norway and England - were easy and frequent, as opposed to creeping around the coast, East Anglia would have been up-to-date with Scandinavian thinking in the seventh century and could have been routinely influenced by it. This was a counter to the prevailing notion that the North Sea in the 'Dark Ages' was a forbidding barrier, and became a thoroughfare only with the Vikings. But, surely, the Sutton Hoo ship could also sail and even cross the sea? Some of these bold convictions were tested by practical experience. In the ship-museum at Oslo are preserved the Viking ships that were excavated at Gokstad, Tune and Oseberg. A replica of Gokstad (*Viking*) had been sailed in 1892 through the ice fields and up the St Lawrence to Chicago, to make a telling appearance at the celebrations to mark the 400th anniversary of the 'discovery' of America by Christopher Columbus. In readiness for 1992, a perfect replica of the Oseberg burial ship, last resting place of the formidable Queen Åse, had been constructed. Up on the icy coast near Ålesund our film crew was to row, sail and witness the disastrous maiden voyage of this beautiful ship, which was named the *Edda*. Here we learnt that sailing in a narrow keel-less boat before the wind is as thrilling a sensation as life has to offer, but, abeam to the wind, the sensation can be perilously short. In the course of our learning how to tack with a single square sail our ship capsized and sank, we crew barely escaping with our lives. If the Anglo-Saxons already knew how to sail and regularly crossed the sea, they would have needed skills of a high order to defeat a head wind - skills we have now nearly lost. Perhaps the Viking gift to history was not the long-ship, but the knowledge of how to tack (**Fig.3.3**).[8]

These adventures, encounters and consultations, and the deliberate policy of sharing the decisions and results with the interested community at every stage (it was small enough), were immensely helpful to the project throughout its life, in particular during the evaluation, when they inspired and guided the project, influencing what was done on the ground and its eventual interpretation. The programme of scholarly exchanges continued until the project's end. In 1989 the seminar series climaxed in Sutton Hoo's 50th anniversary year, with three conferences held at the Universities of Minnesota, Kalamazoo and York. By this time the digging was well advanced and an interim account of what had been found was available to inspire imagination, interpretation and controversy. At the York conference, the last in the series, a mighty feast was held in the Merchant Adventurers Hall. 'Mirth was renewed, laughter rang out and cup-bearers poured wine', and then, by way of entertainment, our own poet spoke in the hall. On his feet among the tables, gesticulating and prowling in an imaginary Dark Age heathland, the actor Julian Glover held 200 diners spellbound in the candlelight, reciting and performing the story of Beowulf, Grendel and Grendel's mother.[9]

THE KINGDOM OF EAST ANGLIA SURVEY

The second theatre of research was to be the geographical region in which Sutton Hoo was situated. In 1986 interested parties from the academic and fieldwork sectors of the archaeology profession gathered at Ipswich to decide how they were going to find the Anglo-Saxon kingdom of East Anglia. It was plain that the most important task was to map its settlements and observe their patterns in the landscape. The shape of a settlement and the size of buildings it contained might be a more reliable indication of social organisation than the form of a cemetery and its graves. A grave might be an investment in the next world, but a settlement would be an investment in this one, and thus reflect more accurately the distribution of resources. The East Anglian region, almost alone in Britain, had used pottery continuously from the Neolithic period to the twentieth century; and, as had been shown by the stunning results of fieldwork at the little village of Witton, Norfolk and Suffolk archaeologists had developed ways of using pottery picked up off the fields to show where earlier settlements were, how big they were and how much land they had under the plough - without doing any digging.[10]

The regional survey designed by the Ipswich seminar divided East Anglia into six sample zones, of which the first to be tackled was the local one, the Deben Valley. The method was straightforward: in each zone, accessible fields were walked in systematic strips and pottery, flint and other materials were picked up off the surface, identified, dated and plotted on a map to the nearest 10m. After covering a number of fields a pattern began to emerge, which showed the settlement areas of different periods. The fields were then walked again, this time with a metal detector; metal finds would help to distinguish the rank of the settlements, since high-quality metalwork should be confined to the more important sites. John Newman, the Suffolk Archaeological Unit field officer who led the survey, already knew the area very well, his negotiations with farmers giving him access to a representative sample of land. After five years spent examining the fields in optimum conditions he was able to reveal the pattern of shifting settlements from the Neolithic period to the Middle Ages (**Fig.3.4**). The prehistoric and Anglo-Saxon settlements in general were located less than 1km from running water, while the Roman and medieval settlements were more widely deployed. Within the Anglo-Saxon period special settlements could be distinguished that were long-lived or had a particularly large spread of pottery on the surface of the fields. Using this evidence, Rendlesham emerged as a chief place of the Anglo-Saxon region.

At the time of the recent campaign the Deben Valley Survey suffered from one disadvantage: little new reconnaissance was possible from the air. Although it was, on the whole, good flat arable land, with excellent cropmark potential, there were problems of access from the air because three sensitive military air bases lay within a few kilometres. The US Air Force offered a little compensation in the form of a flight in a Super Jolly Green Giant, a helicopter with an open back, which provided hair-raising views of the burial mounds in their riverine setting. Other helpful vistas were offered from a hot air balloon, courtesy of Brian Ribbans, a well-known racer. From it one could see the fields stretching east to Rendlesham Forest and Sutton Heath, south to the estuary and the North Sea, north to Wilford Bridge, the first dry crossing point of the Deben, and west to the tree-fringed river with Melton, Woodbridge and Martlesham beyond.

The Deben Valley area also formed the subject of a special documentary study by Peter Warner, in which he examined the early geography of the Wilford Hundred using documents, place-names and maps. The left bank of the Deben opposite Woodbridge was notable for its lack of churches: there were none apart from that at Sutton itself, suggesting a 'pagan enclave' that may have endured around Sutton Hoo beyond the period in which parishes were generally created in the tenth to eleventh centuries. Warner also discovered that the seventeenth green of the Woodbridge Golf Course, situated on an

3.4: (Above) The zones chosen by the East Anglia kingdom survey. Sutton Hoo lies in the one marked 'S. E. Suffolk'. (Below) The four maps show the prehistoric, Roman and Anglo-Saxon settlement patterns as located by John Newman of Suffolk Archaeological Unit.
(J. NEWMAN)

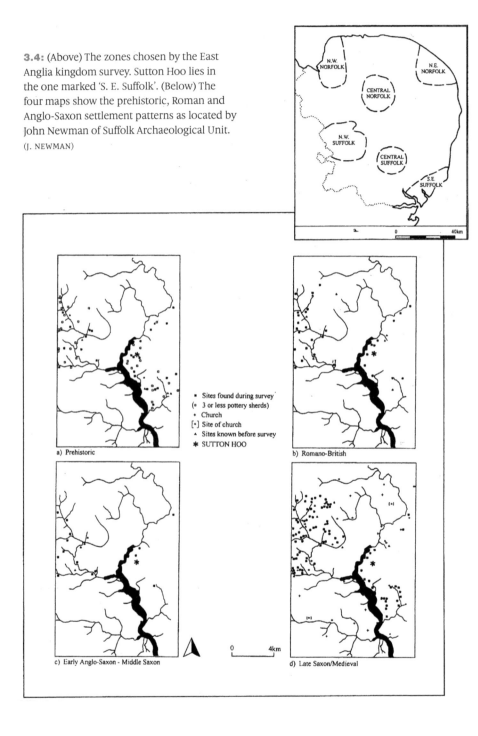

- Sites found during survey
(○ 3 or less pottery sherds)
+ Church
[+] Site of church
▲ Sites known before survey
✳ SUTTON HOO

a) Prehistoric

b) Romano-British

c) Early Anglo-Saxon - Middle Saxon

d) Late Saxon/Medieval

0   4km

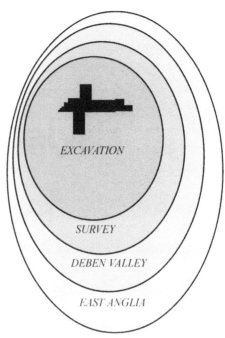

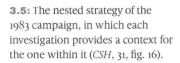

3.5: The nested strategy of the 1983 campaign, in which each investigation provides a context for the one within it (*CSH*, 31, fig. 16).

eminence above Wilford Bridge, was once called Harrow Pightle, an Anglo-Saxon name indicating a temple site. For another, perhaps not unconnected, reason this place was to have an important role in the later interpretation of the site. It was shown on a map of 1601 as 'Gallows Hill' and carried a little drawing of the gallows itself. This identification received some endorsement later during a round of golf with the secretary of the club, when the information was divulged that some years ago, when the land was landscaped (in the service of the world's most exasperating game), several human skeletons had been found. These were presumably the remains of victims who had died on the scaffold.

The wider picture gained from the European experience and the exploration of the Deben Valley and the settlement pattern in Anglo-Saxon East Anglia provided the essential geographic context for Sutton Hoo (**Fig.3.5**). Now to describe the third theatre of the campaign, the investigation of the site itself.

WHAT TO DIG? THE EVALUATION PROGRAMME 1983-86
Work on site began in 1983 with a programme of evaluation, which aimed at answering the following questions: How extensive was the archaeological site? Which periods were represented? How well had evidence for each period survived? What could that evidence tell us?

3.6: The contours of the surface of the Sutton Hoo burial ground brought out by oblique lighting at night. In the foreground is a track that was in use from before 1601. Wooden shuttering protects a pilot excavation in Mound 2. Beyond can be seen the lights of Melton.
(NIGEL MACBETH)

Many techniques for mapping buried and invisible strata were applied in order to look at the surface of the ground, through the ground and under the ground to assess what was left of Sutton Hoo and what it could still tell us without at first exposing or disturbing it. The mapping techniques were chosen and deployed in 'zones' that reflected the current land use: plough soil, pasture and woodland. On the barrow site, the priority was to remove the bracken and gorse, expel the rabbits and clear away the debris.

Soon the mounds emerged clean and tidy, if still marked here and there by the tracked vehicles of the army. The following spring, released from the tyranny of the bracken rhizomes, a hundred different species of plants pushed up through the leathery turf, their selective growth producing a colourful pattern. Dozens of square and circular patches could be discerned, strongly marked by sheep's fescue and moss: these patches were the ghosts of backfilled and overgrown holes dug by farmers, archaeologists - and treasure-hunters. Taking a leaf out of the treasure-hunters' book, a metal detector was used to map the fragments of metal on the surface of the site; most of them consisted of bullets and .303 cartridge cases (some stamped '1942', the year in which Sutton Hoo served as a military training area). In the centre of the site was a mass of bottle tops discarded near the old site-hut used by the British Museum excavation team of 1965-71. The surface of the cemetery itself was mapped with an electronic theodolite, and the results enhanced by computer-generated contours. More vividly still, strong lighting thrown across the

3.7: An early archaeological use of soil-sounding radar. Messrs. Oceanfix using a Japanese instrument on Mound 2 in 1988. (NIGEL MACBETH)

site at night illuminated all the little dips and hollows captured in the newly cleaned surface (**Fig.3.6**).

During the evaluation, before the bustle of the full seasons, with their crews of 50 to 60 diggers, it was imperative to maintain a presence on site in order to guard the mounds, now mown and, with their smooth green sward, as smart as a golf course. Indeed, they looked as though they should host a game of golf, and several local variants of the sport were invented. One consisted of chipping from the top of one mound to the top of another, and on a good day one could play them in numerical order, beginning at Mound 1 and ending at Mound 14. But the finest practice was to play down from the top of Mound 1 on to Mound 12 without hitting the tree which sheltered it, chipping short and hoping the ball would run on under the tree and stay perched up on the slight eminence of Mound 12. It was practically impossible, and I always hooked and left it short, where for some reason it rolled back towards me. In due course the reason was discovered; when the sun was going down behind Top Hat Wood a very faint shadow - two, in fact - could be seen in front of the tree; and in this manner two new mounds, Mound 17 and Mound 18, were found and included in the reckoning.

Seeing through the turf was accomplished by the range of geophysical instruments then current. The different machines were first tested over a trial area that was subsequently excavated: resistivity and fluxgate gradiometry were found to work well and were used in mapping the wide area around the site. The Sutton Hoo evaluation also introduced British archaeology to soil-penetrating radar in the form of a pioneering machine built by Mike Gorman for the Scott Polar Institute, Cambridge, to map mountains under the polar ice. This personable and photogenic yellow tractor was later to be deposed by a more commercial Japanese apparatus. The timed emissions produced by the radar were reflected from soil/sand interfaces and so affected to look deep into the mounds, detecting a burial chamber under Mound 12 and the robber trench through Mound 2 (**Fig.3.7**).

A fair bit was already known about the underground world of the barrow cemetery from the excavations that had taken place in 1938-9 and 1965-71. Further previews were achieved by re-excavating a wartime anti-glider ditch and a silage pit dug in the 1950s, both of which showed the strata of the prehistoric site in varied states of preservation. The bracken had clearly been the biggest single agent of destruction, reaching down into the prehistoric pits and into the burial mounds with rhizomes up to 3m long. Ideally, a preview was also needed within a mound, in order to assess the degree to which the mounds, the burial chambers and the old ground surface had survived and to know whether any special means would be required to understand them. For this, part of Basil Brown's 1938 trench through Mound 2 was reopened and re-excavated to the bottom (**Fig.3.8**). The line of his 'boat' could be seen, dark and gently curving on the sandy floor, with the marker canes still where he had placed them in 1938 to show the location of rivets (Fig. 1.9). It looked unlike an early medieval boat and unlike a burial. Plans were laid for the wholesale dissection of the mound.

The adjoining land, meanwhile, under the plough and bearing a crop of potatoes, was examined by 'fieldwalking', by which method thousands of prehistoric flints and pottery sherds were collected and plotted. The coarse predictions of the geophysical surveys, the air photographs and the fieldwalking were then subjected to 'ground-truthing' by digging transects across the fields (**Fig.3.9**). The ditches of the prehistoric field system duly appeared, together with the pits containing pottery and flint, datable from the Neolithic to the Iron Age. But in one transect, stretching 100m away from the eastern edge of the grassy mounds, a lozenge-shaped pit was located that was not of the common prehistoric form. On lowering the fill it was found to contain a long dark smear, at first thought to be a root; but it soon took the familiar shape of a femur and tibia: it was a grave, containing the stain left by a human body. The remainder of the grave was soon excavated and its inmate revealed.

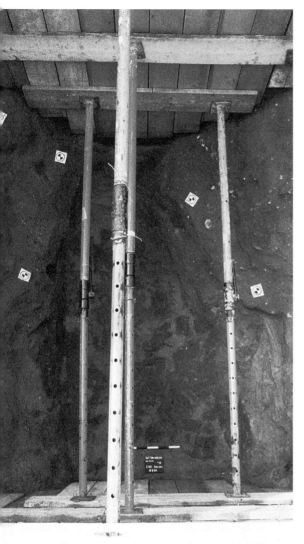

3.8: Pilot excavation in Mound 2 in 1988, encountering Basil Brown's excavation of 1938 (see Fig. 1.8).

3.9: Exploratory trench (Intervention 22) through fields adjacent to the mounds previously surveyed by surface collection.
(NIGEL MACBETH)

There was no skeleton, and little bone; the body had decayed to a hard dark brown crusty sand - our introduction to the 'sandmen'. With gentle trowel and brush, the line of the corpse could be seen or felt for, and so defined in three dimensions: on its back, with its hands together and head tilted forward, in a grave that seemed too small. The grave lay 70m from the nearest known burial mound. A broader area was opened, and at once more graves appeared. A larger extension still was opened to the east, where there were no more graves; and for another 50m still beyond that an absence of graves was gratifyingly, if laboriously, confirmed. In this way an eastern edge to the Sutton Hoo cemetery was located.

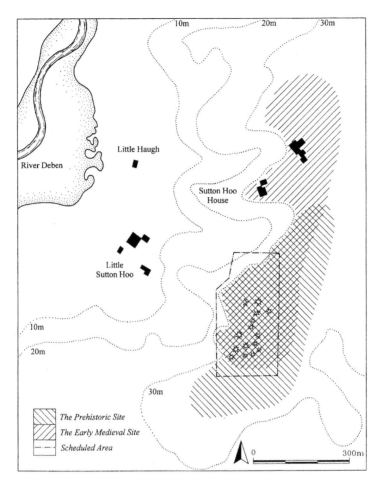

3.10: The extent of the prehistoric settlement and early medieval burial ground at Sutton Hoo as predicted in 1986.

Over, on and through the ground, the techniques of evaluation had endeavoured to present us with a shop window of what lay in store. In the autumn of 1985 we were ready to pronounce on the value of the site. It consisted of a large prehistoric settlement complex stretching for some 10 hectares, on top of which had developed an early medieval mound cemetery of at least 4.5 hectares (**Fig.3.10**). The deposits in the central area generally lay up to 50cm deep, the prehistoric strata being protected by the early medieval burial mounds; even beneath the mounds, however, they had been badly scrambled by plants, animals and man (**Fig.3.11**). Outside the scheduled area, where the land was under the plough, all earthworks had been rubbed out, but the archaeological features were less disturbed because, in recent times at least, they had been protected by cultivation from bracken roots and rabbits. The Anglo-Saxon site seemed to consist largely of graves. There were about

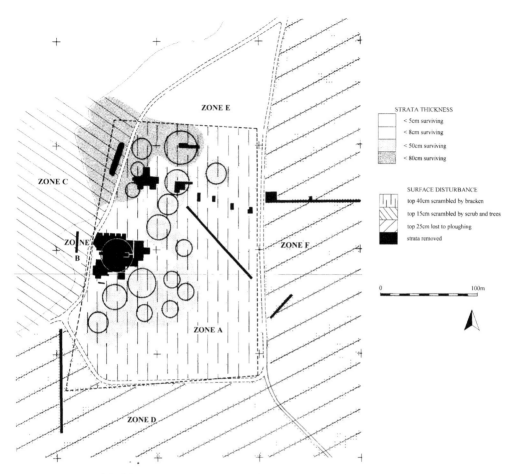

3.11: A model of the archaeological deposit of the mound cemetery and its immediate surroundings, as constructed in the evaluation phase (1986).

18 suspected burial mounds and most should yield some information, even if they had already been excavated. From the contacts made around Mound 5 (in 1970) and now on the eastern periphery, we imagined then that flat graves could be present in large numbers. The condition of bodies was severely degraded; sex determination and pathology would be difficult, but there was enough osseous matter for radiocarbon determination. If the density were to continue between the two burial sites, maybe several hundred graves were there to be found. In this we were to be proved wrong.[11]

DESIGN

This was the picture predicted by the evaluation; the *strategy* now came into play. What could the Sutton Hoo site be persuaded to tell us, out of all we wanted to know? Over the long period of prehistory and the Roman period,

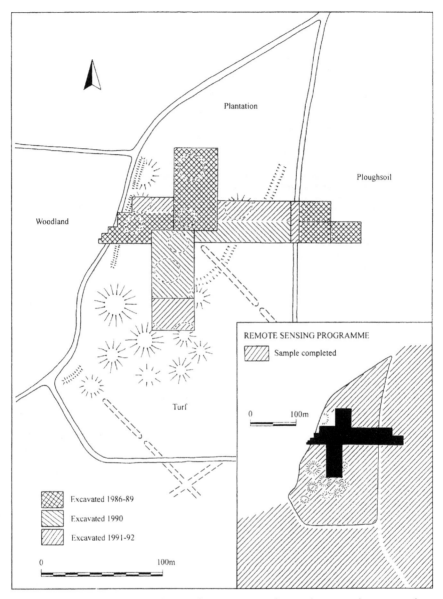

3.12: The excavation strategy. The cruciform transect indicates the area to be excavated: about one hectare in extent. Inset (hatched) is the area to be surveyed by remote mapping.

the best information on offer was the history of land use - how the land had been divided, cultivated and settled. The location of the settlements would come most readily from the Deben Valley Survey, and that of land boundaries from aerial photography. The best use of excavation, therefore, was to get dates on the field boundaries and establish their character. It would be particularly useful to know when the landscape was first partitioned, since this could signal the arrival of landownership in this part of Britain. Pollen taken from under and outside the burial mounds could confirm or modify Geoffrey Dimbleby's sequence of the environment: oak forest (Mesolithic), cleared in the Neolithic, grazing lands occasionally cultivated for arable (wheat) until the Roman period, grazing throughout the Middle Ages and a final reversion to heath in the sixteenth or seventeenth century. Lastly, it would be interesting to learn which prehistoric earthworks (if any) had been standing when the Anglo-Saxons adopted the place for their cemetery.

Now we had to address the question: what to dig? The targets were ambitious: the changes in society and the coming of kings, the contacts, alliances and policies of the people of early East Anglia. Would big questions need a big dig? To 'dig the whole thing', which was the mantra of the age, was a prescription that I personally would never accept. We should dig only to answer questions, and they must be questions important enough to merit the destruction of part of a unique monument. If the questions demanded that we should dig the whole thing, they were the wrong questions, and we should think again.

Our reasoning was as follows: the story of the politics of early England was embedded in the burial rites practised at Sutton Hoo. So the aim would be to obtain a sample of the burial rites practised from the beginning to the end of the use of the cemetery. Although there was no way of knowing for sure where the beginning and end of the cemetery were, there was a certain logic to be drawn from the terrain. The Anglo-Saxons were likely to have begun their cemetery at the edge of the scarp overlooking the River Deben, and the latest burials should be those furthest inland. If this were the case then a transect should be excavated from west to east, west at the edge of the scarp and east where the furthest burials from the mounds had already been located. The transect was to be 32 m wide, wide enough to catch a burial mound should such a thing have been built there. Within this transect, examples of the burial rites from earliest to latest should appear and signs of any major structural phase should be captured.

Needless to say, there was at least one flaw in this argument: supposing the cemetery did not grow inland in that logical way? Do cemeteries develop in a logical manner? The Anglo-Saxons may have begun their burial at the south end and dug a trail of graves wandering northwards along the scarp. Or they may have clustered them in groups belonging to different families. Accordingly, the proposed east-west transect was paired with a north-south one, so that the design would consist of two transects at right angles. The area to be excavated was cruciform: the east-west arms stretched 200m, encompassing the known limits of the cemetery; the north-south transect, at 100m, was just long enough, it was felt, to determine any axis of growth (**Fig.3.12**).

3.13: The excavation as completed in 1992. (JUSTIN GARNER-LAHIRE)

The excavation area, so devised, was to be placed at the north end of the cemetery, because that was where most of the previous digging had been done. Mound 2 had already been trenched, Mound 5 had been started; the British Museum team had dug eight or more trenches in the area. Our cruciform transect was therefore placed with its centre over Mound 5, its arms stretching north over Mound 2 and south over Mound 7, west to embrace the newly discovered Mounds 17 and 18 and east to include those flat graves on the periphery. The proposed excavation area contained eight burial mounds that were to be wholly or partly excavated. The number of flat graves anticipated at that time in the chosen area was 200-300 on the basis of those found. The area to be excavated was 1 hectare, or less than a quarter of the known cemetery. Outside and conserved for the future were nine or ten burial mounds in 3.5 hectares, among them those most likely to be still intact. Conserved for the future would be the best deposits that Sutton Hoo still had to offer. This excavation area was also well suited to the prehistoric strategy: a major ditch system had already been located there by the British Museum archaeologists. There would be buried soils and intact prehistoric strata under the mounds; and there was ample space to map prehistoric features and thus increase the likelihood of producing a good account of land use over 3,000 years.

Now it remained to cost the excavation, fund it and do it. The Sutton Hoo Research Trust received the proposal for six years' work, like a blueprint from an architect, and scrutinised it; then they accepted it, resolving and minuting at the annual general meeting on 15 January 1986 that 'The Trust has received

3.14: Horizon mapping near Mound 5. The surface is prepared with trowel and spray, photographed and the edges of the exposed features tagged and surveyed. In this photograph an early Bronze Age ditch (foreground) and an Iron Age ditch (parallel to it) are cut by the pit of tomb-robbers. Rupert Bruce-Mitford inspects the location of the Mound 5 burial. (NIGEL MACBETH)

the Sutton Hoo Project Design ... and approves it in principle. The Trust states its firm intention to complete the excavation and ... its publication.' This was an enlightened and courageous act of faith by the Trustees, and at the time rather novel. The proposal to undertake a research excavation had been detailed in advance, stating the exact area that was to be opened, why, and with what expected results, how long it would take and how much it was going to cost. This information, integrated into a 'project design', was then published, with the affirmation that it would be supported from beginning to end. It was felt to be a significant moment for British archaeology.[12]

EXCAVATION 1986-92

The excavation programme began in August 1986 and continued, in seven seasons, until the spring of 1992 **(Fig.3.13)**. The cruciform transect was divided into five sectors: north, west, south, east and far east, each of which was stripped and then mapped, and the located features excavated. At every stage the ground was sprinkled with water to improve the colour contrast

3.15: (left)
Area excavation
in progress
over Mound 6
(foreground) and
Mound 7.
(NIGEL MACBETH)

3.16: (opposite)
A 'sandman'. The
body survives as
bars of dark sand
containing flecks
of bone. In this
example (Burial
34) the excavators
encountered a
wooden container
(A) within which lay
the body (B).
(NIGEL MACBETH)

between the subsoil and the pits and graves that had been dug into it. In small areas of 4 × 8m every part of the 10,000 sq. m site was soaked and stroked into its most vivid definition, and then photographed from a tower and surveyed. This procedure, which here acquired the name 'horizon mapping', captured thousands of features, some modern, some early medieval, some prehistoric and some natural (**Fig.3.14**).[13] At first every one of these features was dug, but as our powers of recognition improved it became possible to identify the features of each period and apply selectivity, thus digging less. As a deliberate policy, all the early medieval, a representative sample of the prehistoric and a few of the more puzzling natural features were excavated; so that even in the excavated area many located features, not then germane to the inquiry, await the questions of a future age (**Fig.3.15**).

THE 'SANDMEN'

The first sector to be opened and mapped was on the far eastern periphery, where we had made contact with a cemetery of 'sand bodies' (**Figs 3.16a,**

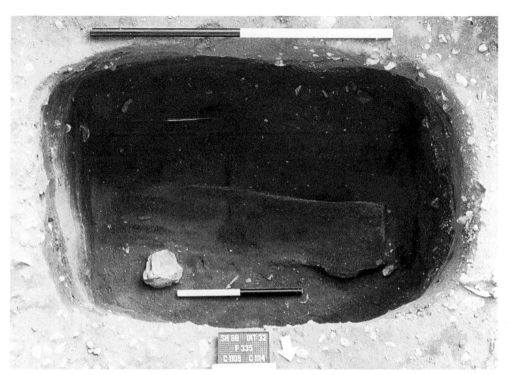

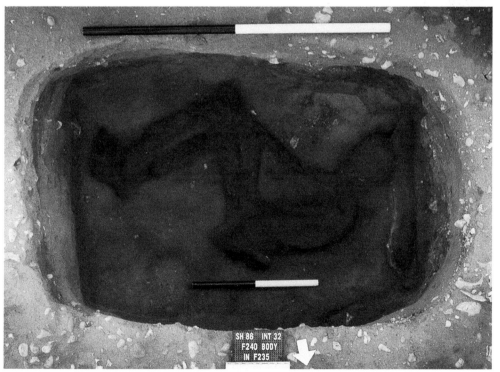

3.17: In Burial 30, the sandy body preserved the shell of the skeleton. (NIGEL MACBETH)

3.16b). When first spotted on the horizon surface the graves were oblong patches of dark sandy fill against the yellow sand and gravel of the subsoil. The mixed fill was then removed in horizontal slices ('stages') until the first anomaly appeared. If this anomaly took the form of a dark straight line, it generally meant that the grave had a wooden coffin, and that this was one of its sides, a decayed board viewed edge-on from the top (**Fig.3.17**). More often, the first thing to appear was a crusty brown lump of sand the consistency of sugar, which looked dark to the eyes, felt rough to the fingers, rasped under the trowel and curved away downwards. This was evidently part of a decayed body. Follow the edges of the surface of the brown crust, taking away the softer fill beside it, and the shape would be revealed: a head, an arm, a pelvis, a leg. The whole sand body was eventually defined like this, not as a skeleton but a brown person. Bone would sometimes survive, but it would be inside the crusty sand jacket, showing that what was being defined was the shape of the flesh itself. Some of these were permanently captured in three dimensions with the use of silicon rubber (**Fig.3.18**).

For most of us the shape of a human body is familiar and more or less predictable, and the excavator feeling for the sand bodies in the grave expected to have an easy time of it. Once you have the skull or a leg, you would know which way round the body lay and could say with reasonable confidence

3.18: Making a mould of a 'sand-body' using silicon rubber. The moulds were used to make fibre-glass casts for display to visitors, who rarely had the chance otherwise to see the evidence for these disconcerting burials at first hand.
(NIGEL MACBETH)

where the rest of a person was going to be. But the Sutton Hoo bodies often played tricks. A pelvis might be the wrong way up. A head would be found by a knee and a foot would rest on a ribcage. Some graves contained two people, and one contained three. It became increasingly clear that most of these bodies were buried in positions that were odd: one was kneeling, head to the floor of the grave; one stretched out, hand above the head; another folded forward, another folded back, another sideways; and, strangest of all, one splayed out in a hurdling position, accompanied by a wooden object that vaguely resembled an ard or primitive type of plough. He soon attracted the epithet of 'the ploughman'. Every burial seemed to be different, and the body positions of most, differing from the peaceful norm of a person laid out on their back, indicated some abuse of the individual that we referred to as 'ritual trauma' or 'deviance'.

3.19: Overview of excavations on Mound 5 (left) and Mound 2 (right), taken by a camera-kite (the photographer, holding the kite-strings, stands on the bank near the track). Mound 5 was excavated by the British Museum using the 'box' method; Mound 2 employs the 'quadrant method', where the boxes are offset to give cumulative sections.
(NIGEL MACBETH)

A number of excavators tried their hands at the definition of these extraordinary graves: old, young, expert or novice, suspended on planks or cradles and sheltered by windbreaks. All carefully followed the lead of their hands and eyes and ears, with spatula and handspray, and after a week or so of intensive work produced burial positions that were believable ... but grotesque. Burial 24 had his head at right angles to the vertebral column, and teeth, hand and wrist had survived to give a tableau that was both ghastly and sad. Those who saw it all came to a similar conclusion, and it was soon being referred to as 'the hanged man'. Could all these people have perished in a similarly brutal way? Were these the victims of war, execution or sacrifice? Or were all these bodies simply dumped without ceremony, the clients of a shoddy undertaker?

The varied postures, the use of coffins, the large size of some graves, seemingly dug to accommodate the posture, the early medieval radiocarbon dates that were soon received – these things seemed to argue at first against an execution cemetery. The group appeared to be Anglo-Saxon, with a ritual air. So could they have been sacrificial and, if so, why here? The sacrifices reported by Adam of Bremen at Gamla Uppsala, where men and animals were hanged on a tree, inevitably came to mind. Obligingly, in the centre of the Sutton Hoo eastern group of graves, a large pit was located, of a kind left by a fallen tree; it was surrounded by a set of post-sockets. These, we surmised, were the traces of a gallows.

A convincing interpretation would depend on seeing the large sample of burials that was anticipated. But now there was a big surprise. Throughout the whole excavation sample between the mounds, there proved to be hardly any graves at all. The total number of flat graves *expected* between the mounds was 200–300. It was in fact 39, and they were tightly disposed in two groups; one group was on the eastern periphery, as just described, and the other was around Mound 5; and not just near it but radially and tangentially clustered around it in a manner that gave rise to the interim term 'satellite burials'. Both groups included 'deviant' burials, victims of hanging, to which could be added some compelling examples of exposure on a gibbet. There was much online debate at the time in both the UK and the USA about whether these could be sacrifices contemporary with the mounds or executions of a later date. The matter was resolved, although not till 20 years later, in favour of execution. Stratigraphically, the earliest graves found around Mound 5 had been dug into its quarry pits, already partially refilled; and, from the radiocarbon dates received, execution was found to continue long after mound-burial had ceased (see Chapter 6).

Between the mounds great stretches of sand and gravel were meticulously examined, but, apart from the two groups already mentioned, only three graves were revealed, modestly furnished and probably of high-status children or adolescents. It seemed that to be buried at Sutton Hoo you had either to be an aristocrat ... or a deviant.

DIGGING MOUNDS

The excavation of every mound was an adventure in itself, and its potential history was complex. A mound was initially a place of burial, but could theoretically become a memorial where meetings took place. It might subsequently attract grave-robbers, who would cut trenches through it, and farmers, who would quarry it for soil. Each mound was not so much an encumbrance to be removed to expose a burial as a monument with a story of its own to tell. The archaeological problem in digging mounds was an old one: how to see in plan and profile at the same time. To discover the use of the mound surface and the cuts made into it would need inspection in plan over a wide area; but the make-up of the mound would be more visible in section, where the subtle distinctions between turf, sand and soil could be seen by looking sideways at a vertical cut through the heap. To try to gain the benefits of both plan and section, the mounds were 'peeled' against a grid of balks carrying a cumulative section. The sections were drawn when the balks stood about 1 m high - about as high as they could stand without risk of collapse - and then the balks were removed so that the new surface of the mound could again be examined in plan. Balks were then reinstated on the same lines and the process repeated (**Fig.3.19**).

The trowellers on a mound were well aware of the opaque mixture of the material they were trying to clean. The upper levels were hairy with root-lets ('like trying to trowel a heap of dead Airedales' was one assessment). The lower levels were streaked with yellow sand, dark turf stains and clusters of pebbles. Most mounds offered up to eight horizons, defined in the following way: *Horizon 0* was the surface of the turf. *Horizon 1* was the first surface under the dark soil that supported the turf: the Second World War slit-trenches were seen at this level. *Horizon 2* was the first level at which mound make-up could be seen: but only just. It was riddled with rabbit burrows betrayed by dark curved bands and huge fans of yellow sand. Scarcely a square metre of any mound was unmarked by rabbit burrows. Our dream of finding ancient activity at this level was frustrated, and was soon abandoned altogether, when we made the discovery that the mounds had been crossed from west to east by parallel grooves of a distinctive kind. The Sutton Hoo burial mounds had in fact been ploughed, and ploughed nearly flat. Once observed, it was hard to see how one could have failed to predict anything so obvious. How could mounds so broad have been at the same time so low? The mounds we were excavating had been very greatly reduced since their construction; perhaps several metres of their height had gone, and the agent of that reduction was (mainly) the plough.

At *Horizon 2* or *3* another common revelation was the second principal agent of any mound's destruction: the so-called 'robber trench'. This was a species of large pit or wide trench cut by earlier excavators whose efforts and discoveries had remained unrecorded or secret. Every mound had been visited at least once by these wanton explorers. In Mounds 6 and 7 the trench took the form of an immense cut 3m or more wide passing west-east almost through the entire mound. At one end was a set of steps cut in the sand, and at the other the splayed walkway of a wheelbarrow run. The steps were presumably used by the antiquary or landowner, and the wheelbarrow run by his labourers.

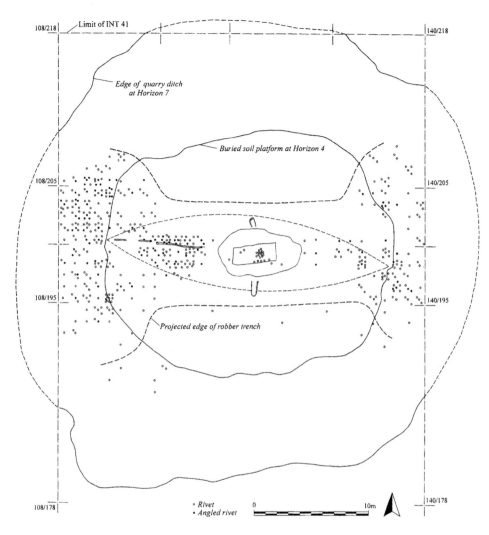

Edge of quarry ditch
at Horizon 7

Buried soil platform at Horizon 4

108/205

140/205

108/195

140/195

Projected edge of robber trench

108/178

140/178

∘ Rivet
• Angled rivet

0   10m

3.20: Plan of Mound 2 showing the pattern of disturbed ship rivets and the likely location of the nineteenth-century excavation trench.

The surface of the soil buried beneath the mound (designated as *Horizon 4*) revealed the edges of the burial chamber, but usually little else. This was because the soil under the mounds had also been ploughed, most recently between the Iron Age and the Anglo-Saxon period, and presented a dark opaque sandy surface littered with prehistoric artefacts disturbed by cultivation. At *Horizon 5* the plough marks could be clearly seen. *Horizon 6* was the surface of the unploughed soil. At *Horizon 7*, on the surface of the sand and gravel subsoil, the remains of the prehistoric settlement could be seen, brown against yellow, in all their busy detail: ditches, fences, houses, hearths (dishing well below ground level), pits, all accompanied by hundreds and thousands of potsherds and flint implements: a rich assemblage and a vivid sequence unconsciously captured and preserved by the barrow-builders of the early years of the seventh century AD.

3.21: The complex of inter-cutting features in the centre of Mound 2. The earliest is a rectangular straight-sided pit that contained the seventh-century burial chamber; the large oval pit is the remains of a vertical shaft used to rob the burial chamber in the seventeenth century. Nineteenth-century excavators arrived via a long trench, cutting a set of steps which can be seen at the edge of the pit, rear centre. Basil Brown's trench, cut in 1938, crossed the chamber at an angle; its square end can be seen in the background. The picture was taken during the final dissection of the mound in 1987.
(NIGEL MACBETH)

A WRECKED SHIP: MOUND 2 DISSECTED

Mound 2 was the first and the largest mound to be excavated, and set the procedure for the rest. The burial rite it revealed was unique. It had clearly included a ship, since at every stage ship rivets were encountered. Not a single one was *in situ*, and the scattered pattern that resulted from plotting them implied that the mound had suffered some immense disturbance (**Fig.3.20**). The quantity, size and shape of the rivets showed that somewhere in or under Mound 2 there had originally been buried a full-sized early medieval ship. In the centre of the river of rivets was a large hole, which had been the site of a burial chamber; but it had been entered twice since - by the robbers, and by Basil Brown in 1938 - it was like a nest of Chinese boxes (**Fig.3.21**). Once the sides of the hole had been fully defined it remained to descend to the bottom and discover the truth about the very curious 'boat' reported by Basil Brown in 1938. In this sandy soil, the besetting sin of the excavator is failing to get to the bottom - everybody stops too soon. And so it proved here. Basil Brown had not entirely emptied the feature he encountered, and he had defined, not an Anglo-Saxon burial pit, but the tread and backfill of a robbers' entry

3.22: The chamber floor of Mound 2 as excavated in 1987, showing the remains of the original deposits and the timber lining. (NIGEL MACBETH)

3.23: Andy Copp taking samples for chemical mapping from the chamber floor. (NIGEL MACBETH)

shaft. Basil Brown's 'boat' was skin deep and its imaginary lines just followed the fans of sand that had washed into the huge hole that the robbers had left open. Behind and under Basil's boat appeared the black shadows of the timber lining of a rectangular burial chamber 5m long, 2m wide and 3m deep in which an Anglo-Saxon had been buried. A ship had indeed featured in the burial rite, but it had been placed not in the hole, but above it, on the old ground surface. Later, the central section of the ship had collapsed, filling the chamber with rivets and wood pieces for later excavators to find and scatter, or to puzzle over.

There was little left on the chamber floor, but a dozen or more objects were recovered from the robber trench or from Brown's earlier excavations. If the body had been missing in Mound 1, here practically everything else was missing too, and it became the site of our most elaborate experiment in the mapping of the invisible (Fig.3.22). A programme funded by the Leverhulme Trust and entitled 'The Decay and Detection of Human Bodies on Archaeological Sites' was under way: Phil Bethel, who was responsible for the research, had worked out that sand-bodies were enriched by concentrations of certain cations - aluminium, lanthanum, strontium and barium - which were held as insoluble compounds in places where a body was, or had been. If these compounds could be mapped, it might be possible to determine if and where a body had lain. Accordingly, supervisor Andy Copp took 600 samples of 30g each from the subsoil floor of the Mound 2 burial chamber (Fig.3.23) and the quantity of each element present in each sample was measured by ICP (Inductively Coupled Plasma) emission spectrometry. The results were spectacular. The tell-tale cations from a body were, gratifyingly, all up at the west end; while at the east end were patterns of sand heavily impregnated with copper and iron, which could have derived from bronze cauldrons or ironbound tubs. A coarse burial tableau had been conjured from an entirely blank patch of natural sand three metres underground (Fig.3.24). Taking it all together, there was enough to identify this as the burial of a high-ranking male, as lavishly equipped, perhaps, in its original glory, as the burial beneath Mound 1.

CREMATIONS UNDER MOUNDS

A further six mounds were dissected following the procedures developed for Mound 2. It was found that Mounds 5, 6, 7 and 18 had originally covered cremation burials, but each had been thoroughly robbed. In most, the cremated bone and the twisted fragments of grave goods burnt in the fire were scattered along a robber trench and in a vestigial pit at the centre. Here it was even more difficult to penetrate the fog of later disorder; but the burial rite - cremation - was still reasonably clear, and the fragments that remained pro-

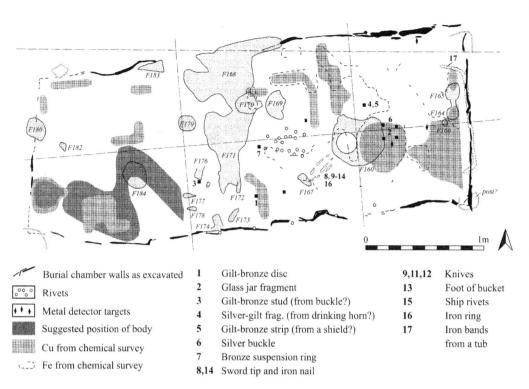

3.24: Chemical map of the Mound 2 chamber floor, showing areas of chemicals associated with the body, with iron and with copper, together with residual deposits and disturbed objects.

vided other clues: the cremated person had been accompanied on the pyre by animals, which included horse, red deer, cattle, sheep and pig. The ashes had been gathered up and placed in a bronze bowl, perhaps first wrapped in cloth; or a cloth (found stuck to the bronze) had been used to cover the bowl. The Mound 5 burial, already special owing to its 'satellite burials', became more special still when it was found that the skull of the cremated person had been cleft with a sword or comparable blade. Mound 5 had been flattened before the twentieth century, but it could still be seen to have had a different style of construction, the make-up being quarried from pits rather than ditches. Some of these pits were cut by the quarry ditches of Mound 2 to the north and Mound 6 to the south. So Mound 5 could have been among the earliest to be built.

HORSE AND BED: MOUNDS 17 AND 14

The last two mounds to be examined had used burial practices that were individual to them. Mound 14 was the only rich burial that could be readily identified as that of a woman. It had a central burial chamber lined with thin planks set on edge and had been robbed by means of a large trench. At the base of this trench, near the chamber floor, the fill became very fine and silty, and was full of little fragments of finds, as though a giant blender had been at work.

3.25: Horizon mapping of Mound 14, showing the quarry ditch and the robbed chamber. (NIGEL MACBETH)

This implied that the robbing team had been interrupted by a rain-storm and, in attempting to complete their ransacking of the chamber during the downpour, had mashed the wet sand of the floor as they groped for the finds that were slipping away from them. Their misfortune was our good luck: the captured assemblage, fragmentary as it was, included parts of a châtelaine (a symbolic key-ring) and allowed us to identify the buried person as a female (**Fig.3.25**).

Mound 17 was the last to be dug, in the last month of the last full season in 1991; apart from Mound 1 it is the only mound-burial at Sutton Hoo so far to have been discovered intact. The mound had hardly shown on the ground surface, and might never have been excavated at all if it had not been for good fortune and the author's persistent hook with a number seven iron (see p.67). The mound had survived as a circular platform of soil about 30cm thick, not quite ploughed to oblivion, but certainly much disturbed. Off came this soil, with shovel and trowel, and beneath it emerged two oval pits each with a bright yellow band around the edge and a rich dark soil centre, like some enormous and luxurious chocolate cut in half. As veterans of encounters with half a dozen robbings, we expected the worst: not one, but two, robber pits to empty and sieve for clues to the original burial. With disciplined resignation, the first and largest pit was tackled first: taken down in spits until, after 30cm or so, a surprising neat brown circle appeared in one corner; it should have derived from wood, and looked like the rim of a small wheel. Annette Roe, the excavator, knew that this was unlikely to figure within a robber pit back-fill and she took out the next shallow spit with the greatest circumspection.

3.26: Annette Roe excavating the Mound 17 burial supported on a cradle. (NIGEL MACBETH)

3.27: Bucket and cauldron (containing pot) *in situ* in the Mound 17 grave. (NIGEL MACBETH)

The brown circle persisted, and could now be guessed to be the rotted fabric of a circular wooden tub. A little lower down, at the other end of the grave, there appeared the curved rim of a bronze bowl. It was a satisfying moment when Madeleine Hummler came to get me: 'Come and look,' she said. 'It's the real thing.' There is, of course, nothing to match the real thing in any of life's moments, and the last few weeks of the campaign were probably the most exciting in all the years of our fieldwork.

Annette Roe lowered the surface of the fill a centimetre at a time, taking out the deposit of the backfilled grave (**Fig.3.26**). No one can say the excavation of a grave is easy, but it is certainly easier to excavate an intact grave than a robbed one: everything is where it should be, one thing warns of another, the excavator is prepared and increasingly alert. The black lines of the coffin edge appeared on each side. Beside the coffin, under the bowl, was a little cluster of bones originating from a handful of lamb chops, which, it could be deduced, had once been in a kind of kit bag, with the bowl on top. Beside it was a small lugged cauldron, and next to that an iron-bound bucket (**Fig.3.27**). In the coffin was the skeleton of a young man, with surprisingly well-preserved bones, and a sword as long as his legs. A tiny fragment of millefiori glass and garnet lay near his ear; had we missed a piece of jewellery? No, next to them

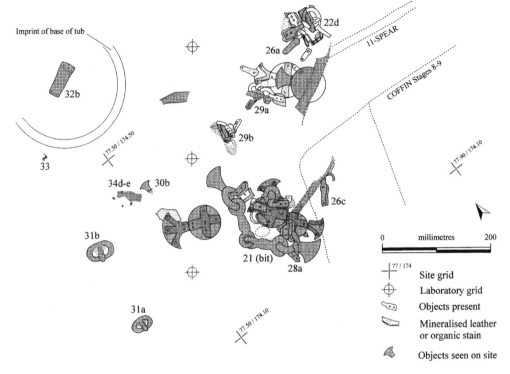

3.28: Plan of the horse harness in the ground.

was a small iron bar showing that a purse or pouch had contained these keep-sakes. Under the coffin lay a shield-boss.

Annette Roe worked on for three weeks with scarcely a break as the light gradually weakened and the weather worsened into winter. She lay on a cot mattress on a board supported by a scaffolding cradle, so that no foot or hand had to put its weight on the funeral deposit. A shelter was built around the grave and a generator provided lighting from 4 or 5 o'clock onwards. The aim was to present the most perfect tableau we could manage, as nearly as possi-ble to reproduce the last view of the mourners before backfilling commenced, with everything showing that was showing then. But some things were too delicate to expose without endangering their survival. The cauldron appeared to be crazed as though ready to break into a thousand fragments; the bucket tottered, its rings of iron held in position only by a jacket of crusty sand.

And at the west end appeared the greatest prize of all: a dark heap of organic traces with the glint of metal peeping out in a half a dozen places. The pieces, where they could be clearly seen, were small plaques of gilded bronze featuring writhing Anglo-Saxon animal ornament; they had little loops and studs with dark ribbons of decayed leather going away from them. It looked like a mass of belts and buckles. Disentangling this was work for a laboratory, not a cold damp dark hole in Suffolk. It was time to call in the British Museum conservation team, which had been standing by during the six years of the excavation for just such moments as these.

3.29: The British Museum team preparing the Mound 17 sword for lifting.

3.30: Man-yee Liu dissecting the bridle block in the British Museum (author).

Meanwhile, the adjacent pit, smaller than the first, was being excavated, and here too it was apparent that there would be a burial that had not been disturbed. But it contained no finds and no human body; instead there was defined, in precise detail, the large folded carcass of a horse, part skeleton and part sand-body. Now it became clear what had been buried at the west end of the human grave: it was a harness, with probably a saddle and, above that, the wooden tub for the horse's bran, now only a dark brown ring (**Fig.3.28**).

After one last photograph in a Force 8 gale, the British Museum conservators swung into action like a team of paramedics at a traffic accident; tub, cauldron and sword were bound up with plaster of Paris bandages and lifted when set (**Fig.3.29**). The shield boss was lifted and the spear was extracted from under the heap of harness. Then the soil cube containing the harness, henceforward known as the 'bridle block', was prepared for lifting. It was first wrapped in cling-film, and then in baking foil. Then polystyrene foam was generated in situ to make a rigid casing. A steel plate was inserted under the block, and then the block was turned over, sealed and lifted out of the grave with the back-actor of a mechanical excavator and loaded on to the tailgate of a Ford Granada. Soon it was on its way to the British Museum, where it would be dissected into its component parts and reassembled: the first complete Anglo-Saxon horse harness to be excavated (**Fig.3.30**). Finally the coffin was dissected, its decayed wood stain revealing a curved convex base which, together with four curved clamps, showed that the young man had been buried in two halves of a tree trunk.

The team returned in the bitterly cold spring of 1992 for a clearing-up season. Still to be investigated was the feature in the centre of Mound 17, which proved to be an unsuccessful robber pit; it had arrived at a point situated between the two burials, thus no doubt puzzling and disappointing those who had dug it. An important group of Beaker-period pits adjacent to Mound 1 was also excavated, and a number of other records had to be completed. Then, suddenly, the digging programme was at its end, and it was time to backfill our excavations and reconstitute the site. With the use of heavy earth-moving machinery all the excavated mounds were rebuilt to the height at which they were first encountered in 1983 – all, that is, except one. Mound 2 was raised to the height to which it would have stood before ploughing had rubbed it down: a magnificent 3.5m high, visible now from Melton across the river and imparting to the visitor the monumental presence once offered by a cemetery of such mounds on an open terrace above the river (**Fig.3.31**).

INTERPRETING THE DISCOVERIES

Making sense of the results took place in three main stages. First, there were a great many routine analyses to undertake: of the objects, the human remains, the pollen and the soils. Then the activities implied by these analyses had to be put into sequence and dated; and from this dated sequence of activities the 'site model' – the story of what had happened on the site – could be compiled. Armed with this story, the archaeologist and the historian could decide on how it fitted into the context of the culture and history of the period; how that context changed the interpretation of what had happened on the site; and how the interpretation of the site might change the current vision of the past that had supplied the context. All this was attempted in 13 years of post-excavation work.

The enormous prehistoric assemblage, some 100,000 finds and hundreds of features, was reduced to comprehensive synthesis by Madeleine Hummler, and is presented in Chapter 4.[14] The examination of the early medieval objects was a simpler task than that faced by the British Museum in 1946, but it had challenges of its own: the robbed burial mounds had produced many frag-

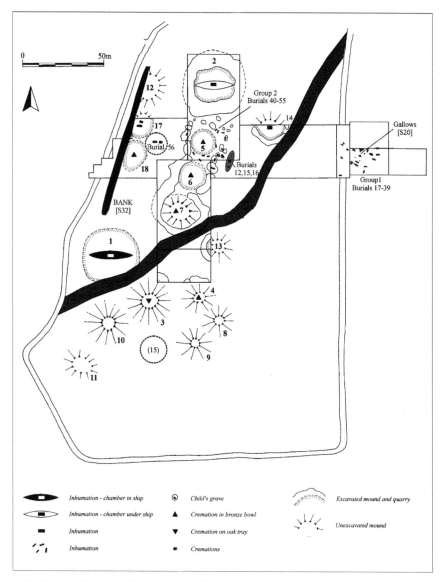

3.31: Map of all early medieval and later features.

ments, often tiny, which derived from objects long since smashed and dispersed; these were scrutinised by Angela Evans, a veteran of Bruce-Mitford's own research team. As a result, the terminal of a drinking horn and the stud of a gilded buckle were soon identified in the Mound 2 assemblage, and the dies of the fittings of the drinking horns in the two great mounds proved to be identical. It was apparent that here was a burial of the top rank, originally sharing many attributes with Mound 1, and almost as wealthy. A fragment of châtelaine was picked out from Mound 14, a find decisive in determining that this had been the burial of a woman. Among the cremated bones dispersed over the scrambled site of Mound 18 was a tiny fragment of a comb, the sole indication that this, like the others, had been a burial of the early Middle Ages (see *Archaeological Records* for lists of all the finds).

The most interesting task was the examination of the finds from Mound 17, this being the only mound burial other than Mound 1 to have been found intact. Sword, bucket and cauldron were X-rayed and unwrapped from their protective bandages. The little purse proved to have been a cloth-lined leather pouch containing seven rough-cut garnets, a single garnet in the form of a bird's beak and a fragment of red and blue millefiori glass. The sword had a pommel of horn and an iron knife in a leather sheath had lain with it. In the laboratory, a corroded iron spear-head became two leaf-shaped spear-blades, and these and the shield-boss, iron-bound bucket, cauldron and a ceramic pot were all conserved and researched. The toughest assignment was the examination and restoration of the harness. The block in which it had reached the museum was first subjected to radiography 'in real time' - that is, placed on a turntable in an X-ray beam, and rotated. The radiographic images obtained at different viewpoints can be seen immediately and directly on a television screen in an adjacent room. Then the conservators began to dissect the block, lifting the 13 strap-distributors, seven buckles, five strap-ends and two pendants, all lying within the soil matrix and crossed by the faint tracks of decayed leather. These pieces then had to be assembled in the imagination and on paper, inspired by such analogies as earlier discoveries in Britain and the Continent could provide.[15]

The horse itself was determined by Terry O'Connor to be a rather thickset male, five to six years old and standing about 14 hands. O'Connor had also identified animal bone in one of the quarry pits of Mound 5 - originally the heads of cattle or horse. Julie Bond found evidence for more animals - horse, red deer, sheep or goat, cattle and pig - among the fragments of cremated bone from the robbed mounds. The precious scraps of decayed human bone, both cremated and inhumed, were searched by Francis Lee for evidence of sex, trauma and age at death - with some measure of success. Most of the execution victims identified were males and mature, but young. In Burial 42 it turned out that two women had been buried face down on a decapitated middle-aged man (see Chapter 6).

The experience of excavating at Sutton Hoo for nine years, and in particular of digging Mound 17, suggested that a return to the evidence for the Mound 1 burial rite might also be fruitful. Knowing what was now known, the form of Mound 1 and the ritual that had preceded its construction might be easier to understand. A model for the burial chamber was devised, drawing on the analogy of the better-preserved example excavated in the Oseberg ship. The evidence for a body was reviewed again in the light of the Leverhulme project on the decay of human remains, and Bruce-Mitford's conclusion – that there had been a body at the west end – was endorsed. The evidence for a coffin (principally the iron clamps), suggested and rejected over the years, was re-examined from first principles, comparing the Mound 1 observations with those made at first hand in Mound 17. The split sides of the Mound 17 coffin, its collapsed lid, pressing all the finds into a thin layer at the base, and its curved iron clamps: all seemed to echo the Mound 1 account.[16] A special analysis of the Mound 1 stratigraphy was then undertaken, in which the objects in the chamber were related stratigraphically to each other. From this study it seemed more certain that the chamber had had a floor and that a coffin had stood upon it.[17] It was deduced that the objects had been placed in the coffin, on the coffin, on the walls and on the floor. The same analysis offered an account of the order in which the chamber had been furnished, and how it had collapsed to result in the tangle that was found. New material originating from Charles Phillips and Guy Maynard also helped to propose how the mound was subsequently reduced by ploughing and robbing.

This 'Mound 1 story' was joined by similar chronicles worked out for each of the ten mounds investigated. Putting the mounds in their order of construction proved to be much harder. There were few instances of definable stratification, and all the objects clustered in date around AD 600. Such indications as there were suggested that the cremations came first, led by Mound 5; then the inhumations, including the Mound 17 horse-burial; then the two ship-burials, Mound 1 and Mound 2. The best fit seemed to be achieved by supposing that the cemetery had grown from two nuclei, the first based on Mound 5, the second on Mound 1 (Chapter 5). Through radiocarbon dating, the sad remnants of the two execution cemeteries were eventually given their dignity and due (Chapter 6). The passing of the Sutton Hoo site into the care of the National Trust (see below) involved the construction of a visitor centre, exhibition hall and tea room. This required prior archaeological investigation to rescue any ancient settlement that lay underground, and one was duly encountered: an Anglo-Saxon cemetery dated to the generations living in the sixth century AD – just before the mounds were built; this provided the Sutton Hoo Story with a prequel (Chapter 4).

NEW OWNERS, NEW FUTURE

It had always occasioned surprise, particularly among foreign visitors, that, in spite of its prominent role in English history and its consequent national importance, Sutton Hoo remained in private ownership. For students of

heritage matters it might not be without interest to consider some aspects of the 14-year struggle to convey the site to an institutional owner, successfully concluded in 1997 with the gift of the whole estate by the Annie Tranmer Charitable Trust to the National Trust.[18]

As a landowner, Mrs Edith Pretty did not require permission to initiate her excavations of 1938, and under the English law of Treasure Trove was determined as the owner of the finds from the great ship-burial and, by implication, from any other graves. Following her donation of the objects to the British Museum the site was *scheduled* – that is, officially protected under ancient monuments legislation originating in 1882.[19] This measure does not oblige the landowner to look after the site, only to desist from destroying it. Neither does it provide for public access. But the long-term conservation and presentation of its historical assets to the public might nevertheless be considered as the natural destiny of such a place. This at any rate was the concern of the 1983 campaign, and to devise a secure future for the site was an integral part of the evaluation with which the 1983 campaign started. The process of evaluation was intended to assign a current value to Sutton Hoo and to express how that value could best be appreciated by means of a research plan and a management plan. The programme of excavation had involved only a part of the site in the firm conviction that the rest would still be there to answer the questions of another generation. Could that long-term conservation be guaranteed and, if so, how? Public access could also be considered part of the duties of a researcher, either because the research was being done in the name of

3.32: (opposite) Members of the Sutton
Hoo Society, a voluntary organisation that
supported the excavation campaign.
(NIGEL MACBETH)

3.33: (above) Members of the
International Society of Anglo-Saxonists
advancing from Mound 1 in 1986.

3.34: (right) Prince Philip, as President of
the Sutton Hoo Society, visiting the site in
1989. (NIGEL MACBETH)

the public or because the presentation of a monument (whose character was
about to change irreversibly) should be considered a part of the publication
programme.

Accordingly, during the excavation campaign temporary measures for
conservation and presentation were put in place. In terms of *conservation*, the
most urgent necessities were to guard the site against treasure-hunters and
to eliminate bracken and rabbits. This custodianship was achieved without
a break from November 1983, including over the Christmas holidays, when
students who wanted to get away from it all (particularly with someone else)
might spend the festive season in the site-hut with a calor gas fire and bottle
of wine or two. In eight years we suffered only three minor attempts at van-
dalism, none very damaging. The rabbits and bracken were eliminated by
the site caretaker, Mr Peter Berry, who became responsible for transforming
the tangled, ugly, neglected surface of the Sutton Hoo burial ground into a
smooth green monument of which any government would have been proud.

Presentation was multi-media in every sense. The treasures from Mound
1 were already on display at the British Museum in a new gallery in the Early

Medieval Room.[20] There was also a small exhibition in Woodbridge Museum, dealing with the history of the exploration of the site. There were books already published. Access to the site itself was agreed with the owners in a limited, controlled way, so that only the dedicated undertook the long walk from the road to the mounds. There they were greeted by volunteer guides from the Sutton Hoo Society, a group that was created locally with the express purpose of making visitors welcome (Fig.3.32). Over and over again, the guides stood on Mound 1 recounting the discovery of the ship-burial, and then took their parties around to see new discoveries being made.

Visitors came from all over the world, from learned societies, from families needing a day out, from schools, from clubs, from town and country, from overseas and from the neighbouring village; among them were day-trippers, professors and royalty (Figs 3.33, 3.34). Eventually, when the excavation campaign was complete, Mound 2 was itself reconstructed as a reminder to the visitor of the imposing monuments that had once stood here, and how they had been reduced and rubbed away by the use of the land. The most important visitor access was provided by BBC television, which made four programmes about the campaign, each of which was shown a number of times. Through this medium, it could be said that more than 13 million people had spent an hour in the company of the Sutton Hoo project (Fig.3.35).

Achieving a long-term future for the site was much more difficult. The right to excavate was still owned by the Pretty family, who had retained it, together with pre-emptive ownership of the finds, under a deed of covenant when they sold Sutton Hoo House. This right was subsequently assigned by Robert Pretty to the Sutton Hoo Research Trust, and under the same agreement the finds from future excavation would continue to be given to the British Museum. In 1983 the Sutton Hoo site lay in the estate of Mrs Annie Tranmer, who, together with her principal trustee, John Miller, had given permission for the research programme and provided a stout bulwark for its aims. Neither were they insensitive to the bigger question of the future of this historically precious piece of land. Within a few months of the project's beginning they opened a dialogue on the possible gift of Sutton Hoo to the nation, partly at least in exchange for relief from estate duty.

It was then that the current mood of English politics became apparent: even if the owner was willing to give the site, the nation did not seem to want it. English Heritage, the government agency designed to manage its publicly owned monuments, was formed in 1983, the year the campaign began. In spite of its own title, English Heritage did not seem to regard the acquisition of the earliest burial ground of English kings as particularly imperative and maintained a stoical lack of interest in acquiring it. After several attempts

3.35: Camera crew filming for the Sutton Hoo series shown on BBC 2, under the direction of Ray Sutcliffe.

at engaging the attention of the agency had failed, an alternative tack was adopted: an approach was made direct to the Capital Transfer Tax Office. This body agreed in principle to accept Sutton Hoo on behalf of the nation provided that we could find someone sensible to give it to and provided that the duty claimed by the Inland Revenue was nevertheless paid. But who would pay it? The next door to knock on was that of the National Heritage Memorial Fund, which had recently paid a handsome sum to prevent the export of the Earl of Warwick's sword. They were most responsive, insisting only that the District Valuer should be consulted as to the real value of Sutton Hoo. The Inland Revenue required £350,000 from the Tranmers; it would be interesting to see whether the state was getting a bargain or not.

According to criteria used by the District Valuer, Sutton Hoo was not so much priceless as worthless. As agricultural land it was obviously most unsatisfactory: it was covered in large hummocks that would impede ploughing, and there was an injunction (that is, the Ancient Monuments Act) that would discourage cultivation in any case. It would fare little better as a recreational place: the hummocks (unless they could be removed, of course) would inhibit a good game of football. It was agreed that it could serve as a picnic area, but the value of such places was not high. The whole site was not expected to reach a value to the community of more than £3,000 - that is, about £300 an acre.

But what about its value as an archaeological site? It appears that it had none; or, if it had a value, it certainly did not have a price. Sutton Hoo, one of the most famous sites in the world and perhaps the second most important one in England after Stonehenge, was not wanted by English Heritage and was apparently worth only £3,000 to a landowner in need of £350,000.

Perhaps someone in another country would appreciate what we were trying to save for our incorrigibly venal nation? J.P. Getty had recently given a large sum of money (and compensation to the developers) to purchase a field the development of which would have spoiled the vista of Ely Cathedral. It was decided that the Getty Trust would be approached, but, to anticipate any questions concerning price, it seemed wise to be ready with our own estimate, which reflected, in money, the worth that we believed it could claim in terms of archaeological value. This would need ingenuity, since the site was in truth simply undulating sand and turf. The graves might contain finds, but by deed of covenant the finds would belong to the British Museum and could bring no financial value to a landowner. What price, then, a field of historic hummocks?

The method used was to draw an analogy. If hummocks were history, so were illuminated manuscripts, in which the Anglo-Saxons had also invested much wealth and labour when they ceased to be pagans and became Christian. A burial-mound was the analogue of a codex, one like the Lindisfarne Gospels in the British Library; and a flat grave might be considered the equivalent of a folio, or perhaps an illuminated initial. But could these be priced? Fortunately, yes; in the shops of Old Bond Street it used to be possible to find illuminated initials for sale, snipped off their parent manuscripts; they could be picked up for £100. And, as for the famous gospel books, some had been lent recently by the British Library to an exhibition in Stockholm, and an insurance figure had had to be quoted for this purpose. Using these data for the equation, and with Sutton Hoo's expected burials in mind, a price could be computed amounting to £7.25 million. It should be a veritable snip at £350,000 (less the finds). But Getty's staff decided against. Sutton Hoo was worthless to the nation and had failed to get itself exported. It seemed that the Sutton Hoo Research Trust would have to remain its informal unpaid guardians for ever more.[21]

Happily there was a second better option - the possibility that the site might pass into the ownership of the National Trust for England and Wales, a charitable organisation dedicated to the protection of English landscapes and buildings, which celebrated its centenary in 1995. Through the good offices of Elisabeth Walters, a member of the National Trust's Executive Committee and a most hospitable resident of neighbouring Sutton village, we solicited the interest of Merlin Waterson, the National Trust's regional director, and contact of a gentle and sympathetic kind was shortly made. In 1993 Mrs Annie Tranmer died and the estate passed to her daughter, Valerie Lewis. The trustees of the Annie Tranmer Charitable Trust, National Trust officers and the Sutton Hoo Research Trust were soon in discussion.

The transfer was finally made feasible in August 1997, when the Heritage Lottery Fund awarded £3.6 million to create public access to the site. The Heritage Lottery Fund, under the wing of the National Heritage Memorial Fund, had accepted that the site was of international importance. Annie Tranmer, her trustee and her daughter had created an opportunity to conserve and present a noble and a precious monument, one fit to stand for the earliest burial ground of English kings. A visitor centre was constructed and opened by Seamus Heaney. Sutton Hoo was at last safe for the future and for international knowledge, in the words of the National Trust centenary aphorism, *for ever, for everyone.*[22] So began a new era for early England's most glittering monument. In accordance with the National Trust principles, a *conservation plan* was soon initiated and a *research plan* later prepared, which collected all the archaeological contacts made up to 2014 intended as a platform for further research. This included plans for the construction of a full-scale replica of the ship found in Mound 1 in a partnership with Woodbridge Riverside Trust named 'The Ship's Company'. In 2012, the Sutton Hoo Centre celebrated the arrival of its one millionth visitor.

Each generation digs into the past for its own reasons: some for treasure, some for status, some for more history, some to rescue history. In the 1930s Edith Pretty and her team were led to the mounds by curiosity, and their reward was a jackpot of splendid objects. In the 1960s Rupert Bruce-Mitford returned to solve specific problems necessary for the definitive publication of the ship-burial. The campaign of the 1980s set out to discover a context for the ship-burial, to see if Sutton Hoo could throw light on the origins of an early English kingdom, and to try to understand the message that the mounds had for those that built them and those who were later to see them in the landscape. In the year 2000 county-based archaeologists recording in advance of the visitor centre had a chance to add a key chapter to the story.[23]

The results are presented in the chapters that follow, in which imagination feeds on science to offer an evocation of the Sutton Hoo Story from the Neolithic to the Middle Ages. No archaeologist can pretend they have the final and definitive picture; not even those attending the seventh-century burials could claim that. What follows is an archaeological picture of the times, after which we will allow ourselves to 'entertain conjecture' and so evoke its wider world.

4 | BEFORE SUTTON HOO
c. 3000 BC to c. AD 600

Putting pots in pits: Neolithic colonists ✦ A Beaker revolution ✦ Iron Age farmers mark the land ✦ Romans at Sutton Hoo ✦ The coming of the English ✦ The Tranmer House cemetery: a precursor

For more than 3,000 years before the Anglo-Saxon burial mounds were raised the ridge above the River Deben at Sutton Hoo had been occupied by hunters, herdsmen and farmers. Their traces were captured in and under the buried soil beneath the mounds (**Fig.4.1**) and gathered off the surface, where many thousands of potsherds and flint tools had been disturbed and dispersed by mound-building and ploughing (**Fig.4.2**). The rich harvest of features beneath the mounds created a palimpsest in which settlement succeeded settlement through the Neolithic, Bronze Age, Iron Age and Roman periods (**Fig.4.3**). It was on this relict landscape - some of it certainly then still visible - that the earliest English were to settle.[1] The first chapter of the Sutton Hoo Story begins in the deep past, but these roots were to remain relevant to the early English (**Fig.4.4**).

PUTTING POTS IN PITS: NEOLITHIC COLONISTS
Pollen grains found in the ancient brown soil show that the Deben Valley was once heavily wooded: there was alder and hazel along the sprawling river banks and oak woodland on the terrace above. Leaf-shaped flint arrowheads and a flint axe were found in the recent excavations, suggesting that this wild country was visited by hunters and woodsmen, and to them and their successors can be attributed the first great artificial change to the landscape before 3000 BC, the early Neolithic period in Britain. The process of agricultural exploitation, which began somewhere in the fertile crescent of the Near East in the eighth millennium BC, had its faint echo here 5,000 years later, with the thinning of the trees and the creation of grass clearings that could be grazed. So began a series of local agricultural experiments that were to continue throughout prehistory.

Opening up the landscape, the people of Neolithic Suffolk may have been aware of the special asset that they were destroying, even then. Here and there

4.1: Under Mound 2. The surface of the platform seen after the removal of the mound is cut by post-holes of a circular building of the early Bronze Age, a post-row of the later Bronze Age and a ditch of the Iron Age. The oval pit marks the position of the Mound 2 burial chamber. (NIGEL MACBETH)

4.2: Prehistoric flint arrowheads of the Neolithic and Bronze Age found on the surface at Sutton Hoo.

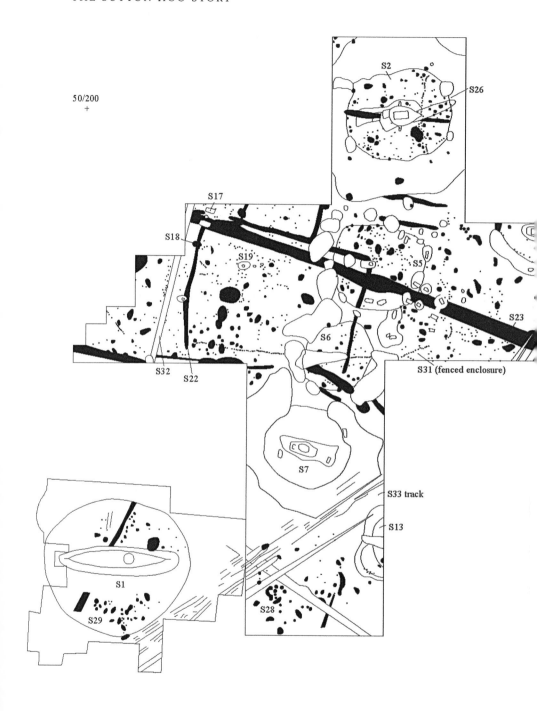

50/200
+

S2

S26

S17

S18

S19

S5

S6

S23

S32   S22

S31 (fenced enclosure)

S7

S33 track

S13

S1

S29

S28

50/50
+

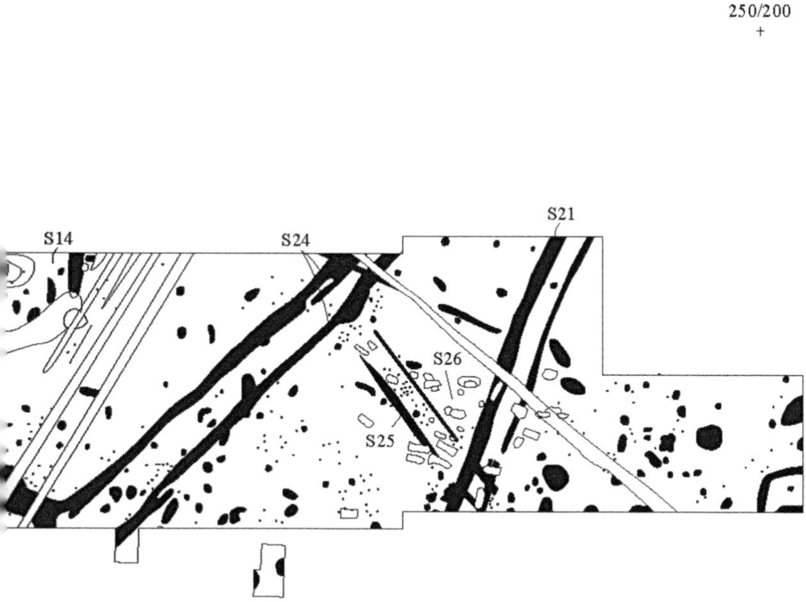
250/200
S21
S14
S24
S26
S25
250/50

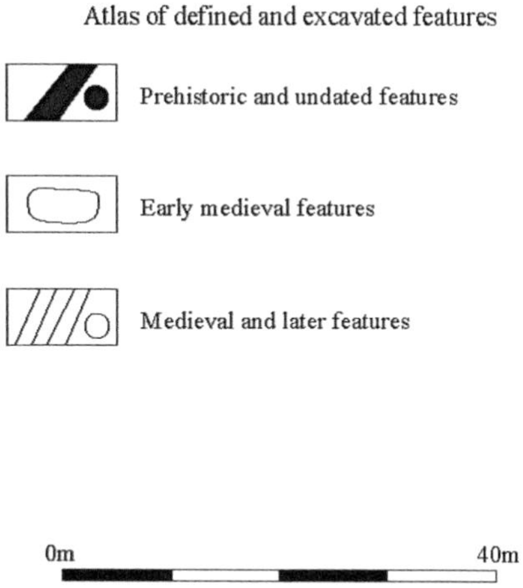
Atlas of defined and excavated features
Prehistoric and undated features
Early medieval features
Medieval and later features
0m
40m

4.3: The total plan of the excavated site, showing features of all periods.

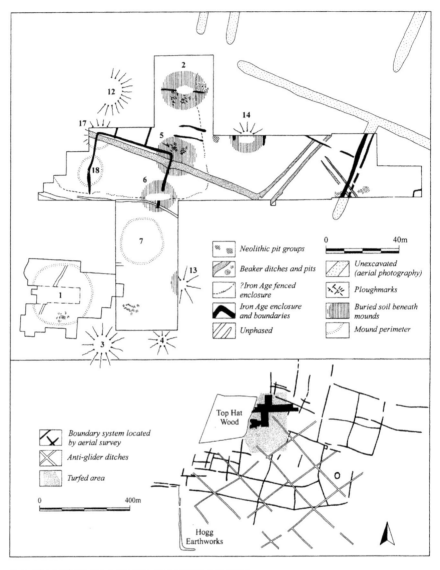

4.4: The prehistoric sequence. (MADELEINE HUMMLER)

on the terrace, small pits have been found containing whole pots of character-istic thick-walled flint-tempered earthenware. The pits are often sited around or near large untidy hollows with half-dark, half-bright coloured fill. These hollows were recognised for what they were following the great storm of 1987, which created a host of new examples of the genre: they are 'tree-pits', formed when a tree is pushed over and uprooted and the root mantle left to rot. The close association of tree-pits with pot-pits is by no means secure; there is no stratification to show if they might be contemporary. The pits are found all along the Sutton Hoo ridge, but do not speak of a village: over a millennium the people who dug them came and went, creating clusters in favourite spots, leaving their flint and burying pots.[2] It seems our first farmers were semi-nomadic, in harmony with their landscape. But this was about to change.

A BEAKER REVOLUTION

Beakers with sinuous profile and geometric ornament are found all over western Europe in inhumation burials containing special grave goods, such as barbed and tanged flint arrowheads. In Matthew Arnold's day these were seen as immigrants from Spain: 'shy traffickers, the dark Iberians' who 'on the beach undid their corded bales'. Now we see this burial rite as rather the harbinger of an ideology that took root widely before 2000 BC, just as Christianity was to do much later in the same European lands. And, not without relevance to this parallel, the new ritual was accompanied by a massive increase in and reorganisation of economic energy. Developers of Stonehenge, which was equipped with its trilithons, the people of this period (the early Bronze Age, around 2000 BC) wrought many changes to life and landscape. Much of the evidence comes from burials and ceremonial centres but in East Anglia there are a number of sites that show the ordinary farmers in action. Sutton Hoo is one of them. These farmers also had middens, which they tidied away into clusters of pits. But now they built dwellings too. Under Mound 2 was a round-house, first contacted by Basil Brown, consisting of a ring of upright posts up to 300mm in diameter, presumably designed to support a superstructure of wattle walls and a thatched roof, although nothing of this remained. A pair of posts suggested an entrance to the south-east (**Fig.4.5**). There was a central hearth, where a coloured faience bead had been dropped. The people used beautifully made and ornamented pots in smooth walnut-brown fabric (**Fig.4.6**), and were cultivators of barley (*hordeum*), oats (*avena*) and wheat (*triticum*). They had access to stands of woodlands and left acorns and hazel-nuts in their pits. Next to the house under Mound 2 was a massive pit, probably owed to the root-mantle of a tree. Under Mound 1 was another round house with a rich cluster of pits adjacent, containing more than 500 sherds of Beaker pottery.

But the most significant development was territorial. In the early Bronze Age, great ditches were cut straight across the land from river scarp to skyline, undeviating irrespective of quirks in the topography (**Fig.4.7**). In this sandy soil, ditches were unnecessary for drainage and, at 3m across and (probably) carrying a hedge on an adjacent bank, were much larger than was needed to keep out the fiercest cow. The size of the land parcels so marked is not known, but, given that no further such large ditches were encountered in the

4.5: (above) Circular building of the early Bronze Age built of upright timber posts, its post-holes and hearth excavated under Mound 2.

4.6: (left) Beaker pottery from Sutton Hoo.

4.7: (opposite) Early Bronze Age boundary ditch, showing recuts.

(NIGEL MACBETH)

excavated area, this was a major boundary that can only have been achieved by a commanding or organising hand.

These 'first wave' linear boundaries probably signal the imposition of the most fundamental arrogation in human history: the ownership of land, or at least its restricted control. The principal boundary at Sutton Hoo crossed the site from north-west to south-east, where it connected with a double-ditched droveway. The Bronze Age landscape may be envisioned as open farmland punctuated by stands of timber – a landscape that was organised and owned. Much of lowland Britain experienced this 'first wave' of carving up the landscape that has been linked to both increased social inequality and to greater intensification and pressure on the land.[3] Numerous recuts show that these boundaries endured.

This fertile region, within easy reach of southern Britain, France, Holland and Scandinavia, could never opt out for long from Europe's drama. It was too easy to reach, quick to clear of brushwood, quick to stock with sheep and quicker to plough. From now on, whatever politics prevailed, the owners were destined to struggle with the acid sand and with each other to maximise their investments, their holdings and their influence. It is in the Middle Bronze Age (around 1500 cal BC) that Sutton Hoo acquires its first funerary 'monument', a small barrow consisting of a ring-ditch and central cremation, radio-

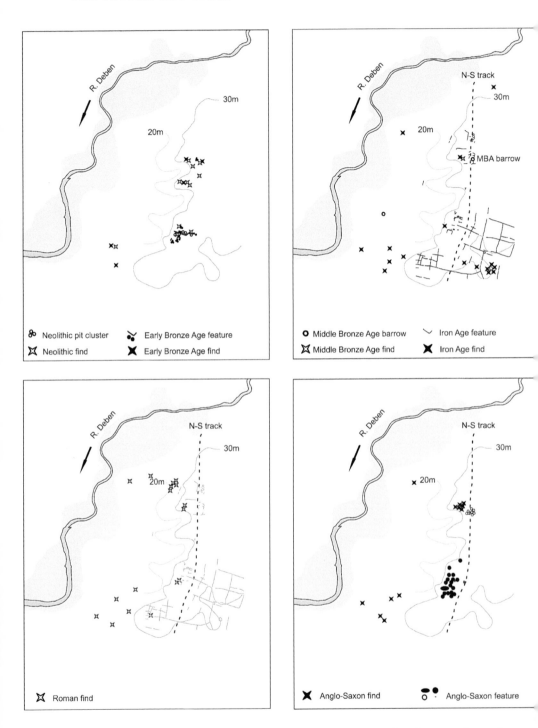

4.8: Neolithic/early Bronze Age, late Bronze Age/Iron Age, Roman and Anglo-Saxon sites and find-spots at Sutton Hoo. (MADELEINE HUMMLER)

carbon-dated to around 1400 cal BC, excavated in the Tranmer House site (see below). At present it is the only undisputed Bronze Age burial at Sutton Hoo, but it is likely that more once existed. This was the first group of people who would use individual burial mounds to show they were here to stay.

Without artificial fertiliser, the acid sand of the Sandlings can tolerate being ploughed only for short periods before becoming leached and infertile: the condition known to soil scientists as a podzol. Then it will support only gorse and brambles, unless and until the grass can be allowed to regenerate and the cycle begin again. The oak trees, pride of Suffolk where they remain, and immortalised in Constable's paintings, did not return to Sutton. As the trees were gradually eliminated by fierce winds and by axes of stone, bronze and iron, the sandy soil had little to retain it and it began to erode and drift through wind-blow and rain-wash into the Deben Valley, where it was taken away to the sea.[4]

IRON AGE FARMERS MARK THE LAND

The early Bronze Age settlement, marking a peak of affluence at Sutton Hoo, was eventually abandoned, the boundary ditches silted up, and the debris from the houses was swept into open pits or the hollows left by uprooted trees. After the 'first wave' linear boundaries went out of use, an enclosure was built of close-set posts about 200mm (8in) in diameter, set the same distance apart and enclosing an area of c.4,800 sq. m. Its purpose is not known, but such a palisade may have had as much to do with keeping animals out as in, perhaps at a time when the impoverished podsolized soil meant that more reliance had to be placed on pastoralism. Display may also have played a part.[5]

But grain fever returned, probably in the Middle Iron Age (c. 500 BC), and with it a new type of enclosure, known elsewhere as the 'Celtic field', which spread in a rectilinear network over the terrace (**Fig. 4.8**). These were the boundary ditches that had been seen from the air. The soil within some of the fields was ploughed, the marks of the ard preserved in a criss-cross pattern scratched on the surface of the relict brown earth. In others there were narrow trenches reminiscent of the cultivation of vines, and in others small pockets of dark soil suggesting rows of currant bushes or cabbages. These represent the last episodes of cultivation before the mounds were built and are probably Roman in date.

Etched into their landscape was the north-south ridge-top track that has endured to today. It certainly influenced the siting of the Anglo-Saxon burials, both at Tranmer House and at the royal burial ground, where at least four of its barrows (Mounds 17, 18, 5 and 6) were placed on banked Iron Age boundaries (Fig.4.4). The track still acted as a major line of travel in the eighth century AD, when the execution cemetery to the east of the royal burial ground (Group 1) was laid out alongside it. By then the ditch was partly filled in and burials (Burial 31 of Group 1 and Burial 20 of the Tranmer House cemetery) were laid within the ditch and aligned to it. Thus it was not the Iron Age *ditch* itself that was particularly long-lived, but the axis it marked, perhaps flanked by a bank and fence or hedge, and accompanied by a trackway, enduring for a millennium or more.[6]

ROMANS AT SUTTON HOO

The use of these fields continued into the Roman period, for a few fragments of Roman pottery and a fibula were dropped and incorporated into cultivated soil. Insatiable colonisers, the Romans worked every piece of land and water in Europe. Settlement in Suffolk for the previous 3,000 years had been consistently established within 1km of running water. Now it crept up on to the clay land and down on to the alluvium. Roman occupation is well attested in Suffolk and along both banks of the River Deben, but the Roman and sub-Roman periods (the first five centuries AD) are so far represented only in a muted form in the area of the Sutton Hoo estate (Fig.4.9). Roman finds have been located by surface collection outside the estate, both to the north and the south of it, and within the estate in its northern part, with a dense concentration in the north-west of the Garden Field north of the visitor centre. The foreshore also saw Roman activity on the floodplain, perhaps linked to temporarily better climatic conditions; in the Foreshore survey of 2002-3 and 2009 the pottery picked up was mainly Roman greyware, while samples of wood (some from a wattle structure) produced radiocarbon dates of the late Roman-early Saxon period (fourth-sixth centuries AD). Some cultivation of the fields of the Iron Age system may have continued, since cultivation marks of possibly Roman date were found under Mounds 2 and 5. A camp-fire lit in the part-filled hollow of the south-north axis ditch on the Tranmer House site was radiocarbon-dated to the third-sixth centuries AD.[7] The main axial north-south track continued in use from the Iron Age through the Roman period, and was to influence the layout of the Anglo-Saxon cemeteries.

At a larger scale, the Deben Valley Survey showed sites of Neolithic to Bronze Age date clinging to the left bank of the Deben with some penetration up its tributary to the west, the River Fynn. Iron Age sites colonised both banks of the Deben and its tributaries to north and west, while the Romans show an increased presence here and up on to the clay uplands that separate south-east from north-west Suffolk (Fig.4.10).

We can expect the soil of Sutton Hoo to have been worked hard, as long as

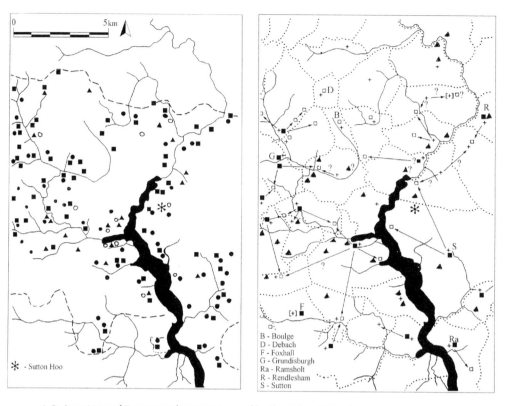

4.9: Iron Age and Roman settlements mapped by the Deben Valley Survey. (JOHN NEWMAN)

4.10: Early, middle and late Saxon settlements mapped by the Deben Valley Survey. (JOHN NEWMAN)

it could bear the load; but the recommencement of the cycle of degradation was inevitable. Soil loss seems not to have been prevented by the embanked enclosures, and by the middle of the first millennium AD, as the fiscal system of the Roman empire collapsed, up to a metre of soil had disappeared. Turf or scrub grew on an infertile sand 400mm thick. A few trees, among them alder, hazel, oak and beech, stood here and there on the slope. The farmers had gone, but their earthworks were still visible: a network of low banks along the terrace looking out over the ancient tidal breathing of the Deben.

And that is how the Anglo-Saxons found it.

THE COMING OF THE ENGLISH

Current research has tracked the earliest English immigrants as arriving via the Wash in the early fifth century and moving up rivers into Lincolnshire, west into the Midlands and south into Norfolk. The incomers came across the North Sea from north Germany and southern Denmark, where they used

113

similar pots and burial rites. South-east Suffolk has its own set of estuaries, the Alde, the Deben, the Orwell and the Stour, and no doubt attracted its own group of pioneers. The area they colonised was an extensive stretch of acid grassland laced with rivers and creeks known today as the 'sandlings', propitious for settlement, rich in pasture and also suitable for cultivation, as the Beaker and Iron Age farmers had already shown. The first phases of English settlement favoured both banks of the Deben and inland via Martlesham Creek up the River Fynn and into the Lark Valley. By the eighth century new settlements had been established on the upland between the rivers, at, for example, Sutton and Rendlesham, east of the Deben, and at Foxhall and Grundisburgh to the west. These sites are marked by pottery made in Ipswich ('Ipswich Ware') that has been generally found near a church, so these are places that probably formed part of the early Christian landscape.[8] On John Newmans's model, new villages budded off from these centres in the ninth and tenth centuries.[9] At the Sutton Hoo site itself the activity so far defined is clustered on the ridge above the 30m contour. The Deben and its riverside has been richly chronicled by Tom Williamson, showing that the left bank was marked by a series of headlands carrying settlements served by an inner strip of fertile land including ploughland, with water-meadows on the low ground by the river and an upland platform of heath where sheep grazed. The use of the word 'heath' is confusing, because nowadays we think it to mean gorse, broom, bracken and shrubland rather than grass. But sheep graze on the grassy patches of moorland and this in turn helps to generate more pasture.[10]

Current terminology designates as 'Anglo-Saxon' the people who were living in the eastern and southern parts of the island of Britain from the fifth to the eleventh century AD, their presence marked by distinctive kinds of artefact, settlement and cemetery. The Venerable Bede believed that there had been a migration of folk from Denmark (Angles) and North Germany (Saxons), and that these people had settled on the eastern side of Britain, and had become the English: one race (the English) had dispossessed another (the Britons).[11] In our own time, the ethnicity of the Anglo-Saxons is seen more as a matter of assumed identity than of biological fact. Thus the pendulum of expectation has swung from visualizing a large influx of foreigners to a small but influential group and back again. The latest work, especially inspired by the publication of the Spong Hill cemetery in Norfolk, is that immigrants from a number of regions in continental north Europe did arrive in quite large numbers from the early fifth century onwards, coming in via the Wash and spreading up its rivers to north and west.[12] Linguistic and cultural areas began to be defined in the sixth century, by which time many 'Anglo-Saxons' were probably mongrels of mixed Scandinavian, north German and British parentage, but anxious, for all that, to be seen as a community with a past (even if it meant making it up) and a future (even if it must be fought for). Then, as now, the world was not a park for wanderers to settle where they might, but a hard school in which people competed for recognition and control of territory using force of argument, force of arms, diplomacy, deception, imaginary family connections, imaginary origins or whatever instrument or contrivance proved most effective. Early England, alas, was no garden of Eden: it seems to have been a bragging, bustling, competitive world.

The result of the competition was the kingdoms with which we are familiar: Wessex, Sussex, Essex proclaiming a Saxon origin, and Mercia and Northumbria considering themselves as Angles. Exactly when these kingdoms formed is not recorded, but it was probably late in the sixth and into the seventh century – the kingdom of East Anglia would not have acquired its name until incomers had become established further west. By Bede's day (he was writing in the early eighth century) all these people were the English, speaking a common language and disputing or adopting similar policies. It is legitimate, or at least less disputatious, and certainly easier of reference, to call the people buried at Sutton Hoo neither Saxon nor Angle, but 'early English'.

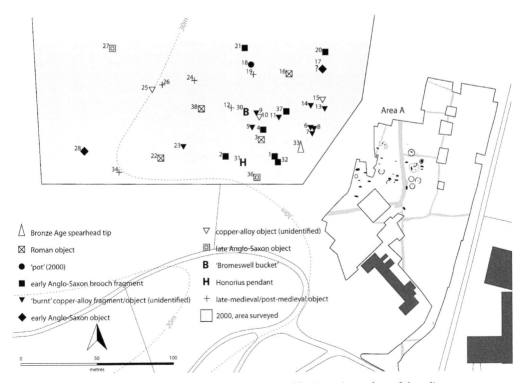

4.11: Excavations at Tranmer House with location of finds on the surface of the adjacent field. (COURTESY OF CHRIS FERN AND JENNY GLAZEBROOK)

THE TRANMER HOUSE CEMETERY: A PRECURSOR

Our earliest local encounter with the early English to date was in the cemetery discovered during excavations in advance of the construction of the visitor centre at Tranmer House, some 500m north of the monumental burial
mounds (**Fig.4.11**).[14] Here the archaeologists renewed their acquaintance
with the prehistoric landscape, encountering Neolithic pot-pits, a Bronze Age
burial mound, the Iron Age counterpane of enclosures and the continuation
of the long-lived ridge-top track. The early English were conscious of this
landscape: the bank and ditch of the Iron Age earthworks formed boundaries
for burial, and the Bronze Age barrow became a focus for the burial plot of a
prominent family group (Plot II; **Fig.4.12**).[15] In the area excavated there were
13 cremations, of which one was in a hanging bowl (Cr 8), and 10 were in pots,
of which two were dug into the Bronze Age barrow and five were under small
mounds. There were 19 inhumations in among the cremations, of which 13
were signified as male, being equipped with a spear, shield (**Fig.4.13**), knife
and buckle; two also had a sword (Burials 21 and 27). Of the remaining six,
four had annular brooches and amber beads with knife and buckle (Burials
19, 26, 30, 31), one had only a pot and a buckle (Burial 15) and one had only
an iron object (Burial 22). From their grave goods, at least four of these graves
should have remembered women.

Using radiocarbon dating on both cremated bone and skeletons, and
taking note of the date of objects, the researcher placed all the cremations in
the bracket 530-585 and the inhumations in three overlapping groups: one
510-570 (Phase A), six in 550-600 (Phase B) and one in 580-610 (Phase C). It
was noted that both migration (early) and conversion-period (later) artefacts
were missing, and the verdict was a date in the second half of the sixth century for most of the burials.[16] These were people who had settled and died
over 100 years after the first incomers had arrived via the Wash.

The dated burials suggested no particular axis of growth, so it looked as
though the cemetery was organised in family plots. Among the most prominent of these was 'Plot II', which had formed around the Bronze Age barrow
that stood beside the north-south ridge-top track. It had a majority of the ring
ditches (six out of nine), and a majority of the cremations (eight out of 12), and
four out of the five horses. Plot II also had one of the earliest inhumations (Inh
23) and also the latest (Inh 27), implying a history of use through the later sixth
century and just into the seventh - so, chronologically close to the first burials
at Sutton Hoo, modelled to lie around 600.[17]

In the unexcavated adjacent land (known to the National Trust as 'Garden
Field') several objects have been found on the surface that indicate that the
Tranmer House cemetery extends westwards towards the river and contains

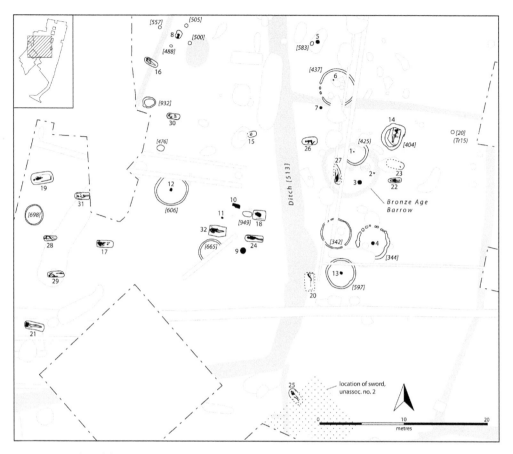

4.12: Plan of the excavated cemetery at Tranmer House, marking cremations (black spots) and inhumations. (COURTESY OF CHRIS FERN AND JENNY GLAZEBROOK)

both earlier graves and rich ones: seven fragments of brooches dating from the mid/late fifth to mid-sixth centuries, a pendant reusing a gold coin of the early fifth-century Roman emperor Honorius, and a copper-alloy Byzantine bucket probably made in Antioch around AD 500.[18]

This last object, which may have been used as a container for a cremation, was discovered when the Garden Field was harrowed in 1986. It shows images of a pair of warriors wearing 'corn-row' African-styled hair, armed with shields, swords, spears and arrows and accompanied by a hound. In the surviving parts of the frieze the two are seen attacking a lion, lionesses (?) and a griffin, although plenty of other game animals race around the rim (**Fig. 4.14**). The inscription in Greek reads 'Use this in good health, Master Count, for many happy years'. The story on the bucket has been decoded by Marlia Mango and her colleagues as depicting Atalanta and Meleager, characters known in the Greek myths. Atalanta, known for her running skills and fondness for apples,

4.13: Shield from Inh. 21 in the Tranmer House cemetery. (COURTESY OF THE BRITISH MUSEUM)

4.14: The incised frieze around the neck of the Bromeswell bucket.
(BRITISH MUSEUM; DRAWING BY JIM FARRANT)

was the only woman Argonaut. She repudiated marriage and dedicated her life to hunting (especially lions). Although Meleager was married, he yearned for Atalanta and, despite opposition from the all-male band of heroes, let her join the hunt for the Calydonian boar then ravaging southern Greece. Atalanta was the first to hit the murderous boar with an arrow, before Meleager scored with his javelin and finished it off with his spear. He then awarded the hide to Atalanta, a gesture that pricked the pride of rival males and ended in a family bloodbath. Although the characters depicted on this and other buckets of the group attack lions and a griffin, and one is armed with a sword and a Roman shield, the vignette is thought to incorporate a number of iconographic ideas which together stand for the exhilaration of the hunt, with perhaps the added zest of a heterosexual team working together - appropriate to the new mood generated by the joint reign of Justinian and Theodora at the time the bucket was made. Such buckets are known generally to belong to high-ranking officials or army officers, who used them in the baths.[19]

Like Sutton Hoo itself, the Tranmer House cemetery lies on the traditional border between Essex and East Anglia, where objects of both Saxon and Anglian cultural type have been encountered.[20] The strongest references are seen as Anglian with some Scandinavian influence. We note some particular funeral themes here: use of prehistoric earthworks, cremation in a bronze bowl, cremations under mounds and a preponderance of warrior graves. We will meet all of these attributes further south in the 'burial ground of kings', and it entitles us to the verdict that these sixth-century people belonged to the community, or even the families, that were to build the great mounds.

5 | BURIAL GROUND OF KINGS
AD590 to 650

The Sutton Hoo Cemetery and its sequence ♦ Cremations (Mounds 3-17, 18) ♦
A horse and rider (Mound 17) ♦ The Mound 2 ship-burial ♦ The Mound 1
ship-burial ♦ The youngsters ♦ The dowager ♦ A political theatre

THE SUTTON HOO CEMETERY AND ITS SEQUENCE

Up on the terrace on the east bank of the River Deben, in open grassland, in the decade around AD600, the people of the Sandlings began the development of a new and special cemetery. Was it then a remote spot? The new site had been used for agriculture, but not for some time, it seems. The Iron Age field banks were still visible and the surface was probably an acid grassland pasture. The River Deben would have been busy with boats, of both local and sea-going traffic. Opposite Sutton Hoo, the river swelled into a stretch of open water up to 250m across, where ships could gather and turn when the tide was full. At intervals alongside the river were well-established settlements - probably small farmsteads - and at certain places a kind of 'manorial' centre was being created, where the emerging aristocracy could draw tribute and hold court: sites located at Rendlesham, Sutton, Coddenham, Grundisburgh and Foxall are candidates. The people that lay in the Tranmer House cemetery had no doubt lived in a settlement nearby - not yet located, but possibly at a point on the Sutton Hoo promontory itself, where Tranmer House would later stand. The occupants of some of the new, wealthier centres may also have created small cemeteries of burial mounds, which in due course would be replaced by churches. Sutton Hoo was probably not the only new foundation to be seen on the banks of the Deben in the early seventh century.[1]

The Iron Age field system stretched along the 30m ridge, and it was on the corners of some of these relic fields that the first mounds were raised. At least 17 mounds were to be erected during the short life of the royal cemetery, in general commanding their own space and not touching each other (**Fig.5.1**). Precise evidence for the chronological order of their building therefore remains equivocal, and the sequence is not obvious from the layout. Which came first: Mounds 12, 17 and 18 because they are nearest to the river? Or Mound 2 because it is on the highest point? Or Mound 1 because it is the biggest *and* near the river edge? There are some clues from stratification. The Mound 2 quarry ditch cut a Mound 5 quarry pit, and another Mound 5 quarry pit was cut by one of Mound 6's quarry ditches. Mound 6 and 7 seem to have shared a quarry ditch system and could have been laid out at the same time. At the south end of Mound 7 the quarry ditch curves round. The building method varied between mounds: Mound 5 was quarried from a ring of pits. Mound 2 had a broad continuous encircling quarry ditch. Mound 1 had no quarry ditch (see Chapter 3, Fig. 3.32). This might indicate a 'learning process', from fiddly to smooth.

This implies that Mound 5 was first and Mounds 6 and 7 followed hard after, but no more mounds were immediately planned here. An empty space, in which no burials were found, lies between Mounds 1, 7, 13, 4 and 3, while another space, not yet proved blank by excavation, lies north of Mound 1. Mound 14, sited some way to the east, appears to be an afterthought. The finds and radiocarbon dates allow the cremations to precede the horse-burial (dated c.600), and are followed by the ship-burials (dated around 630) and then the battered Mound 14 (dated c.650). The juvenile burials (12, 15, 16) are focused on the eastern side of Mound 5. We can say little about the unexcavated Mounds 8, 9, 10, 11 and 15.

From these observations, a model can be constructed. Mounds 5, 6 and 7 (all cremations) appear to be the first burials at Sutton Hoo, with Mound 5 leading. Another cremation (Mound 18) and the horse-burial (Mound 17) came next, being at the front of the scarp. Two great ship-burials followed: Mound 2 in the north (ship over chamber) and Mound 1 in the south (chamber in ship). The children (Burials 12, 15 and 16) and a rich female (Mound 14) were interred further east and may have been among the latest. Another inhumation (Burial 56) was certainly late - it was radiocarbon-dated to the eighth century.[2] However, it is represented only by a detached skull and it is not impossible that it is a relic of an execution and belongs in Chapter 6.

Although this sequence has something of an eastward trend, the lesson from the Tranmer House cemetery is that the early English buried in family plots. Sutton Hoo is on a grander scale, with a great variety of burial sizes and rituals, so it is hard to see how such a contingency could be allowed for in advance. All the same, looking at the plan, at least two such groups present themselves as perhaps representing two families, or branches of the same family. In the north part, and marginally the highest part, a suite of three cremations in bronze bowls (Mounds 5, 6, 7) were followed by a horse-burial (17), a ship-burial (2), the children and a woman's chamber grave (14); in the south, two cremations may have initiated the second series (see Fig.5.1, where these groups are stippled).

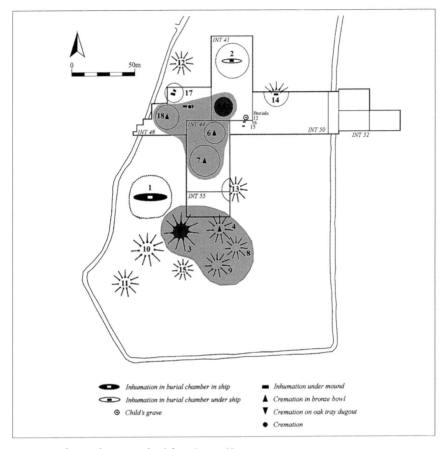

5.1: Map of seventh-century burials at Sutton Hoo.

The empty space east and north of Mound 1 may have had an initial role as an assembly area superseded or embellished by the mound that contained a prominent figure. Naturally, over a time span of 60 years, scarcely two generations, the memory of who was in each mound would stay fresh, and it is likely that some burials were added in retrospect in the gravitational field of a revered ancestor. The juvenile graves (Burials 12, 15 and 16) may have fallen into this category. The memory of who was in the mounds would surely have been retained even a century later, so that the placing of the two execution cemeteries, beginning in the eighth century, will be significant.

The overall Sutton Hoo sequence is therefore proposed to have been as follows: the Tranmer House cemetery was active in the mid-sixth century and discontinued in the early seventh (Phase 1). The Sutton Hoo burials begin in the late sixth or early seventh century (590-610), led by cremations in bronze bowls in a group of three mounds (5, 6, and 7), of which Mound 5 is stratigraphically the first (Phase 2). The horse and rider grave comes next (Phase 3).

Then the two ship-burials, Mound 2 and Mound 1, both of the early seventh century (Phase 4). The furnished graves of three juveniles were added east of Mound 5 at an unspecified time. The latest burial, dated by its silver ornaments, is Mound 14, probably datable to the mid-seventh century (Phase 5). This order of building will be used to present the events that unfolded in the Sutton Hoo princely burial ground. It is not a complete picture. The remaining excavated mounds (3, 4, 18) were cremations and so may belong to the initial phase. Of the undug mounds (8, 9, 10, 11, 12, 13, 15) we can guess little, and as a consequence our story cannot claim to be more than a convergent hypothesis. But this is the price one pays for leaving archaeological assets for the future: one will eventually, at some time, and in some measure, be shown to have been mistaken.[3]

CREMATIONS (MOUNDS 3-7, 18)

The person remembered in Mound 5 had died a violent death: the skull had been cut at least nine times by a sword or similar blade, with no sign of subsequent healing. The body was cremated, together with animals in the 'large ungulate category' (i.e. horses and cattle), and the ashes wrapped in cloth and gathered into a bronze bowl (**Fig.5.2**). The bowl was then placed in a pit and unburnt trinkets added: a dozen delicate bone gaming pieces, a pair of iron shears, silver-mounting from a type of cup used to contain tots of liquor, a piece of an ivory box with a sliding lid, like a little pencil case - perhaps intended to house a stylus - and probably much else besides, since lost to tomb-robbers.[4] Such grave goods as we have indicate a man.[5] The burial pit was then sealed or backfilled and a mound heaped upon it. To this end, three groups of mound-builders had extracted turf, soil and sand from a ring of quarry pits. The most energetic were on the west side, while those to the north dug small pits that were scarcely more than gestures. To the east, horses and cattle were killed, and - whether or not feasting followed - the heads of the animals found their way into the open quarry pits. Around Mound 5 were a series of traumatic inhumations, at first thought to have been victims sacrificed as part of the rituals enacted at the Mound 5 obsequies, but shown in the event to have been executions carried out some 100 years later, as the quarry pits were beginning to refill. Nevertheless, the use of Mound 5 alone for this form of retribution, practised subsequently over two centuries, indicates that it was then remembered as notable or notorious.

The rite of cremation continued to be practised in the line of mounds that had begun with Mound 5, all of them also subsequently robbed. The adult buried in Mound 6 had been cremated with a number of animals including a large ungulate (horse or cattle), a whole sheep and joints of pig.[6] Once again,

5.2: Cremated bone is placed in a bronze bowl, covered with a cloth and laid in a pit before being covered by a mound. Artist's impression by Victor Ambrus of the burial rite used in Mounds 5, 6 and 7.

5.3: (opposite) Mound 17: plan of the graves with the robber-pit between them.

the burnt remains were wrapped in a cloth before being placed in a bronze bowl. In addition to fragments of the bowl and the textile that had covered it, the surviving finds were a bronze inlaid pyramid from a sword suspension system, a bone comb, fragments of bone facings from a box and gaming counters. In Mound 7 horse, cattle, red deer, sheep or goat and pig accompanied the adult onto the pyre, and the finds included a large multicoloured bead with a hole through it, also perhaps from a sword suspension system, together with bone gaming pieces and fragments from a cauldron, from an iron-bound bucket and from a silver-mounted drinking horn or cup. In Mound 4 the burial contained cremated bone from both a man and a woman, together with horse and (possibly) dog. They were accompanied by gaming pieces. In Mound 3 the cremated remains of an adult man and a horse had been placed probably on a wooden trough, bier or dug-out boat, and lowered into a pit. Here were placed also a Frankish iron axe-head, burnt fragments from the facing of a bone casket that had carried a Christian chi-rho inscription, a bronze ewer from Nubia and a limestone plaque with a winged victory

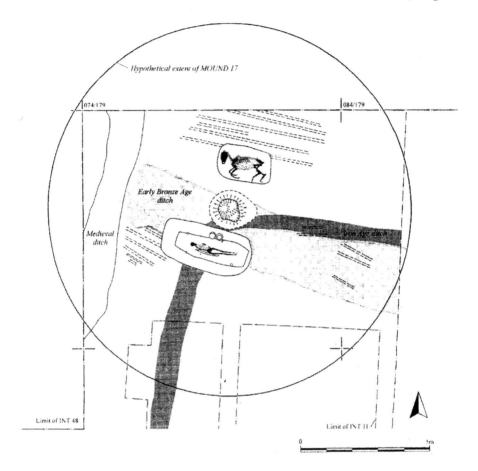

or angel from Alexandria.[7] An outlier to the west was Mound 18, a memorial to a young adult who had been cremated, and whose remains had been wrapped in cloth and placed in a bronze bowl. Only a fragment of a comb survived from the grave goods. None of the cremated remains could be sexed, but the grave goods have a male flavour to them.[8]

These cremations were in every case disfigured by later plundering, and left a strange assortment of objects, but they nevertheless seem to share a leitmotif. This was a group of individuals who were young, male, vain, belligerent and fond of board games; we could also guess that they rode, feasted, fought and, in at least one case, had died in an armed struggle. They had access to domestic animals and game and to classy imports. They were the new aristocracy of the seventh century.

A HORSE AND RIDER (MOUND 17)

Not out of place in their company was a young man buried, but in a very different way, under Mound 17 (**Figs 5.3, 5.4**). The place chosen was the north-

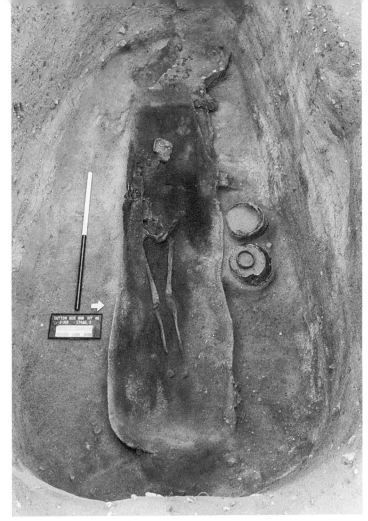

west corner of the old earthwork which carried Mound 5, 6 and 18, near the edge of the scarp that overlooked the river. Two pits were dug side by side, the turf, soil and sand being thrown up in heaps to east, west, north and south. Some of the sand was washed back in, perhaps overnight, before the funeral cortège arrived. Then the larger of the two pits was furnished, perhaps with the aid of a pole sloping into the pit like a ladder.[9] Two spears were laid on the base of the pit, and upon them a shield, laid flat with its iron boss uppermost. An iron-bound bucket and a bronze cauldron were placed along the north edge of the pit. The cauldron must have contained some perishable material, such as grain, since an earthenware pot was found sitting within it, the grain replaced by sand. Next to the cauldron, on the east side, was a haversack, in the shape of a small kit bag, containing lamb chops and probably some other foodstuffs of an eternal picnic (bread? or apples?) all trace of which had unfortunately vanished, apart from a stain; but these items had propped up a bronze bowl, which remained at the mouth of the bag (Fig.5.5).

A splendid harness was deposited at the west end; a snaffle bit with

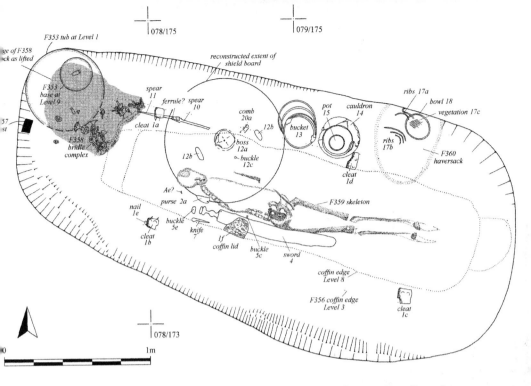

5.5: Mound 17: plan of the human grave with its contents. Note the two pairs of iron cleats (or clamps) either side of the wooden coffin.

ornamented gilt-bronze cheekpieces was originally joined to reins, and by leather (calf-skin) straps to a browband and noseband; all were connected by strap-distributors covered with gilded bronze disks ornamented with writhing animals (**Fig.5.6**). And, just as the strap ends of human garments so often carry animal ornament, in a neat reversal of the norm the gilded strap-ends of this harness carried little human icons, a set of anxious faces with moustaches. The strap connectors of the bridle were enlivened with axe-shaped gilded pendants, while a set of small axe-shaped bronze pendants, covered with silver sheet, probably came from a body harness (**Fig.5.7**). Leather, wood fragments, bronze pins and a buckle above the bridle probably originated as part of a saddle and a girth strap. On the top of the heap was a tapering tub made of solid wood, the sort of receptacle in which to give a horse his bran. And in an adjacent pit to the north lay the body of the horse, killed, we must suppose, to accompany his master. It was a stallion or gelding, five or six years old, which stood at around 14 hands (c.1.44m at the shoulder)[10] (**Fig. 5.8**). Reconstructing the harness as a whole shows what splendour and status might have been achieved in the seventh century by dressing one's horse (**Fig.5.9**).[11]

The moment came for the coffin to be placed in the grave. It was a bisected tree-trunk, the lid joined to the sides with four large curved iron clamps with two nails at each side, hammered into the wood (**Fig.5.10**). Inside the coffin

127

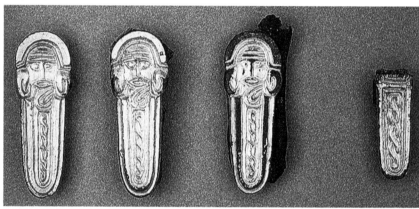

5.6: Mound 17: parts of the horse harness: (top row) strap-distributors with axe-shaped pendants from the bridle; (centre) strap-ends or pendants from the bridle; (bottom) the iron snaffle bit with gilded cheek piece terminals.
(BRITISH MUSEUM)

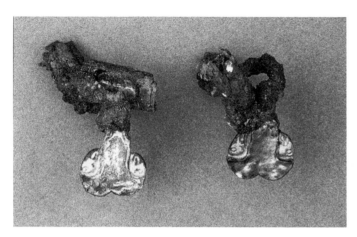

5.7: Silver gilt pendants and strap-connectors, probably from the body harness.
(BRITISH MUSEUM)

was the body of a young man, about 25 years old, his sword at his side and a purse by his shoulder. The sword had a pommel of horn, and the sword belt a buckle of bronze inlaid with leaf-shaped garnets (**Fig.5.11**). The purse contained mementoes or lucky keepsakes: a piece of millefiori, some garnets, a pebble. Whether by accident or perforce, the coffin was lowered on to the stud of the shield and canted over. Inside the coffin, the body of the young man rolled against his sword. Now the grave would be filled in; the spades dug into the heaps of earth on the east and west sides and the sand and pebbles rattled on to the coffin lid. But there was one more object to come, a personal one. A comb seems to have been dropped or placed on the coffin-lid, since it ended up standing almost vertically against its side. One of the mourners had no doubt remembered, probably not for the first time, an unkempt youth, liable to forget his comb (**Fig.5.12**).

Whether dressed like this for life, or just for his journey into the other world, the Mound 17 person conjures up an image worthy of a young Siegfried: mounted on his stallion, with gold and silver roundels, strap-ends and pendants dangling and catching the light; the horn-pommelled sword in its sheath, right arm holding the spears, left arm through the shield strap and left hand holding the reins; and, behind, attached to the saddle or body harness, the camping kit: bucket, cauldron and pot, and the haversack with iron rations and a bronze bowl to fill at forest stream or spring. His early death was mourned through an evocation of every young man's dream: to ride out well-equipped and self-sufficient on a favourite mount, on a sunny morning, free of relatives, free of love, free of responsibility and ready for any adventure.

THE MOUND 2 SHIP-BURIAL

From these burials of high rank and varied ritual we now approach Sutton Hoo's funerary climax, Mound 1 and Mound 2, which represent not only still

5.8: The Mound 17 horse, buried in a separate pit alongside its rider. The form of the animal survived partly as bone, partly as sand-stain. (NIGEL MACBETH)

higher rank and more idiosyncratic ritual but the most extravagant funerary investments so far known from Britain.

The land where the Mound 2 burial was to be made had been ploughed, but was now under grass; an Iron Age boundary was seemingly still visible and had been used to locate the mound and align the ship.[12] The party responsible for planning the burial laid out an exceptionally large memorial. On what was locally the highest point on the terrace overlooking the River Deben they reserved an oval area measuring about 20m north-south and 25m east-west. Then the turf was stripped and stacked, ready to be used later in the construction of the mound.

In the centre of this reserved area a rectangular burial chamber was dug: it was to be 1.2m wide, 3.6m long and 1.8m deep from the old ground surface, now stripped of its turf. The brown soil and yellow subsoil excavated from the chamber was heaped up on the north side. Once dug, the deep pit was lined with overlapping vertical planks along its north and south sides, probably held in place with horizontal shoring planks secured by struts jammed across the chamber pit. The short walls to east and west appear to have been formed by horizontal planks dropped behind the ends of the long sides. In this way the burial party contrived an underground room (**Fig.5.13**).

The chamber was now ready to be furnished, and it was furnished richly. Unfortunately its richness proved irresistible to later visitors, leaving us only

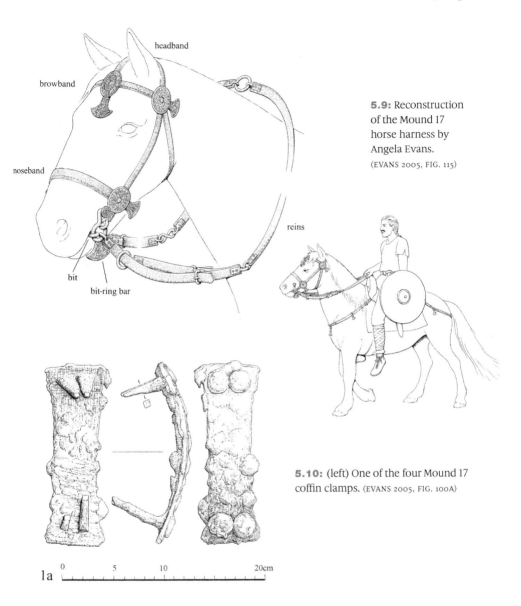

5.9: Reconstruction of the Mound 17 horse harness by Angela Evans. (EVANS 2005, FIG. 115)

5.10: (left) One of the four Mound 17 coffin clamps. (EVANS 2005, FIG. 100A)

scraps and stains to guess at its original tableau. With the enhancement of chemical mapping (see p.87, Fig. 3.24), this much can be said: the burial was equipped with a sword, a spear, a shield with gilt bronze mounts and a baldric which included a gilded bronze buckle. There were drinking horns, a blue glass jar, a bronze bowl and a silver-mounted box. There were five knives, including two in a double sheath. At the east end was an iron-bound bucket and, perhaps, a cauldron with a chain. The dead man lay at the west end; the rest our imagination must supply - and with the example of Mound 1 before us who knows what treasures would have been among them.[13]

5.11: The sword harness from the Mound 17 burial. From the top: two pyramids used as strap-ends for the straps that secured the sword in its scabbard; the belt buckle; a linear mount from the scabbard; and a small buckle. It was employed in the suspension of the scabbard. (BRITISH MUSEUM)

So far, the burial was splendid, but conventional - a chamber grave. But what came next was, so far as we know, a 'first' for the western world. A stout beam was laid across the open chamber - it also probably served to prop up a ladder used to furnish the tomb. The burial party said its last farewells. And then a ship, about 20m long, was dragged across the oval platform and over the chamber, brushing past the spoil heap, the centre of its keel-plank resting on the beam. It would need to have been propped by raking timbers to north and south to prevent it 'capsizing' when it was being filled with earth. If

5.12: Mound 17: the day of burial. (ARTIST'S IMPRESSION BY VICTOR AMBRUS)

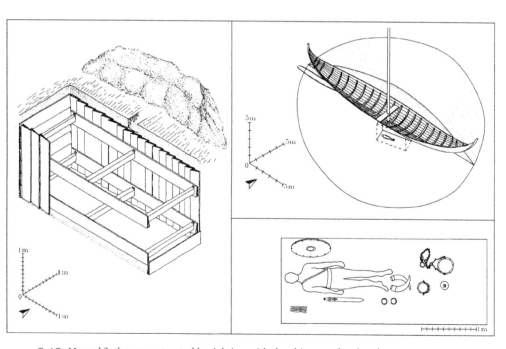

5.13: Mound 2: the reconstructed burial rite, with the ship over the chamber.
(DRAWN BY JAMES BRENNAN)

there was a mast it could have remained in place; if there were figurehead and sternpost, they too could remain. So now the chamber had been sealed - by the hull of a large clinker-built vessel (**Fig.5.14**).[14]

How much time elapsed between the placing of the ship and the building of the mound is not known. One imagines that this kind of investment - a richly furnished underground chamber, a ship and a mound - was not a thing to be done in a corner or done in a hurry. It was meant to be seen, and remembered, by friends, allies, subjects and enemies, as an extravagant demonstration of recognition in heaven and continuing power on earth. It is even possible that the ship stood for some years, until, perhaps at some anniversary, a new memorial service was convened at which the mound was constructed.

The position of the ship itself guided the mound-builders; their spoil was taken from a broad if ragged quarry ditch. Two causeways were left, to east and west, to ease loading. Many hundreds of tons of turf, soil and then sand and gravel subsoil were lifted into the ship and around it, and then piled upon it. The mound would have risen against the skyline until only the prow and sternposts, and a mast if there was one, still showed. Last to be added were probably those stacked turves that had been stripped from the mound platform and could be used to prevent large-scale slippage. The stones from the final loads of sand and gravel rolled down into the quarry ditch; and surplus soil, now mixed from transportation, found its way back into the quarries.

Because the quarry ditch had survived at Mound 2 it was possible to calculate how much soil had been taken out of it from the level of the old ground surface. From this the volume (or cross-section area) of the mound could be estimated and, since the diameter was known (22.30m), the original height of the dome. This worked out as 2.7-3.8m. Assuming that the volume of the soil dug out from the quarry ditch was 790 cu. m and the volume of a wheelbarrow is 0.1 cu. m, and that it takes one person five minutes to dig out soil, fill a barrow and take it up a ramp to add to a mound, it would have taken about 660 man-hours to build Mound 2 (assuming they had wheelbarrows); carrying sacks would take longer. From this one can calculate that it would take at least ten man-weeks - that is, ten men working a ten-hour day for a six- or seven-day week - to build a mound this size. This represents a considerable investment of labour, perhaps the equivalent workload of an additional harvest. In 1992 we used the less strenuous method of an earth-moving machine to reconstruct Mound 2. It now stands to a height of around 3m and is visible from across the River Deben, showing that it acted as a memorial, a monument and a landmark.

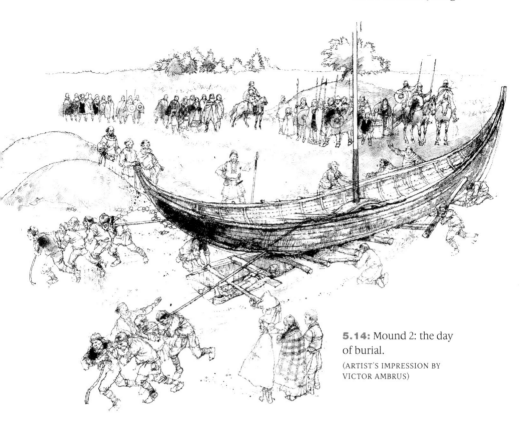

5.14: Mound 2: the day of burial.
(ARTIST'S IMPRESSION BY VICTOR AMBRUS)

THE MOUND 1 SHIP-BURIAL

Mound 2 was one of the largest and richest burials known from Sutton Hoo; but not the largest or the richest. This honour belongs to Mound 1, the other and more famous ship-burial - most famous perhaps because it has come to us intact. But, given its highly unusual content, it was probably famous then, too. Even though it was unrobbed, the uneven survival of materials within the chamber and the circumstances of their discovery mean that several important aspects of the burial rite remain uncertain: the route taken by the burial ship, the structure of the chamber, whether there was a coffin. Our inferences will always be limited, and some details will never be known, since we cannot now return to the 1939 excavation, or indeed the seventh century. But our task here is to draw the maximum from the encounter, using imagination built on science.

The site chosen was on flat ground on a promontory facing the river, suggested above as the assembly point for the two families and their followers. There was to be no dug chamber and no quarry ditch. Turf was stripped and stacked (since some would be used in the mound make-up). A trench 28m long and up to 6m wide was laid out east-west and excavated: descending to

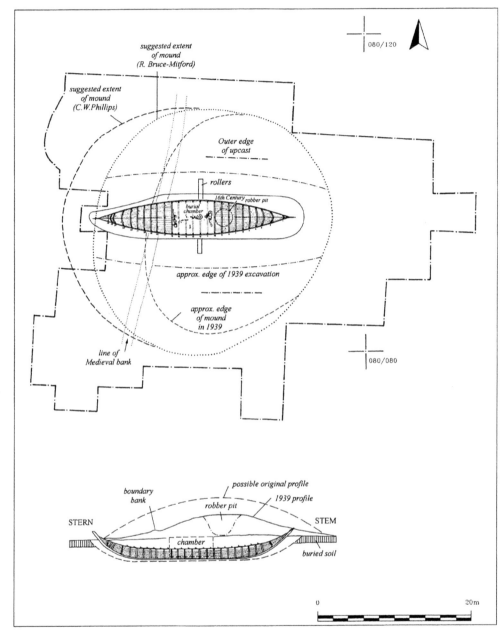

Labels on the plan:
suggested extent of mound (R. Bruce-Mitford)
suggested extent of mound (C.W.Phillips)
Outer edge of upcast
rollers
16th Century robber pit
burial chamber
approx. edge of 1939 excavation
approx. edge of mound in 1939
line of Medieval bank
080/120
080/080

Labels on the section:
boundary bank
possible original profile
1939 profile
robber pit
STERN
STEM
chamber
buried soil
0   20m

5.15: (above) Mound 1: plan of the ship in mound as recorded in the 1939 and 1965-71 excavations. (COMPOSITE DRAWING BY ANNETTE ROE AND ELIZABETH HOOPER)

5.16: (opposite) The terrace on the left bank of the River Deben, showing the cemeteries and the possible routes used to drag ships to Mounds 1 and 2 (*CSH*, Fig. 220).

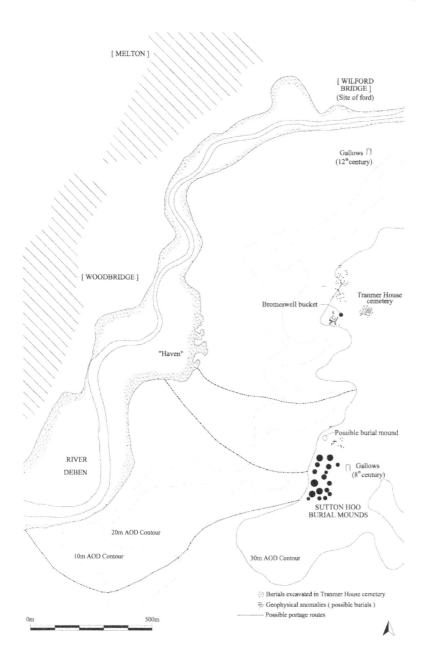

[MELTON]

[WILFORD
BRIDGE]
(Site of ford)

Gallows
(12ᵗʰ century)

[WOODBRIDGE]

Bromeswell bucket

Tranmer House
cemetery

"Haven"

Possible burial mound

RIVER

DEBEN

Gallows
(8ᵗʰ century)

SUTTON HOO
BURIAL MOUNDS

20m AOD Contour

10m AOD Contour

30m AOD Contour

Burials excavated in Tranmer House cemetery
Geophysical anomalies (possible burials)
Possible portage routes

0m   500m

3.5m below the Anglo-Saxon ground surface, it was the biggest hole yet dug
in the burial ground. Nearly 600 cu. m of soil and subsoil were excavated and
piled up in two large spoil heaps to north and south. These were then cut back
to give a clearance of 4.5m to the north and 7m to the south, to allow access
for the ship and the burial party. A whole ship was to be buried below ground,
and the burial chamber placed inside the vessel, amidships (**Fig.5.15**).

Although little is known about how the ship made its way to its grave, the rivet pattern on the hull indicated that it had been patched and was thus a working vessel, not one especially built for burial. The task of bringing such a huge ship out of the water and up onto the heath seems formidable to us, but must have been a feasible procedure to those accustomed to transporting vessels over land, following 'portage' routes from one stretch of water to another. Experiments with some of these land journeys show how they might have been achieved.[16] The Sutton Hoo ships were probably brought up from the river on rollers via re-entrant valleys opposite the burial ground, or perhaps from even further south, so as to follow a gentler approach northwards to the burial site (Fig.5.16). Putting a long ship into a trench cut to size would seem to be no easy matter. In one possible procedure, it would be dragged prow-first on rollers up to the 30m contour and then led between the spoil heaps on until it was over the prepared trench. Then a group of men would put their weight on the back end of the ship so the rollers could be eased out at the front; once their weight was removed, the stem could tilt down into the trench. The free rollers removed, those still bearing load would be hammered back towards the stern, lowering the length of the ship, the last one slipping round the curved stern and out. The ship now lay in its trench without signs of a struggle, albeit heeling over at a slight angle. At 27m long, it was the longest ship so far known from Europe before the Viking era.[17] It was clinker built, with a hull formed from nine strakes per side, held together by some 3,000 iron rivets. A frame of 26 ribs was pegged to the hull. The massive timber ship may have been carved with an ornamental figurehead, and perhaps decorated with shallow-carved interlinked animals all the way down the prow and sternposts, like the later Oseberg ship (pp. 61, 202). This imagined decoration is lost to us, but Anglo-Saxons were surely just as adroit at carving wood as they were shortly to become at illuminating manuscripts.

During the excavation a mass of corky wood was found in the centre of the ship, covering a long low hump 'like a blanket'.[18] The grave goods were mostly found beneath this blanket, which must therefore have belonged to a roof, this implying in turn a supporting structure. Sixty years later, further analysis, enlightened by analogies with the coffin in Mound 17 and with the chamber in the Oseberg ship-burial, has resolved this woody heap into a chamber, a floor and a coffin (Fig.5.17).[19] In this model, a series of joists was first laid across the width of the hull from north to south, coincident with ribs. Then a floor of planks was laid on these joists, to run east-west, parallel with the keel, stretching from rib 10 to rib 16, a distance of 5.5m. The floor was approximately level with the horizontal junction between strakes 5 and 6, and the clearance over the keel was about 30cm.

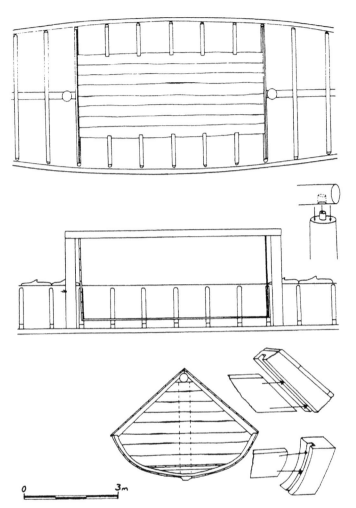

5.17: Mound 1: reconstruction of the possible form of the burial chamber.
(DRAWN BY JAMES BRENNAN)

The existence of a tree-trunk coffin was argued mainly from the two rows of iron clamps, some curved, and the analogy provided by the coffin in Mound 17. Judging from the extent of the heap and the distribution of objects, such a coffin would have been at least 1m wide and more than 3m long: large enough to contain a body at one end and a pile of personal effects at the other (**Figs 5.18, 5.19**). Such massive containers, made from hollowed-out tree trunks and placed in wooden chambers, are well known in early medieval Europe, although, as with other constructions involving very decayed wood, the details are often elusive. The well-preserved wood at the German cemetery at Oberflacht shows an astonishing variety of containers, including a tree-trunk coffin with a double-headed serpent carved on the roof (**Fig.5.20**).[20] If such things have evaded us at Sutton Hoo, the grandeur of a coffin, especially a carved one, is arguably more in keeping with the status of Mound 1 in the top

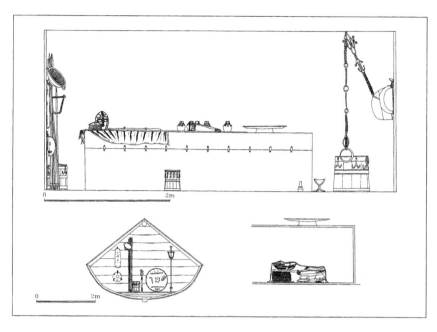

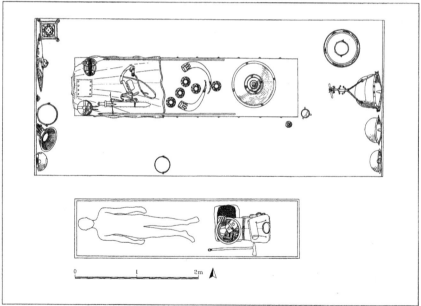

5.18: Mound 1: reconstruction of the furnished chamber, in profile and elevation.
(DRAWN BY JAMES BRENNAN)

5.19: Mound 1: reconstruction of the furnished chamber, in plan.
(DRAWN BY JAMES BRENNAN)

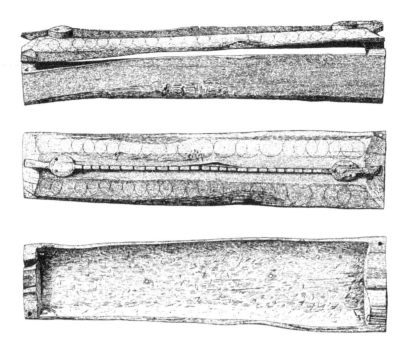

5.20: Preserved dug-out tree-trunk wooden coffins found at the sixth-/seventh-century cemetery at Oberflacht, Baden-Würtemberg, Germany. (CARVER AND FERN 2005, FIG.134; AFTER SCHIEK 1992, TAF. 11).

rank of contemporary European memorials.[21] Given its size, the coffin was probably dragged in and placed on the floor before the end walls were built.

Two large upright posts were founded on the keel outside the floor at each end, their upper ends presumably tenoned into a ridge beam. Against the upright posts and on top of the floor, horizontal planks about 2.5cm thick were placed on edge one above the other to make the end walls; they may have been secured in a groove in the rib. As in Oseberg, the rafters may have been cut so that they lay with their lower ends 'beaked' on the gunwale and their upper ends resting on the ridge beam. The end walls were continued upwards above the gunwale, each wall plank let into a groove cut in the inside face of the end rafters. The end walls would thus be completely secured by ribs and rafters. The lowest plank was secured to the floor by a few nails. The roof was made of planks laid edge to edge and running east-west over the rafters.

The end walls were standing when the chamber was furnished, as objects were stacked against them or hung on them with nails. So, part of the structure, most conveniently perhaps one side of the roof, must have been left incomplete, both to load the chamber and to allow mourners to view the tableau from the surface of the ground. The furnishing was carried out as methodically as a new room in a house (**Fig.5.21**). Textiles were hung on the

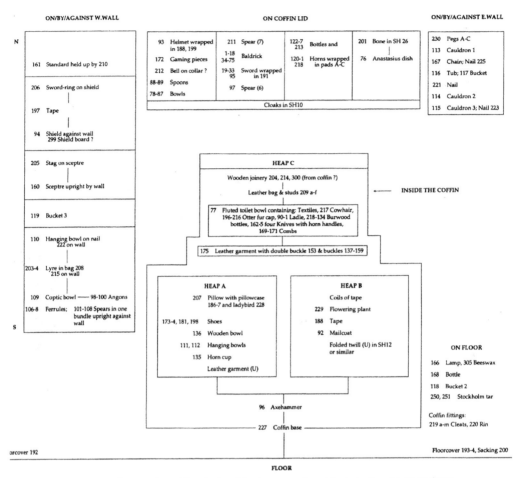

5.21: Mound 1: Stratigraphic relationships between the objects in the chamber, from which the order of furnishing was deduced.

walls and a carpet lay on the floor.[22] Next to be furnished was probably the east wall, which carried two large oak pegs. On these were hung a cauldron, empty, but with a working capacity of 100 litres, its chain looped up onto a nail, together with two smaller cauldrons and a tub, which completed the food and kitchen provision.[23] The west wall was laden with the symbols of office. An iron standard was wedged between floor and roof (**Fig.5.22**). The shield, carrying its dragon and hawk or falcon motifs, stood upright against the west wall (**Fig.23**). On the south side hung a lyre in a beaver-skin bag, and just below it a large and luxurious hanging bowl (**Fig.5.24**). Further to the south, a bunch of five spears and three angons (a weapon resembling the later pike) were threaded through the handle of a 'Coptic' bowl and leant up against the wall. The bowl, an exotic item from North Africa, carried images of a camel, a lion and a donkey.

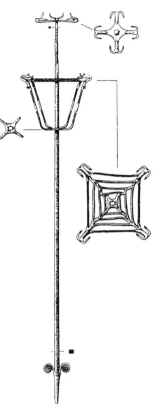

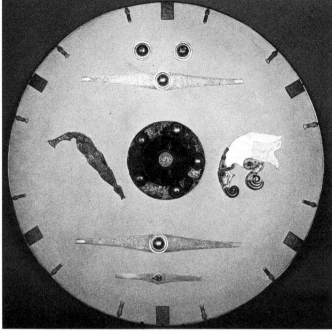

5.22: Mound 1: the iron standard. (BRITISH MUSEUM)

5.23: Mound 1: the shield. (BRITISH MUSEUM)

The putative coffin stood towards one end of the chamber, its lid at this point off and lying on the floor. The dead man, probably wrapped in a shroud, was laid out at its west end. Into the space at the east end of the coffin, by the dead man's feet, were piled objects of a mainly personal kind. An axe-hammer lay at the base. Then two heaps were begun. That furthest from the dead man's feet ('Heap A') consisted of a leather garment, a horn cup and two little hanging bowls, a wooden bowl and, on top, a goose-down pillow in its pillow case. A ladybird had contrived to find its way into the pillow (although not out of it). On either side of the pillow were placed two pairs of indoor shoes, the length of one measurable at size 7 (or size 40 continental): was the Mound 1 hero short and stocky? (**Fig.5.25**) The heap nearer to the feet ('Heap B') began with a piece of folded twill on which a mailcoat was placed, together with many coils of tape, perhaps for fastening garments. Here a flower was laid.

Both heaps together were now covered by a third ('Heap C'), which began with a large leather garment with a double buckle and a number of single buckles. On this lay the toiletries: a fluted silver bowl (**Fig.5.26**) containing several combs, four knives with horn handles, seven burrwood bottles presumably containing various ointments, a silver ladle, fragments of textile and

5.24: Mound 1: Hanging bowl 1, with detail of the enamel and glass escutcheon: diameter of bowl 310 mm; of escutcheon 62 mm.
(BRITISH MUSEUM)

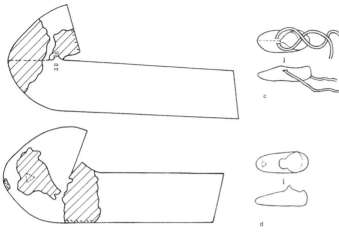

5.25: (left) Mound 1: reconstruction of the shoes (length 272 mm).

(SHSB III, FIG. 574, C & D)

5.26: (below) Mound 1: fluted silver bowl (diameter 410 mm).

(BRITISH MUSEUM; SHSB III, PLATE 2)

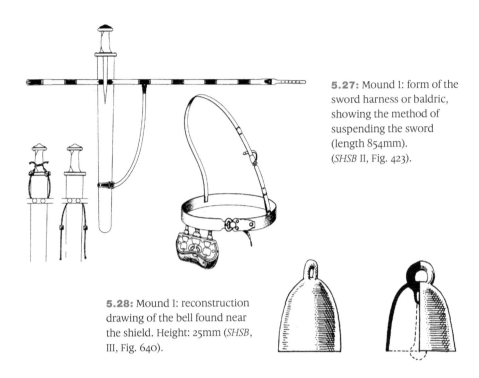

5.27: Mound 1: form of the sword harness or baldric, showing the method of suspending the sword (length 854mm). (*SHSB* II, Fig. 423).

5.28: Mound 1: reconstruction drawing of the bell found near the shield. Height: 25mm (*SHSB*, III, Fig. 640).

an otter-fur cap. On top of the now tottering heap contained (on this analysis) by the coffin walls was a leather object with studs, perhaps the equivalent of a travelling bag or suitcase, and on top of that a fine yellow cloak.

Now it was time to say goodbye to the person as an individual and replace the coffin lid, hammering home ten cleats on each side to secure it. But outside and on top of the coffin the celebration of the person as a statesman was to continue. The remaining two of the three yellow cloaks were thrown over the coffin lid. On them at the east end was placed a great silver dish, imported from Constantinople and bearing the stamp of the emperor Anastasius. On it were food or burnt offerings. In the centre was a group of maplewood drinking bottles and two huge drinking-horns, wrapped in cloth to keep them clean until ready for use. Still further west were placed two spears, one along each edge to guard the parade gear that was deposited in the centre of the west end of the coffin. This comprised a baldric with a buckle of solid gold and connectors of gold and garnet; the shoulder clasps resembled those of a Roman officer, as splendid and individual as anything worn by a centurion (see Fig. 2.5). The baldric supported a purse with a gold frame, its lid guarded by ornamental gold and garnet animals. It contained 37 gold coins, three blanks and two little ingots.[24] On a separate belt was a sword with a pattern-welded blade 85cm long and a wooden scabbard, lined inside with wool. The scabbard carried two little hemispherical bosses, elaborate studs which

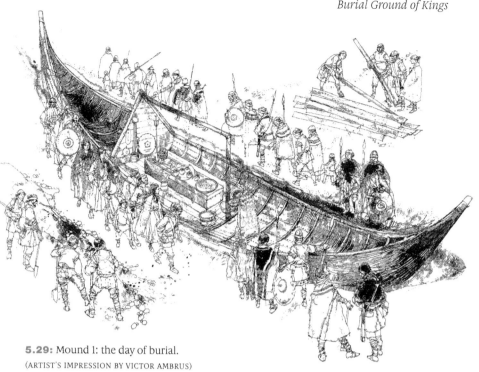

5.29: Mound 1: the day of burial.
(ARTIST'S IMPRESSION BY VICTOR AMBRUS)

secured the sword-belt to the scabbard. A connecting strap secured by a triangular buckle led from the end of the scabbard to a swivel on the sword-belt. When the sword was sheathed the sword pommel was secured with tapes or thongs that had carried little pyramids at the ends, one of which had provided the excavators with the first glimpse of gold (see Fig. 1.13). Pommel, connectors, bosses, buckles and pyramids were all of gold, inlaid with cut garnets: East Anglia's finest jewellery, in a matching set (**Fig.5.27**).

Most of the weapons and drinking vessels seem to have been wrapped in cloth to keep them in serviceable condition during the metaphorical voyage.[25] At the very end of the coffin, and still on its lid, was a nest of silver bowls ornamented with crosses, originally perhaps finger-bowls for the feasting of Christian diners, and two silver spoons. On the coffin lid too was the helmet wrapped up in cloth, and a set of gaming pieces (no one in the Anglo-Saxon world was ever too grand for board games). There was also a little bell on a collar (**Fig.5.28**), perhaps from a favourite falcon, whose mortal remains were to disappear into the dark sand in which all the contents of the chamber were eventually to be immersed.

Now the tableau of the dead man was almost ready. There was still space to circulate and admire all these treasures and gifts, which may have been brought together for the first and last time. A few more items were put on the floor: a bucket by the west wall and another by the south gunwale; near the

5.30: Mound 1: drawing of the iron lamp, restored to its original shape. It stands 160mm high (*SHSB* III, 847, Fig. 605).

east end of the coffin was an iron lamp with its beeswax cake of fuel. A little bottle containing, perhaps, honey or a condiment ended up on the floor, but may have started on or near the silver dish. At the west end in the centre, in the midst of the regalia, the whetstone sceptre stood in an upright position.

The time arrived when enough people had filed along the side of the ship and peered into the chamber; enough speeches had been made and dirges sung; those who were to weep had wept; and those who wished to walk away had gone and the obsequies were finished (**Fig.5.29**). Then the remaining half of the roof could be put in place. Before the rafters were in, someone could slip down and light the lamp (**Fig.5.30**). If so, it did not burn for long, since the cake of beeswax fuel was little used. The roof planks were laid in position, and then possibly turfed over for security. It is unlikely that the boat was filled in and the mound constructed immediately. Indeed, it would have been a colossal task, suitable to celebrate an anniversary or a victory in the struggle for survival of the young East Anglian state. But the task was eventually faced, for the ship and its trench were filled in and a mound several metres high was raised. The burial chamber, its roof wedged tightly shut by the pressure of earth bearing via the rafters against the hull in its trench, was of enormous strength. It would be many decades, perhaps centuries, before it collapsed and compressed the grandly furnished chamber into a fragmented sandwich of rotten wood and metal - the form in which it was to be found.

The Mound 1 finds form a wonderful assemblage: many and varied were the objects assembled in this chamber, and the references suggested by them are diverse and complex and operate at many levels in the mind, then and now. The man is a warrior, equipped for war with helmet, mailcoat, sword, shield and spears. He is a host, ready to put on a feast, with cauldrons, tub, bowls of bronze and silver, drinking horns, wooden bottles, a great silver dish - and entertainment from the lyre-player. He is a leader, dressed in glittering parade dress with highly symbolic accoutrements, his office marked by a standard and a sceptre. For all that, he is a man, with washing and shaving kit, a selection of clothing and shoes, and a soft pillow at the end of the day.

The placing of the burial in a 'cabin' on board a ship evokes the allegory of a voyage, in this case that voyage from which no traveller returns. It puts us in mind of the poetry of the Anglo-Saxons, and of the old English poem *Beowulf* in particular, which refers to the deeds of early heroes and their deaths and burial ceremonies involving ships (p.28). Dead heroes go well-equipped to eternal encounters across the sea. Is this Mound 1's simple message? Perhaps, but the funeral was also a public spectacle, an event of the real world, and political reality must keep breaking in. The burial makes references to practices in Scandinavia, where ship-burial in the seventh century and later is best known. It includes coins from France, silver from the Byzantine eastern Mediterranean and objects from Italy and the Near East. And every item of jewellery and weaponry included was the result of earlier manufacture, earlier use, earlier choice.

But we should not rely on any one of these factors to explain the Mound 1 ship-burial, for this kind of deliberate deposition is unlikely to have been a direct reflection either of real life or of belief. It was a huge investment suggesting deep feeling and bringing forth, from the burial party and its sponsors, a composition that tries to express the fundamentals of loss and hope. In short, the burial is itself a poem, full of references that are interlaced with each other: references to life in the hall, to how a ship is stowed, to the status of the dead person, in reality or aspiration, and at a more personal level to the foibles and achievements of the individual. Looked at in this way, such a burial is a web of allusions, and does not permit a simple or a single explanation; like poetry it will continue to intrigue us and we shall continue to find within it new meanings to suit our own times. Like poetry its meaning at the time depends heavily on the historical context in which it was enacted. In the interpretation presented here, the Sutton Hoo burial ground as a whole can be presented as a theatre, in which each burial is a composition, offering, with greater or lesser authority, a metaphor for its age. The cemetery is an anthology of statements, connected by certain themes, some of which perhaps can be read clearly enough to allow us to make history from them.

THE YOUNGSTERS

The inhumation rite was used for other burials that lay east and west of the main axis of cremations. One (Burial 12) was the grave of a child, in a coffin less than 1.2m long. The child could not have been more than seven years old, but he had already been given arms: he wore a small belt buckle and dress pin, and a miniature spear lay inside the coffin. The grave was originally covered by a mini-mound less than 2m across, indicated by a shallow circular groove around the outside of the grave. Here was evidence that Anglo-Saxon society at Sutton Hoo, as elsewhere, had reached the stage in which status could be inherited, as opposed to achieved. Two other inhumations (Burials 15 and 16)

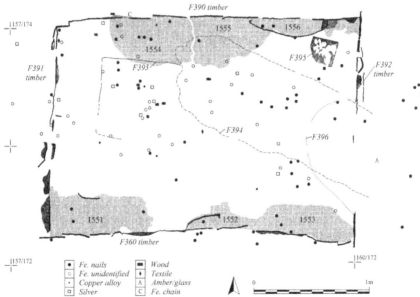

5.31: Mound 14: Photograph of the burial chamber floor (above) and the drawn plan of the anomalies (below). (SUTTON HOO ARCHIVE; *CSH*, FIG. 46)

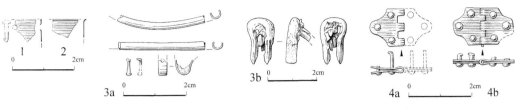

5.32: Silver fragments from Mound 14, with possible identifications: (1) rim of a bowl; (2) rim of a cup; (3) parts of a purse frame; (4) hinges from a casket. (EVANS 2005, 211-14)

made a row with Burial 12 and may also have been covered by small mounds, although no trace of these remained. The person in Burial 15 appears to have been laid on a small boat or section of a boat, wore a leather belt with two bronze buckles, one with a tiny gold cell containing a flat circular garnet at the base of the tongue, and carried a knife in a sheath. The Burial 16 person lay in, on or under a rectangular container with cross-members, which may have been a plank coffin or box-bed. The occupant wore a belt carrying an iron châtelaine, the emblem of the well-bred woman, and a leather pouch with draw-strings. The châtelaine included three latch-lifters and a small knife. By the left ear was a hair tie - a leather loop with a pin and a tiny white bead.[26] Although the remains were almost past recognition, Burials 15 and 16 probably represent, respectively, the bodies of a teenage boy and girl.

THE DOWAGER

Still further to the east lay Mound 14, greatly intriguing as the tomb of the only high-ranking woman so far found at Sutton Hoo. The mound had covered a chamber 2.65 × 1.90 m in size, its edges originally lined with thin slats. The grave had been ransacked during a thunderstorm, and interpretation of the findings in 1991 was dependent on scraps of broken objects and shadows seen in the sand on the floor of the chamber (Chapter 3, pp. 87-8). The largest of these shadows was caused by the robber trench, but this had obscured a second rectangular form that suggests a coffin or bed (**Fig. 5.31**). A number of iron tacks (87 of them) were found, some associated with the chamber walls but most scattered in the centre of the chamber with some fragments of wood. The tacks were short and stubby, so leading to the idea that they had been used to upholster a coffin, box-bed or couch.[27]

Found in the chamber were fragments implying the one-time presence of silver fittings for a purse, a silver bowl, a least one wooden drinking vessel with silver rim-mounts and facings, silver hinges, perhaps from a casket, a silver dress-fastener, two or three silver buckles, some tiny lengths of silver wire from a foxtail chain, and an iron knife (**Fig. 5.32**). Decisive for the identification of the burial as that of a woman was the discovery of a châtelaine, damaged beyond restoration but including rods, links and rings of bronze or iron.[28]

5.33: Textiles from Mound 14 A: embroidery (*CSH*, FIG. 99) B Tablet bands. (WALTON ROGERS 2005, 262-8)

Also in the chamber, and indicative of a woman of the highest status, were pieces of textile, preserved through their contact with metal. Their crumpled condition suggested that the clothes were buried on a person, rather than placed in the grave.[29] The most informative fragment, attached to the châtelaine, revealed a sequence of four layers, the first being actually a trace of human skin, followed by an inner gown of medium-weight linen, an outer gown of fine linen and, outermost, a fragment of a wool blanket or cloak. The textiles included embroidery and tablet-weave, each making ornamental bands worn probably around the sleeves (**Fig.5.33**). The embroidery was similar to that found on Bathild, the Anglo-Saxon wife of the Frankish king Clovis II, who died 680/1; and the tablet-woven bands recall the ornamental cuffs found on the forearms of Queen Arnegunde, who died c. AD 600 and was buried at St Denis in France. Researcher Penelope Walton Rogers concluded that the woman had worn an inner chemise of medium-weight linen with long sleeves and embroidered cuffs, and over it a gown of fine linen also long-sleeved and also with patterned cuffs, this time tablet-woven. The Mound 14 textiles were made locally but using techniques known in Scandinavia.[30]

This is the only rich mound burial so far discovered at Sutton Hoo that is certainly dedicated to a powerful or favoured female. Peering through the confusion created by the pillaging operation, it is possible to discern the tableau of a wealthy person, richly robed, decked with silver ornaments, with purse and casket and symbols of status and perhaps laid on an upholstered couch in a timber-lined chamber. Such indications as we have from the artefacts, the burial rites and the position of Mound 14 in the cemetery point to a date around the middle of the seventh century.[31] We mourn the loss of a mass of material special to women and to the age. The chamber was thoroughly ransacked in five frantic incidents, reflecting neither the central pit of the seventeenth-century excavators nor the east-west trench of those digging in the nineteenth century. It is not excluded that this relatively small mound had attracted hostile attention in its own day. If the imagination is allowed free rein, here is one of the last of the princely clan, a dowager who outlived the heroes she had commemorated.

A POLITICAL THEATRE

The monumental theatre that is the Sutton Hoo mound cemetery seems to have been in use for less than a hundred years - perhaps less than half a century. The objects in Mound 1 can all be dated on stylistic grounds to the late sixth or early seventh century, and this is also true of the Mound 17 assemblage and of the fragments of finds from the other mounds. The coins, which were Merovingian *tremisses*, provide some more exact indications of date: five out of the 37 coins carry the names of identifiable rulers, and the gold content of this type of coin has been found to vary with time. Both kinds of evidence suggest that at least some of the coins were minted after AD 595 and all may have been minted before AD 613.[32] There is little independent scientific dating because all the burials had poor preservation of bone and organic materials. Radiocarbon dates for Mound 1 were taken from the beeswax in the lamp, which was AD 523 ± 45, and a piece of oak from the bottom of the ship, which was AD 694 ± 45.[33] None of the other furnished graves produced suitable materials; much of the bone had been calcified by cremation, or had decayed in the inhumations, leaving only a stain.

However, the arguments presented here invite the conclusion that, even during this short timespan, allegiance and politics changed. The first burials were expressed by cremation, placed in a bronze bowl and under a mound: burial rites already old and strongly reminiscent of pagan Scandinavia. The horse-burial makes reference to the Rhineland. The ship-burials find their closest parallels in Sweden. In the first half of the seventh century Sutton Hoo and indeed East Anglia as a whole had its eyes fixed on Scandinavia. Given that the people were burying only a selection of their cultural treasures it must be concluded that the emerging kingdom and the Sandlings region in particular was outstandingly wealthy. The presence of symbolic items that could be construed as instruments of government (the standard and the sceptre) increases the impression that wealth means power, and that the initial reaction to Sutton Hoo from 1939 onwards - that this was the burial ground of East Anglia's kings - seems eminently reasonable. Certainly the researches of the last 60 years have done nothing to diminish that impression (Chapter 7, pp.195-6). Through that framework of increasingly demonstrative wealth and power runs a leitmotiv of mounds, horses, boats and symbolic ornament that is markedly non-Christian. Nevertheless, there are signs within the sequence of monuments, their Mediterranean imports and their martial gear, of a wide variety of responses to the times, including the turning of the face from the North Sea towards the Mediterranean, from heroic Germania to Rome and ultimately towards the new opportunities promised by Christianity. Among the aristocracy these trends need be seen as neither progressive nor sequential, since men and women of successive generations, then as now, can proclaim political allegiance either in the name of tradition or of change. The situation can be epitomised by the 'Roman'-style parade gear adopted by the Mound 1 'imperial warrior' and the Scandinavian dress style of the dowager buried a generation later.[34]

Sutton Hoo can be termed 'royal' in so far as that word can be given precision in seventh-century England: it is the cemetery of an aristocracy (implied by its wealth), which was dynastic (implied by the suite of cremations in bronze bowls) and which claimed both a regional supremacy (implied by the symbolic apparatus in Mound 1) and international recognition (implied by the exotic objects). The cemetery lay in the territory of the East Angles, since Rendlesham (to the north) and Ipswich and Felixstowe (to the south) all relate to that province. Since the earliest kings of East Anglia are recorded to have died in the late sixth century, the Sutton Hoo cemetery was initiated at, or just before, the local adoption of kingship itself.[35]

From the choice of burial rite - cremation under mound and ship-burial - it can be deduced that this was a kingdom that was being created in a pagan mode, in alignment with Scandinavia. This is in contrast to contemporary France, Kent or Northumbria, where kingship was being developed with a Christian ideology and within an alliance of Christian peoples, resulting in a material culture that was markedly different. Of personal belief we know little, any more than we know what our neighbours really think about the other world today. Archaeology does not often report what people believed, only their communal attitudes and formally declared allegiance. For the East Angles, the question of official and institutional conversion to Christianity must have constituted the most agonising dilemma of the day - not so much a question of faith as one of allegiance and political judgement. On the one hand, there were the advantages of a large continental market; on the other, the potential loss of autonomy, loss of contact with kin and allies in Scandinavia and the threat to deeply held convictions about how life should be lived. Such anxieties are not without analogies for our own times.

6 | THE GALLOWS AND THE GENTRY
AD650 to 1938

The executions ♦ The gallows by the track ♦ Execution on Mound 5 ♦ Dating ♦
Rituals ♦ The later Christian Ages ♦ Inquisitive landowners

THE EXECUTIONS

The first sighting of burials outside the mounds was puzzling: they lacked skeletons but retained the rounded form of human flesh in dark sand that could be followed with a trowel. Thus the 'sandmen of Sutton Hoo' (**Fig.6.1**).

But once the shape was determined it was seldom conventional: the bodies lay on their side, or on their front, or folded in half; some graves contained two people, one contained three. Burial appeared hasty, the buried persons contorted. The total tally was 39 graves, disposed in two groups (**Fig.6.2**). Group 1, the first to be discovered, lay beyond the mounds to the east beside the ridge-top track that had endured since the Iron Age (p.112). Here were 23 graves arranged around a space containing a set of post-holes. Group 2, with 16 graves, was focused on Mound 5, the bodies buried in or beside its quarry pits. Who were these people? Why were they buried there? Why in two groups? At first it seemed, especially in the case of Mound 5, that they must be closely connected with the princely burial ground - sacrificial victims, in effect (Chapter 3, p.80). Twenty-five years after their

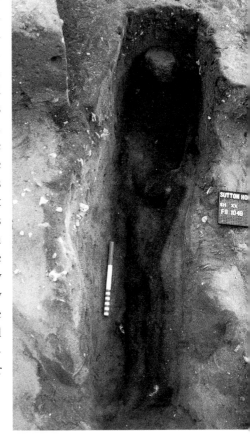

6.1: Burial 17: the excavated sand-body.
(NIGEL MACBETH)

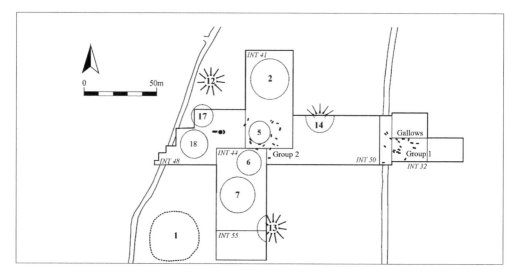

6.2: (above) Location of the execution cemeteries (Groups 1 and 2).

6.3: (left) Group 1: overview of the execution site during excavation. The area in the foreground contained no burials.

6.4: (opposite) Group 1: plan of graves and all other features (*CSH*, Fig. 141).

discovery we have the confidence to say that they were not sacrifices but judicial executions, all of which took place after the building of monumental mounds had been discontinued.[1] Here we will visit each of the execution cemeteries, consider their forms of burial and their dates and surmise what kind of misfortunes or changes in circumstance had led them to death.

THE GALLOWS BY THE TRACK

The burials of Group 1 were found in an area opened to the east of the mounds originally in an attempt to locate the limit of mound burial (**Fig. 6.3**). They were arranged in two arcs around an open space and exhibited a variety of postures (**Fig. 6.4**). The bodies in Burials 19, 25, 32 and 33 were buried face down,

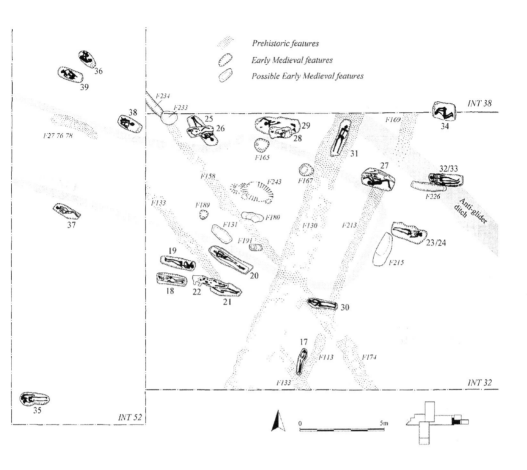

with the wrists or ankles laid over each other as though tied. In Burial 19 one arm was behind the back. In Burial 29 the arms had been stretched above the head. Burials 24, 28 and 39 were buried kneeling or crouching. In Burial 21 the head had been removed and replaced in the grave of Burial 22 that followed. In Burial 35 the head had been removed and laid on the shoulder (**Fig.6.5**). In Burial 23 the neck had been broken and the head and vertebrae were at right angles. The body in Burial 38 was buried on the back with the knees drawn right up to the shoulder. Burial 27 was spread-eagled on the floor of a large grave and accompanied by timber pieces reminiscent of a primitive plough (and was thus nicknamed 'the ploughman'). These timber shadows may have derived rather from some instrument connected with execution or burial, such as a hurdle, spades or even the gallows itself.[2] Some burials seemed to provide echoes of a less desolate end: the bodies in Burials 17, 18 and 20 were laid on their backs, two of them (18 and 20) in coffins. In Burial 34 the body had been placed in a chest or square container of some kind, revealed as a layer of wood shadow over the sand-body (Fig.3.16).

The open space between the graves was approached by a kind of avenue terminating in an arena in which there was a central pit and a cluster of post-holes.[3] The central pit was undated but resembled in its shape and fill the pits encountered here and there on the site left by blown-down trees (Chapter 4, p.106). The four post-holes were arranged in a rectangle, suggesting a structure with four posts or two pairs of two. The post-holes were all similar in size and shape, and one retained the silhouette of a squared timber post cut from birch. The pairs of posts stood 2–5m apart. The position of these features, in an open space surrounded by graves containing bodies that had met a violent end, suggested that they belonged to instruments of execution: perhaps in the first place a tree and then a four-post gallows, or a succession of two-post gallows. One such is depicted in a late Saxon manuscript (**Fig.6.7**).[4]

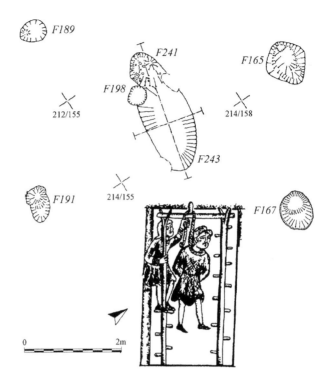

6.5: (opposite, top) Group 1: Burial 25, with the skull on the right shoulder.
(NIGEL MACBETH)

6.6: (opposite, below) Group 1: Burial 27, 'The ploughman'. For interpretation see text.
(NIGEL MACBETH)

6.7: (right) Group 1: plan of features interpreted as belonging to gallows of the eighth to tenth century, with (inset) a picture of a late Saxon hanging depicted in Aelfric's Pentateuch.
(BL MS COTTON CLAUDIUS B.IV F. 59V)

EXECUTION ON MOUND 5

The 16 burials of Group 2 were found mostly to the east and south of Mound 5, five of them cut into partially backfilled quarry pits, the remainder cut into buried soil at the foot of the mound (**Fig.6.8**). One outlier lay on the west side in a quarry pit (Burial 53), and further west still a detached skull was found in an isolated pit (Burial 56).[5] The overall disposition is untidy but there is little doubt that they were focused on Mound 5, on top of which, by analogy with Group 1, the instrument of execution would have stood. Burial 53 lay on the base of a large quarry pit, not so much buried as covered with planks and branches. But the corpse was so decomposed that even its identity as a human is in doubt, and it may have been the remains of an animal. All was covered up when soil surplus to mound-building was returned to the pit. Graves were later added to the east and south sides of Mound 5. Four of them (Burials 44, 45, 50 and 51) were tangential to the mound and against its original edge. The occupant of one of these (45) was buried face down, but the others were relatively normal in the way they lay. The next series of burials was added a little further out, radial to the mound or in its eastern quarry pits (Burials 40, 41, 42/3, 46, 48 and 49). Burial 48 had its head detached and placed below the knee. Burial 40's head had also been removed but replaced askew at the neck end. In the extraordinary Burial 42 a mature male lay on his back, decapitated, and on top of him lay two women, face down (**Fig.6.9**). Burials 41 and 46 had

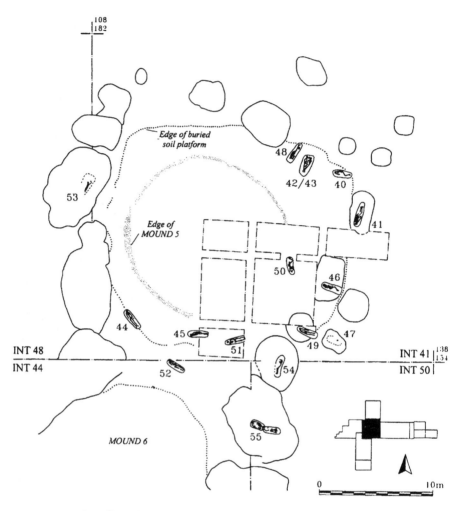

6.8: Group 2: plan of burials and quarry pits around Mound 5.

been cut into quarry pits that had been partially refilled and turfed over. Both the wrists and ankles of Burial 41 had seemingly been tied. Burial 49, also in a quarry pit, lay with a 'collar' of dark soil around his neck - seemingly the remains of a rope from the gallows.[7] A third series, furthest away, were Burials 52, 54 and 55, all badly mutilated: Burial 52 had been decapitated and the head replaced at the neck end, although rotated through 180 degrees. The lower left leg was broken. Burial 54 had been decapitated too, but the head was not present. Burial 55 was folded over backwards, and had possibly been quartered. Eight individuals in Group 1 were identified as probably men, and none as women; in Group 2 there were five probable men and two women (in Burial 42). All were young except the mature male in Burial 42 and perhaps that in Burial 39. Defying authority was apparently a young man's game.

DATING

Five burials to the east of Mound 5 were cut into partially refilled quarry pits, so these executions took place after the mound was built. None encroached on the mound platform, implying the mound was already there. Only Burial 53 could have followed very soon after the mound's construction, but this was less certainly the remains of a human, and may have been an animal. Radiocarbon has been the most decisive way of dating the burials, although, of the 39 burials, only eight gave reliable results: Burial 17 AD570-890; Burial 22 AD640-990; Burial 30 AD980-1220; Burial 35 AD640-980; and Burial 39 AD880-1030 in Group 1, and Burial 40 AD890-

6.9: Group 2: triple burial, 42A, 42B and 43. (NIGEL MACBETH)

1160; Burial 42b AD640-780; and Burial 45 AD880-1040 in Group 2. Wood from a gallows post in Group 1a gave a date of 680-990.[8] These dates suggest that the cemetery had a span of 300 years or so. They have prompted the verdict that it started in the late seventh or early eighth century and ended after the Norman Conquest, though no burial need be later than the eleventh century. The burials of both groups contained both early and later examples, showing that they must have been concurrent, although it is not impossible that execution began around Mound 5 and later migrated to the eastern site. Together the Sutton Hoo burials cover the complete period in which execution burial was practised by the Anglo-Saxons, a timespan matched only at Staines and Walkington Wold.

RITUALS

In both groups the people in the graves had been hanged or beheaded. There were some cases of severe mutilation that could have formed part of a ritual killing or may have resulted from the suspension of the corpse on a gibbet and its subsequent decomposition before burial (**Fig.6.10**).[9] Why were they killed? The distinction between human sacrifice and capital punishment as possible explanations of these cemeteries has been much discussed, and it is not a distinction that would necessarily be clear to the victim or the onlookers, or to morality or reason. The *weregild* system implies that as a response to murder the pagan Anglo-Saxons preferred payment of compensation to vindictive moralising, since an executed person cannot mend their ways. Given that there is no certain example of human sacrifice in Anglo-Saxon England and bearing in mind the likely date, we should more sensibly look to the much better-documented examples of judicial killing of the seventh to eleventh century collected and assessed by Andrew Reynolds.[10]

Here we find numerous examples of prone burials, bodies folded backwards or forwards, hands tied to the front or at the back, ankles tied, displaced heads and missing heads. These are the signs of death by strangulation; the struggles of hand or feet, if free, merely prolong the agony. The gallows depicted in the eleventh-century manuscript requires the victim to climb to the noose and then swing, as opposed to the swifter and more compassionate drop. Example of double and triple burials are also known from elsewhere in eighth- to eleventh-century England. At the execution site in Staines double burials were focused on the same spot over an extended period. In one of these, the limbs of an adult male were intertwined with those of a younger person (aged 14-22). There are other examples of threesomes in addition to Burial 42 at Sutton Hoo. At Galley Hill a women was buried with two men. At Staines a young person (aged 16-20) lay with left and right hands on the crotch of an adult on either side. The sins of these young people, if recorded in their burial tableaux, would seem to refer to sexual misdemeanours.[11] As well as murder and theft, the laws speak of false trading, adultery and intercourse with nuns as capital offences, and it was known that marrying one's widowed stepmother was a practice condemned by Christians that took some time to be stamped out.[12] Other heinous crimes were fighting in the king's hall and, most serious of all, treason. Some examples of coffined burial at Sutton Hoo and elsewhere suggest there was room for sympathy of another kind, understandable among people who probably knew each other and found themselves on opposite sides of the law. The punishment of judicial killing is thought to be the due of those that oppose the law, and its sentence the prerogative of the king. Pagan kings may have exercised this prerogative, and it is not impossible that they did so at Sutton Hoo. On the other hand, the date and siting of the gallows suggests that they resulted from a change of attitude and regime.[13] The executions align with a time in which mound burial had ceased and East Anglia's kings were largely Christian.

Historically, gallows and gibbets are sited at visible locations, along major routes and at the edges of kingdoms, both to deter local delinquents and to proclaim local jurisdiction to incomers.[14] For the later Anglo-Saxon period at

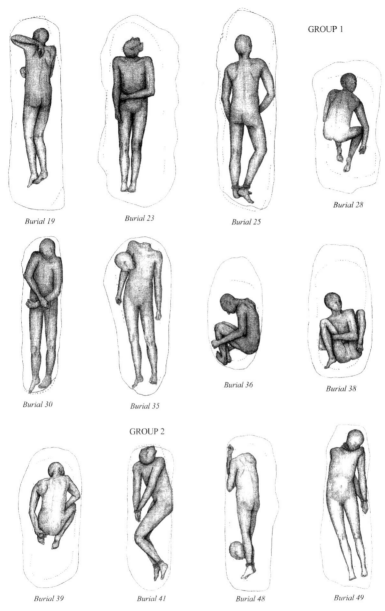

GROUP 1

Burial 19

Burial 23

Burial 25

Burial 28

Burial 30

Burial 35

Burial 36

Burial 38

GROUP 2

Burial 39

Burial 41

Burial 48

Burial 49

6.10: Execution victims: positions of victims in their graves. (DRAWN BY JULIET REEVES)

least, Andrew Reynolds has worked out a 'landscape of judgment': those that fell foul of the law would follow an itinerary from initial confinement at the farmstead of a local lord (i.e. a manor), to the court for judgment and then to the church to undergo the system of appeal, the ordeal by hot iron, boiling water or drowning - rapid recovery from which supported his protestations of innocence and showed his conscience to be clear. Those that failed the test made the melancholy trip to the gallows with the final alienation of burial outside a churchyard.[15] Reynolds argues that the landscape of judgment changes when society changes: while the social rejection of individuals might be signalled in the cemeteries of early kin-based Anglo-Saxon communities, execution was rare. But there came a moment in the later seventh and eighth centuries when the consolidation of power resulted in execution sites being placed at key crossing points at the borders.[16] Such a site was Sutton Hoo, lying on the border between the fledgling kingdoms of Essex and East Anglia (Chapter 7, p.190).

Using the old royal burial ground as a place of execution would be particularly apposite, especially for rebels against the new regime. Victims of the gallows in this case had not only sinned against the authority of the ruler but against the Christian god, and a pagan cemetery was a proper place to dispose of them. Some, perhaps declared and unrepentant pagans, would be executed and buried next to the mound that had contained, or was thought to have contained, the ancestral founder of pagan kingship. Others, Christians who had strayed or rebelled, would be dispatched at the cemetery's edge and near the track. Although they were not permitted to enter consecrated ground at nearby Sutton church, they could be placed in coffins and perhaps even be aligned with the rising sun in the Christian manner. In any event, the new generation of kings struck at both body and soul of a dissident and his family. The Beowulf poet speaks of:

> the misery endured by an old man
> who has lived to see his son's body
> swing on the gallows ... .
> The wisdom of age is worthless to him.
> Morning after morning, he wakes to remember his child is gone.[17]

The Christian leaders of East Anglia were now investing in other ceremonial centres and sites: churches at Rendlesham, and probably at Sutton; monasteries at Iken, the probable site of St Botolph's *Ikenhoe*, Burgh Castle, founded by the Irishman Fursa, and probably at Felixstowe, the holy place of Felix, a churchman from Burgundy who became bishop of the East Angles. Felix had an episcopal headquarters at Dunwich, a site now alas vanished beneath the North Sea. The riverside settlement at Ipswich expanded into a great port, bringing in wine from the new market opened through Christian alliance with the sunny heartland of Europe.

The ideological pendulum had swung in favour of the Christian community and its new principles and customs. But Sutton Hoo lived on, a dark interlude but a long one. This grim place with its tall mounds and gibbets remained a landmark, visited intermittently throughout the later Anglo-Saxon period by execution parties. A track reinstated a droveway, which had begun perhaps as early as the Bronze Age, leading from a ferry point on the river inland to the villages of the Sandlings between the Deben and the Alde. Sutton Hoo was the landmark for which the track aimed; it then turned east to Eyke and Orford and north to Wilford. The carts using this track probably trundled back and forth, providing a ferry service of their own, run by carters shifting the produce of the Sandlings to the ports on the Deben and the Orwell. On certain mornings some of these carts carried the victims of the current morality, on their way to the new Christian killing-place in the old pagan burial ground of kings.

THE LATER CHRISTIAN AGES

Probably some time between the eleventh and the twelfth century the Sutton Hoo gallows moved. The most likely new execution site was further up river, overlooking Wilford Bridge at the appropriately named Gallows Hill, noted in the seventeenth century. A map of the Stanhope estates made in 1601 by John Norden shows the place, and provides a little pen and ink sketch of the instrument itself: two posts carrying a cross-beam, as drawn by an Anglo-Saxon artist of the eleventh century (**Figs 6.7; 6.11**). The shift of execution site probably coincided with a change in the routeways. The old route, as stated on the same map, went from the ferry through the Sutton Hoo burial ground, where it would have passed hanging bodies on either side (see Fig. 3.31). But once the bridge had been built at Wilford all the traffic could go over the bridge and keep dry. The Wilford turn became the new crossroads of the region, and so the gallows was re-established there. Redundant routes fade slowly in the countryside; the Sutton Hoo track was still in existence in 1783, and presumably the ferry was too. But by 1836, when the Ordnance Surveyors compiled their notes for the area, the ferry track had gone - or, if not vanished from the site (it is still visible now as a shallow earthwork), it had become obsolete. A new route passed on the west side of the mounds, following along the crest northwards to Wilford, a track that can still be followed through bush and briar along the edges of fields.

During the Middle Ages the area had become sheepwalk, and shepherds had sheltered in the hollows of the grassed-over quarries, cooking on open hearths and leaving sherds of coarse pots to be found in the quarry ditches beside Mound 2, Mound 6 and Mound 14.[18] At certain times, especially when the land had grown too sour to support grazing or the root crops on which sheep relied to get through the winter, the demand for meat was met by the obligingly prolific rabbit, which was farmed in large warrens. The rabbit colonies would be established in specially constructed earth mounds, or better

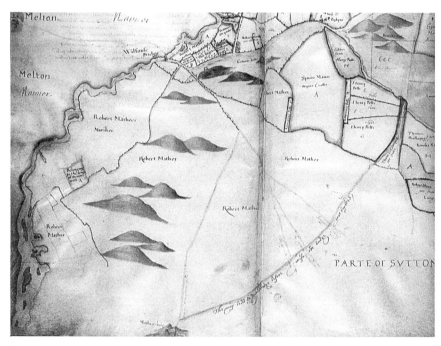

6.11: The early seventeent-century Norden map, showing part of the Mather estate on the left bank of the Deben. Sutton Hoo is labelled 'Mathershoe' and shown in detail (lower, right). Gallow Hill is situated on a promontory overlooking Wilford Bridge, and shown in detail (lower left). The 'cocked hats' shown along the river bank may be intended as promontories, mounds or rabbit warrens. (SUFFOLK COUNTY RECORD OFFICE V6/22/1)

still, contrived out of the existing burial mounds that littered the countryside. The excavated Sutton Hoo mounds proved to be riddled with rabbit holes. On his map of 1601 John Norden uses a characteristic 'cocked hat' shape to indicate warrens.[19] There are numerous examples sited along the Deben, and some of these may have been former burial mounds.

The mounds were not, as far as we could tell, robbed during the Middle Ages. Why not? Preliminary study of this subject suggests that very few burial mounds were robbed during the Middle Ages, but things were different from the Reformation onwards. In Italy a similar surge in tomb-robbing occurred at the Renaissance. This would seem to indicate that the main inhibition to robbing burials was superstition, and people were released from it only when there was change in the relationship between God and man.[20]

INQUISITIVE LANDOWNERS

The period around 1600 proved to be pivotal for the story of Sutton Hoo, just as the period around 600 had been. Two major forces, one old and one new, were about to wake the mounds from their long-respected sleep: agriculture and archaeology. In every quarry pit and ditch of the old Anglo-Saxon earthworks a thick layer of pale sand was deposited over the turf, as though a heathy soil had been pushed in, filling up every hollow. It could perhaps have been blown there - the area has a famous capacity for dust storms, especially after the turf has been stripped and the sandy soil exposed. But the pit-fills contained no 'lensing', the thin laminar discolourations which would indicate that layers of sand had been laid down by successive episodes of wind-blow. Neither were there traces of slumping - such as might be seen if the mounds were to erode and fall into the pits and ditches by natural processes. The observed reduction of the height of the mounds and the homogeneous pale filling of the quarries is most readily explained as being due to the mechanical agency of ploughing.

There were also later attempts to plough and cultivate land that, as Arthur Young pointed out in his classic late eighteenth-century work *General View of the Agriculture of the County of Suffolk*, was really more appropriately tended as pasture.[21] When the price of grain went up, as during a war, every piece of land that could bear a crop was ploughed. This happened during the Napoleonic wars of the early nineteenth century and again during the Crimean War, when the prices made it a 'golden age' for grain growers. It happened again when Britain joined the Common Market, and the high subsidies for grain led ploughs back on to old acid heaths and humpy slopes which could be persuaded to yield wheat in exchange for a dose of chemicals. The land could not recover easily or quickly from these cereal binges, and the result in the later nineteenth century at least was exodus to Canada and America. On 8 January 1862 Charles Cody of Trimley St Mary wrote to his brother in New Zealand: 'The year 1860 from its extreme wetness was most disastrous to all heavy land farmers and pretty well emptied the pockets of the already needy tenants. At the same time the competition for land is so great that young men generally will be wise to seek their fortunes in one or other of our colonies.'[22] Crag, the fossil shells found under the sand, was ploughed into the soil; and coprolites, supposed fossil reptile excrement, were treated with sulphuric acid to provide superphosphate, in a process successfully exploited locally by a Mr Fison. But before the days of mass production of chemical fertilisers, the land had to be left fallow and resuscitated with root crops, those turnips and carrots to which Suffolk sheep were fortunately partial, which had been grown on this sandy soil since at least the sixteenth century.

The archaeological evidence and the maps show that the old Sutton Hoo burial ground was ploughed again in the nineteenth century. The plough was even used on the slopes up to the cemetery from the flood plain (gradient held no terrors for these stalwart cultivators) and a lynchet was built up over the eroded surfaces of Mounds 1, 17 and 12. This happened before 1843, when the area is shown as arable on the tithe map (Fig.6.12). There may even have been a third episode before the site returned to bracken heath in the early twentieth century; but that depends on the date at which Sutton Hoo had its earliest experiences of archaeological excavation.[23]

Like agriculture, capital punishment and the erection of burial mounds, archaeological investigation is a sign of the needs and beliefs of society and it has a history of its own which reflects them. Sutton Hoo, we can be reasonably sure, was subjected to systematic campaigns of excavation on no fewer than five occasions between the sixteenth century and the late twentieth; it offers us a history of archaeology in a single English field. From the evidence collected, it would appear that the first campaign was the most comprehensive and prodigal of them all. The first hint of the operations was provided by a few sherds of Bellarmine flask (a sixteenth-century gin bottle) found by Basil Brown in a deep pit that had been dug through Mound 1. It was not in fact deep enough to reach the burial, which lay in the centre of the ship nearly 4m below the old ground surface and as much again below the top of the mound. It was also off centre, a possible indication that the ploughing of the mounds had already taken place when this robber pit was tried. The pit would most probably have collapsed, leaving abandoned debris at its base. Another unsuccessful hole was dug through Mound 17; unsuccessful on this occasion because it was placed central to the mound and thus arrived at a point midway between the two graves that lay beneath.

It is highly probable that every other mound at Sutton Hoo was successfully pillaged at this time with a central pit. An example had been encountered in Mound 3, Redstone's 'dew-pond', and an oval pit appeared to have been used in Mound 14. A great oval opening marks the mouth of the chamber grave in Mound 2. This cannot be attributed to the ship and would be an extravagant access for the later excavators (who came by trench). It would, however, be a credible legacy of tomb-robbers who descended from the top, as seems to have been the sixteenth-century way. Similar pits were found in the very messy Mound 5, which suffered at least two contemporary attacks

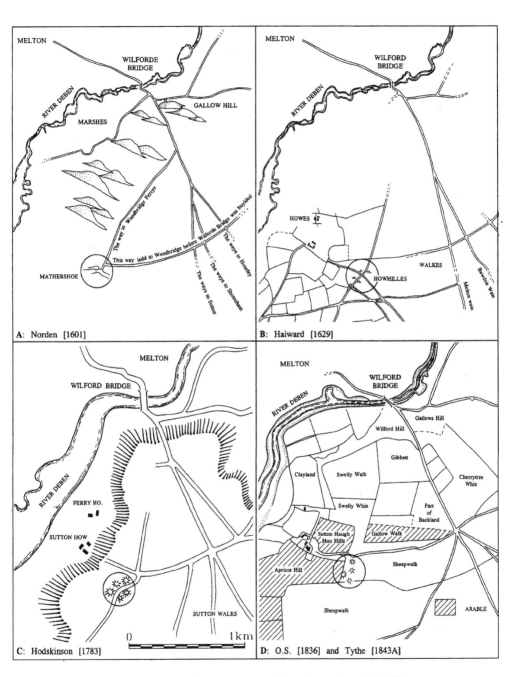

6.12: Estates in the Sutton Hoo shown on maps of 1601, 1629, 1783 and 1836/1843.
(ANNETTE ROE)

by pit. But the most convincing evidence for a campaign of the sixteenth century is the lack of finds recorded from the much better-documented excavation campaign that was to follow in the nineteenth century. We do not know what would have been found during the first campaign, but from the scraps encountered by later excavators one must imagine that it would have included very considerable quantities of gold and silver.

The sixteenth century was a time of known interest in burial mounds, a new kind of interest, neither religious nor scientific. Throughout the Middle Ages burial mounds seem to have been protected by the kind of superstition that discouraged people from robbing a mound in case they met a dragon or worse. If the thinking of the Reformation reduced such inhibitions, the redistribution of religious land after 1540 must have lessened them still further. The new rich who were receiving the estates of abbeys at the hands of the king were liberated from religious subservience and turned their privatised benefits into capital by the fastest possible route; and if this meant melting down a chalice or pyx or turning illuminated vellum into gloves, so be it. The new owners of burial mounds were unlikely to have shown less restraint in 'mining' them for treasure. Burial mounds were recognised and understood, in this case perhaps better than we have done, in that they and their contents were assessed as Crown property, whatever their date. The new owners of Sutton Hoo, the Mathers by 1601, could have easily applied for and won a licence to extract some of the capital value of their holding, for the sake of its development and ultimately for the more widespread creation of wealth.[24]

The second campaign to leave its mark on Sutton Hoo belongs to the mid-nineteenth century. On 24 November 1860 the following item appeared in a local newspaper, the *Ipswich Journal*:

> ROMAN MOUNDS or BARROWS - It is not known by many that not less than five Roman Barrows, lying close to each other, may be seen on a farm occupied by Mr Barritt, at Sutton, about 500 yards from the banks of the Deben, immediately opposite Woodbridge. One of these mounds was recently opened, when a considerable number (nearly two bushels) of iron screw bolts were found, all of which were sent to the blacksmith to be converted into horse shoes! It is hoped, when leave is granted to open the others, some more important antiquities may be discovered. These barrows were laid down in the Admiralty surveys by Captain Stanley during the stay of the Blazer, when taking soundings of the above-named river some years since.[25]

Which mound was excavated in 1860, and what was found? The iron screw bolts must have been ship rivets, and their likely source was Mound 2, since

6.13: Gentlemen antiquaries at work. Artist's impression of the nineteenth-century excavation of Mound 7. (VICTOR AMBRUS)

only two ship-burials are known thus far from Sutton Hoo, and Mound 1 was intact. The early maps suggest that only four or five mounds were easily seen in the nineteenth century, presumably because the others had been so lowered by ploughing as to be scarcely visible in the undergrowth. These should be the five most prominent: Mounds 1, 2, 3, 7 and 10. Mound 2, standing on the highest ground at the end of the row next to the track junction, would have been a natural target. Moreover, it was discovered on excavation in 1987 to have had a trench cut through it from west to east. Ship rivets were clustered along the length of this trench and spread on either side of it. If 'two bushels' (perhaps 2,000 rivets) were recovered for the blacksmith, 500 still remained for collection in 1987. In the centre of the mound the nineteenth-century excavators would have found the great pit - dug, it is suggested, in the sixteenth century - and followed it down. Steps were cut on the west side to gain access to the pit, which was then explored. They seem to have stopped excavating near the base of the chamber, where the earlier robbers had trod. Compacted soil was left against the corners and along the sides. Some scraps of metalwork remained in the chamber, but apart from rivets we must suppose that they found nothing of interest. Disappointed, they left the hole open for a short time, in which it collected copious amounts of silt washed down the steps to create a dished depression, pointed at the west end. It was this that the next excavator (Basil Brown) was to find in 1938, believing he had defined a boat.

It seems that that leave *was* subsequently granted, presumably from Mr

Barritt's landlord, to open other mounds. Trenches very similar in design to that traced in Mound 2 were found in Mounds 6 and 7. Entry in Mound 6 was from the west and stopped after the half-way point, where access steps descended to a small ledge, on which presumably the antiquary stood. The west end of the trench splayed out to provide ingress and egress for the labourers removing the soil. The tableau in Mound 7 was more graphic still (Fig.6.13). This time the trench was driven in from the east, and the splayed east entrance was scored by the wheels of the labourers' wheelbarrows. The antiquary's stance was at the foot of steps on the west side, just above the pit that had contained the burial. In the pit was a cremation, contained in a bowl. The bowl itself had vanished but had left its shape on the little mound of burnt bone impatiently ejected by the excavator. From his stance, the antiquary could lean over, in top hat and morning coat, eager to see what the earth had added to academia, hoping for precious objects to put on the mantelpiece or to sell or to exhibit and impress his acquaintances from other parts of the county, even from London itself. The standard of excavation had risen since the trench cut into Mound 2; here everything was sieved and little remained for those that were to come after. Next in line would have been Mound 1. Did they trench that too? Or was the experience of three robbed cremations in a row too dispiriting? If Maynard's description can be credited, there may well have been a trench cut through Mound 1, but it was too high up to touch either ship or chamber.

The backfilled excavations in Mounds 6 and 7 left a characteristically shaped 'dent' in the top of the mound - not 'ship-dents' as Bruce-Mitford had hoped, but 'trench-dents'. How successful were these diggers of trenches? If they found precious Anglo-Saxon objects, what did they do with them? It is, of course, possible that Mr Barritt or his collaborators had found a heap of treasure and decided to keep quiet about it, because he was a tenant and wished in his turn to escape the rat-race and become a millionaire. But there are several reasons for thinking that he had been unlucky and so had all who were with him. The newspaper article itself makes it likely that the first mound at least had been something of a dud. The burial was not recognised as that of a ship, because the 'iron screw bolts' were not then identified, in their dispersed locations, as ship rivets. The Snape excavators, digging a less disturbed boat below ground two years later, were more perceptive. If precious objects had been found here, or in the mounds that were later trenched, then it does not seem credible that they could long remain a secret. To put the discoveries of this period into context, 1860 was something of an *annus mirabilis* for the antiquary, who was rapidly being accepted as part of the new scientific vanguard. Sir Austen Henry Layard's *Nineveh and its Remains* had appeared in 1854, swiftly becoming a best-seller, and Charles Darwin's *Origin of Species*, published in 1859, seemed to make a remote past possible everywhere. It was a time for the formation of antiquarian societies, and vicars, lawyers, army officers and gentleman farmers were among the first to join. There was probably more social advantage in flourishing an Anglo-Saxon buckle at such a gathering than in having it melted down for a few guineas of bullion.

Moreover, the learned societies of England and Suffolk were no strangers to the Sutton area. In 1860 the autumn meeting of the Suffolk Institute of Archaeology and Natural History convened at Woodbridge, and Roman and Saxon jewellery was exhibited in the lecture hall by Messrs Whincopp, Spalding, Loder, Baker 'and many others'. This was on 24 October, one month before the discoveries were made on Mr Barritt's farm. It does not seem possible for the Suffolk Institute to have remained ignorant of the excavations in 1860, or those that followed, presumably in the spring of the next year, had they discovered anything of value. For in 1864 the British Archaeological Association met at Ipswich, and no mention was made of Sutton Hoo. On that occasion Mr Whincopp was again an exhibitor, as he had been at these gatherings since 1851, when he exhibited to the Archaeological Institute a gold and garnet buckle found at Melton in 1833.[26]

The reporting of these casual finds was unsystematic, and not too much should be made of a failure to mention others. But it is hard to see that a major discovery at Sutton Hoo in the mid-nineteenth century would have escaped the notice of Mr Whincopp or the entire membership and readership of the *Gentleman's Magazine*, the Archaeological Institute, the British Archaeological Association and the Suffolk Institute. We must conclude that there was no major discovery. The mounds had either been well turned over by the sixteenth-century campaign or contained cremations in which little appeared to be glorious. Mr Barritt did not get rich, but his campaign was certainly followed by a last ploughing: the backfilled trench of Mound 7 showed that a plough had been dragged east-west across the mound. But it was a half-hearted effort; the track to the east remained visible. The price of grain had presumably fallen again.

The sixteenth century had gobbled up everything it found; the nineteenth century was ready to share objects of beauty and curiosity, but had found little of this character to reward its considerable exertions. In the twentieth century, as the Sutton Hoo site turned to heathland and Europe turned once more to war, the burial ground still kept its secret. And it might have done so for many more centuries had it not been for the construction in 1910 of a new country house on the promontory to the north and the arrival there in 1926 of Mrs Edith Pretty.

7 | *Now entertain conjecture of a time*
PAINTING A PICTURE OF THE SEVENTH CENTURY

Fact, evidence, interpretation and opinion ♦ The emergence of English society ♦ Signs of the times at Sutton Hoo ♦ A mind of one's own ♦ In the hall ♦ East Anglia and its kings ♦ Wars of the Angles ♦ Who was in the mounds? ♦ Looking outwards ♦ The Company of Illustrious Mound Builders ♦ Envoi

The Sutton Hoo Story is the story of a piece of England, the long life of a landscape in which the singular drama of an early medieval cemetery provides a climactic moment. This was a drama in three acts placed consecutively in the sixth, seventh and eighth centuries and in three scenes: at a gathering of family plots, at a princely burial ground and at twin places of execution. Even if the burials at Tranmer House and those on the princely burial ground do not belong to the same continuous cemetery, they are plainly related: cremations in bronze bowls and warrior inhumations are already part of the Tranmer House repertoire, and the timing sees the burials here coming to an end just as the monumental mounds start to appear further south. The savagery of the executions in the final phase, which might seem at odds with the glittering artistry of the princes' memorials, is also connected with what went before. The hangings follow soon after the last of the burial mounds was built, and the choice of Mound 5 for the gallows will have some significance: the executioners must have recognised its primacy and would know who was in it.

The burials are diverse and they changed with time. They provide one of the most vivid narratives in early medieval archaeology, and we can put them in context by reference to what other Europeans were doing. But maybe there is still more to it. Over the period of Sutton Hoo there were no signs that one people replaced another - so it must be their minds that changed. How far does the sequence reflect the thinking of the day, the emergence of an English kingdom, its interconnections and its politics? In brief, what do the Sutton Hoo discoveries mean? In this chapter we look at Sutton Hoo in its region, in the kingdom of East Anglia and in a global perspective, highlighting some new discoveries and comparing new theories. 'Theories' about Sutton Hoo are numerous, and rightly so, but can range broadly in their plausibility, from the generally acceptable to the quite eccentric. So, before we start, it may be as well (in this sceptical age) to consider how we may assess them.

FACT, EVIDENCE, INTERPRETATION AND OPINION

Sutton Hoo has generated a large and stimulating literature, featuring many controversies and disagreements, as scholars struggle to mould what has been found into a coherent narrative. Unsurprisingly these narratives may differ, which can be annoying for those wanting straight answers to simple questions. Readers will appreciate that our Anglo-Saxons have generated a vast range of attractive but often inscrutable material. Interpretations of sites and objects vary and scientists may change their minds. Archaeology is not just a matter of digging things up, finding parallels and putting them in a museum. It is a dynamic, developing study and examples multiply, year by year. So as time goes on we know more clearly what earlier discoveries might mean. This can be easily seen in the Sutton Hoo story: what was identified in Mound 2 in 1938 as a small dinghy was shown in 1998 to have been a major ship-burial. An axe-hammer long thought to be for fighting or for mending the ship had by 2006 become a ritual instrument for sacrificing cattle. Victims around Mound 5 suggested as human sacrifices in 1993 were by 2005 shown to be judicial executions.

Readers and visitors would like historians and scientists to deliver facts, but facts from this long-ago world are actually quite few. We can be mostly sure of what was found, and where, and roughly what date it is - these are our facts. Seeking parallels and analogies helps to weave these facts into evidence for past human behaviour - our real goal. When the streams of evidence converge, confidence rises that we can address the key questions: what happened here, and why? It is a difficult debate, one open to many opinions. But to contribute to a useful history, archaeologists must strive to create pictures of the past supported by convergent evidence, and so gain consensus for our time.

Sutton Hoo belongs to everyone, from experts to dreamers, from emeritus professors to young children; how can they all be served? Everyone is different and naturally want different things. Some want all the data, others just a nice clear account. But others again want more than either of those things: they want to know why these distant events occurred and why we care. For this we need to enter into a realm where the imagination can be exercised, and conjecture is permitted. Thus the title of this chapter. The quote is a plea by Shakespeare to his audience to allow him to sketch the real world inhabited by the actors on the stage; to paint them a picture.[1] Sutton Hoo deserves this too.

The evidence and the scientific verdicts drawn from it so far are summarised in Chapters 4 to 6, backed by the Research Report (*CSH*) and the online archive (SHOLA). Here, supported by references to new research, is a picture of Sutton Hoo as it might have been, its place in history, who built the mounds, who was in them, their links with a kingdom, their connections with the rest of Britain, Europe and the wider world. This exercise will show how much has already sprung from this remarkable discovery and how much more is to come.

THE EMERGENCE OF ENGLISH SOCIETY

Who were the Anglo-Saxons? When did they arrive in Britain? Why did they build Sutton Hoo? And what did they mean by it? To address such questions we need some background. In the first century AD the Romans conquered Britain and proceeded to 'Romanise' it, adopting the tribal areas of the indigenous Iron Age Britons and turning them into 'Romano-British' *civitates*, regions of government based on cities. The area they exploited was mainly the fertile lowlands, the Jurassic plain of the southern and eastern parts of the island where arable and dairy farming could flourish and a surplus be created to enrich and enlarge the empire.

After the empire collapsed in the early fifth century, the Anglo-Saxons, also immigrants, travelled across the North Sea and entered Britain via the estuaries of the east coast. The Wash was the big front door for seafarers and probably the earliest and most popular entry point. According to the similarity of their pots and burial practices, the immigrants came from parts of north Germany, Denmark and Norway and made their way in small, fast boats through the Fens and up its many rivers, making landfalls in fertile East Anglia.[2] What became of the Roman-British population is still something of a mystery; probably many fled west to Wales, while others stayed put. But the eastern area was soon well 'Anglicised', just as it had been previously 'Romanised', and the incomers set about reviving the fertility of Roman industrial farming in numerous smallholdings.

During the next two centuries the nature of the new society would change. In the sixth century the settled areas began to establish their own identities, in territories not so different from their Iron Age and Roman predecessors, but named after Germanic folk groups: the 'Angles' and the 'Saxons' especially were taken into the names of territories to the south (Essex, Wessex, Sussex) and east (East Anglia, Middle Anglia). Further west was Mercia - the 'March', the border area with Wales. To the north was Lincolnshire, still carrying its Roman name, and, north of the Humber, Northumbria. As the settlement spread further from the Wash into the fertile midlands, so the population appeared to be more British (and was no doubt actually more genetically mixed). As farmers succeeded or failed the land began to be divided into ever larger estates, now managed by a landed aristocracy. These claimed the country and its ancestors as their own, and from their midst rose powerful leaders. By the early seventh century, the time of Sutton Hoo, the people had acquired kings and kingdoms, and the Anglo-Saxons became English.[3]

7.1: Early Anglo-
Saxon cremations urns
excavated at Spong Hill.
(CATHERINE HILLS)

This narrative was not written down at the time and it has many fuzzy
edges. It is the product of convergent evidence, worked out and illuminated
by more than a century of archaeological research – among the most ingenious and fruitful that conducted by the archaeologists of East Anglia. Some of
the sites they have dug can serve as stepping stones, showing how early English society changed in the years leading up to Sutton Hoo; and these sites can
also serve to introduce newcomers to some of the historic assets of the region.

Our first stop, *Spong Hill* in Norfolk, is one of the few Anglo-Saxon cemeteries that has been excavated in its entirety, as well as being one of the earliest.
It was used intensively throughout the fifth century for the burial of cremations in pots (**Fig.7.1**), but in the first part of the sixth century the rate of burial
slowed down and inhumations appeared along the north-eastern flank of the
site, including four grandly furnished graves, male and female, under mounds.
Altogether 2,323 cremations and 57 inhumations were recorded at Spong Hill,
together with seven sunken-featured buildings and four post-hole structures.
The cemetery served a community of around 850 persons for its first 70 years
and around 150 for the next 60.[4] The changes here seem to indicate a rising

7.2: West Stow: view of reconstructed buildings in the early Anglo-Saxon village (author).

awareness of rank (or of the need to proclaim it) as the immigrants in their third generation began to have an idea of themselves as landowners.

West Stow, a village of the fifth to seventh centuries near Bury St Edmunds, showed the kind of place they lived in. It consisted of a succession of rectangular houses, each accompanied by one or two huts dedicated to weaving and other 'cottage industries'.[5] The last house in the sequence sat in its own enclosure, a sign of the way things were going: a fenced property. Today some of the houses and sheds have been experimentally reconstructed, offering a vision of homely dwellings, robustly carpentered and cosy, lived in by small-holders keeping cattle and sheep and growing spelt wheat (**Fig. 7.2**).

The early English farmers would appear to have inherited some of Rome's former crops and stock.[6] But in the late sixth and seventh centuries food waste from settlements shows the adoption of a new strategy, with intensive stock rearing and the cultivation of rye – signs that a surplus was being created. This produce was gathered into new large 'magnate' farmsteads such as that at *Brandon*, with residential halls, craft areas and agricultural buildings where harvests could be processed and stored. These places could provide extra food to support an emergent upper class, at the head of which we can envisage the kings of East Anglia.[7] The process of increasing productivity was seen in the long-term survey at *Witton*, where the amount of land under arable in that part of Norfolk doubled every 150 years.[8] It was also visible in the large-scale excavations at *Bloodmoor Hill*, Carleton Colville, where a sixth-century hamlet of seven houses and a few huts (and their nearby midden heaps) spoke of a farming family with a sideline in textiles and iron-working. In the seventh century the same settlement acquired a cluster of attendant huts and the midden showed evidence for increased productivity: crop processing, metal-working, butchery, spinning, weaving and the working of antlers.[9] In the later seventh century the village acquired a small cemetery dominated by wealthy women - something we now appreciate as a characteristic of this age.

Other cemeteries also report social changes. The recent excavations at *Snape*, near Aldeburgh, enlarged the tally of burials already found there in the nineteenth century (Chapter 2, p.42) and produced a sequence comparable to that at Sutton Hoo, but lasting a little longer. Cremation was practised from the fifth century, and furnished inhumations from the mid-sixth into the seventh century. There were two dugout boats of the early seventh century used for burial, with a pair of drinking horns in one and the other associated with a horse's head with a bridle. The large clinker-built ship in a mound excavated in 1862 had contained a gold ring and a cloak, and there would seem to have been another nine or ten large mounds visible at that time.[10] Another rich seventh-century burial ground has been investigated at *Coddenham*, upriver from Ipswich. Here 50 burials were focused on a prehistoric barrow, three of them under mounds. Another burial took the form of a timber-lined chamber containing a woman on a bed and perhaps covered by a piece of a boat; others contained bronze bowls.[11] The Snape and Coddenham excavations enlarged the repertoire of bed-, boat- and horse-burials, and raise the likelihood of other wealthy early seventh-century mound clusters developing from early family cemeteries. The early English aristocracy clearly had a number of resting places, of which Suttton Hoo is, up to now, only a first among equals.

The contributions of metal detectorists to the Portable Antiquities Scheme have revealed a number of sixth-/seventh-century rural sites with rich scatters of coins and metal objects, without clear signs of settlements. These could be open-air market sites, showing that the creation and movement of wealth was on the increase.[12] In the eighth century produce and trade were centralised in ports or *wics* - the predominant example in our area being *Ipswich*. The ideal place for a *wic* was on a tidal river, so that ships - not yet equipped with a deep keel - could float on and off a beach for unloading, using the tide. For example, at 'Lundenwic', the beach in question was The Strand, and excavations at the Royal Opera House nearby have turned up huts, wells and fences. Behind their waterfronts, *wics* were equipped with residential areas, light industry and warehousing. At Ipswich, the Buttermarket cemetery with its wealthy burials began about AD600 and was abandoned in about AD700, when the trading settlement expanded from 6 hectares to 50 hectares, over-running the cemetery.[13] The selective food remains raise the possibility that the early occupants of the *wics* might be beholden to an authority that fed them in exchange for services. A total of 80% of the faunal supplies at Hamwich (Southampton), Ipswich and Eoforwic (York) were beef cuts from older animals, and Ipswich received cleaned grain from outside the settlement. But low-value bulk commodities show that there was a supply and demand relationship with the local farmers too.[14] So English society evolved from families in scattered hamlets to aristocrats in magnate farms and then to trading places and ports. Underpinning this social change was a steady increase in portable wealth generated by farming, industry and trade.

SIGNS OF THE TIMES AT SUTTON HOO

We can see that, quite independently of Sutton Hoo, the archaeological discoveries elsewhere in East Anglia paint a picture of rising productivity, larger estates and increasing wealth in fewer hands towards the end of the sixth century. The wealth of our cemetery, if outstanding, is not unique. How was this wealth used in remembering the dead, and why in this way?

On our site we begin in the mid-sixth century, more than a century after the first immigrants arrived. The cremations show a link with the earliest settlers. Grave goods of both Saxon and Anglian cultural type have been found at the Tranmer House site, although the excavator argues for a mainly Anglian affiliation. A high proportion of the inhumations were armed with spear and shield, exhibiting a warrior culture, even if we need not believe that every man buried with a spear knew how to use it.[15] The family that commandeered Plot II used an old Bronze Age mound as its focus, placing burials in the mound and beside it, so claiming roots in the past. Although found by chance, Plot II seems to indicate a family on the rise.

Meanwhile, on a new patch of ground further south, the first monumental mound burials were being erected. Building these large mounds was a new venture that required a major investment of labour, implying the need for a powerful message. The mound idea may have come from the ubiquitous Bronze Age barrows, some huge, that are found all over the land that became England. Digging into them, it would have been obvious to the English that they were used for burial, and their often prominent locations showed that they were intended to mark the landscape. They therefore appeared as the graves of distant ancestors, to be emulated and embraced by the new landowners.[16]

The first type of burial rite in the new cemetery appears to have been one already encountered at Tranmer House cemetery: humans cremated and placed in a bronze bowl together with cremated animals, including horse, dog, cattle and sheep. Although dated here to the late sixth or early seventh century, the use of a bronze bowl for cremation seems to have been a throwback to a practice of people of the second century AD living in Germany beyond the frontier of the Roman empire. Romans and Byzantines made luxury bronze buckets for use in baths of the officer class. When the Germans acquired them they put them to use in drinking rituals, and many ended their days as receptacles for cremations. The Bromeswell bucket and the hanging bowl from Tranmer House (Cremation 8) echoed this type of funerary rite nearly 500 years later, but perhaps repeated a similar message - proclaiming status by expropriating the chattels of a rival people.[17]

The young men buried in this way under Mounds 5, 6, 7, 3, 4 and 18 were the upwardly mobile members of a new heroic age. Under their mounds we glimpse the jubilant belligerence of a young aristocracy, the extrovert champions of early England. Certainly they were inebriated by wine and beer, swigged from silver-rimmed cups, but more so by their new riches and leisure, by the beauty of their weapons, horses, clothes and the prizes - even immortality - to be won from daring deeds. In this they resembled the young aristocratic cavalry officers who were to be their successors through the ages. But the ambition and opportunities of the seventh century, and the brilliance of its rewards, must have generated an adventurous spirit of unusual intensity.

In his life's work, the great scholar Hector Munro Chadwick (whom we met in Chapter 1) compared the heroic ages of ancient Greece and early medieval Germany in similar terms:

> That which they prize above all else is the ability to indulge their desires to the full - in feasting and every form of enjoyment for themselves, in unlimited generosity to their friends, in ferocious vindictiveness towards their foes. The hero of the Odyssey, when his opportunity arrives, sets no limit to the vengeance which he exacts, from prince, goatherd or maidservant.[18]

Perhaps, as we gaze at their scattered ashes and upturned bowls, it is good to call to mind the explosive passions of these early medieval Suffolk lads.

In Mound 17 our young 'Siegfried' was buried beside his horse using a rite that existed in continental Europe in the Iron Age. The revival of the practice has been traced to the funeral of the Frankish king Childeric in AD482 at Tournai, in which a horse with a decorated bridle accompanied the dead king and 21 other horses were killed and buried in pits around his tomb.[19] By the later sixth century horse burial was practised in the upper Rhine, Weser and Elbe rivers, and it spread from there to Scandinavia. In the early first millennium the horse was buried wearing its bridle in the same grave as the rider; but, after AD600, horse and man are placed in separate pits, the bridle being placed with the rider, as in Mound 17. In England, the sacrifice of horses was common in early cremation burials, but from around AD600 horses are found with inhumations, with important examples in East Anglia.[20] Horses gave a

7.3: An image of a mounted spear-carrying warrior riding down a swordsman, as featured on Design 2 plaques on the Mound 1 helmet (*SHSB* II, Fig. 143).

big advantage in a battle - both in attack and in running away to fight another day (**Fig. 7.3**). They consequently carried status: beautifully caparisoned horses appear in Beowulf: 'The king ordered eight horses with gold bridles to be brought through the yard into the hall. The harness of one included a saddle of sumptuous design ... .'[21] Horses were also perceived as having magical or even divine properties, perhaps especially in the early Anglo-Saxon period, when they may have been eaten at the funeral feast. Racing and fighting stallions are likely to have formed part of the leisure activities of the new aristocracy, and the early kings claimed to have had equine blood in their veins.[22]

The two great ship-burials of Mound 2 and Mound 1 find their best parallels in Scandinavia, in the early medieval Swedish cemeteries at Vendel, Valsgärde, Tune in Badelunda and Tune in Alsike. In these northern lands the ship had already long featured in the monumental landscape. Skin boats are depicted in rock art (for example at Bohuslän) and there are ship-shaped stone settings (for example at Anundshøg). The earliest medieval examples of buried wooden boats seem to be of the Roman Iron Age (0–AD 400), at Slusegård on Bornholm in the Baltic and at Fallward on the coast between the Elbe and the Weser. There is little doubt about the status of boats and ships at the time of Sutton Hoo - they were the most important machines of their age and the burial of even an old boat represents a considerable sacrifice. It must also be significant that the wealth of burials and the size of a ship increase together. All the known British ship-burials before AD 800 are in East Anglia. Those after

AD 800 are found in northern Scotland and the Isle of Man and belong to the Viking outbreak – being memorials of a later wave of aggressive incomers across the North Sea. The adoption of ship-burial has no real precedents in England and few enough across the Channel and the North Sea, although here we must contend with the visibility of the boats. The wood vanishes, so most of the ships are detected by the pattern of their iron clench nails, as at Sutton Hoo, while those built with oak pegs are hard to see.[23] Like the horse, the ship had its religious role, delivering the dead to lands across the sea in northern Europe from at least the Bronze Age.[24] The little we know about pre-Christian religion in northern Europe suggests that it is reasonably sophisticated, not only in its range of divinities but in its multiple references to different kinds of virtue, protection and propitiation, and its repertoire of rituals and symbols. Mound-burial, cremation in a bronze bowl, horse-burial and ship-burial were all practices already ancient when re-employed at Sutton Hoo. It seems that these ideas stay in the corporate memory over long periods, but are enacted and made real only at certain moments, when a particular ritual is thought necessary to praise a hero or avert a present danger.

Bed-burial is also likely to be an evocation of an early practice: apart from early Iron Age examples, we know of at least one in fifth-century Sweden at Högom in Medelpad, where the bed and its male occupant were excavated under the mound and lifted whole.[25] In England bed-burials are mid- to late seventh century in date and mainly dedicated to women, and can be splendid when they survive intact. The young woman at Swallowcliffe Down in Wiltshire was found in 'Possa's mound' situated beside an ancient ridgeway (now the A30). She was accompanied by a mass of costly things. Her box-bed was made of ash wood with a sloping headboard at one end and an iron rail on each side. On the bed beside her left thigh was a maple-wood casket shaped like a miniature trunk with a curved lid, bronze hinges and a lockplate. Inside was a silver gilt spoon, four silver brooches like safety pins, two beads, two knives and a comb; and there was a bronze sprinkler that took the form of a sphere perforated with little holes and attached to a long hollow tube; something that you could dip into a bucket of rose water and sprinkle around the room or over yourself. On her other side lay an ornamented leather satchel, stiff-sided and shaped like a sporran, made to contain something precious and flat. At the head end of the bed were an iron-bound yew-wood bucket and an iron pan; at its foot a bronze-mounted bucket that might have contained wine, beer or milk, or butter or apples. And on the bed, close to the right forearm, were two little shallow glass cups of a bluey-green colour, evoking perhaps signs of desperate remedies administered during a last illness.[26]

Owing to its near demolition by tomb robbers, Mound 14's possible bed-burial is not very certain, but it qualifies in four particulars: it was the burial of a woman, of high status as indicated by her silver fittings and fine garments, and dated to the mid-seventh century; and the large number of tiny nails are thought to have implied upholstery, if not a bed of a more conventional kind. The bed-burial rite originates long before the Christian mission and before the first monasteries and nunneries are recorded in England.[27] Of the various theories designed to explain this striking celebration of late seventh-century women, one of the most attractive is that women were accorded an enhanced pagan rite to emphasise their continuing responsibility for family and land in changing times.[28]

The third and last phase of the cemetery is very different from all that had gone before: here corpses were tipped untidily into roughly cut graves with indications that they had died violently from hanging, decapitation or exposure on a gibbet, sometime between the eighth and tenth centuries. The evidence is gathered and summarised in Chapter 6, where it is argued that these are victims of executions carried out after mound-burial had ceased: the burial ground of kings had become a place of capital punishment, where later kings despatched their dissidents. Such a change of direction can hardly be attributed to the whim of a potentate: it is better explained as a fundamental revision of ideology, morality and the right to life. From other sources we know of one such change that took place in the later seventh and early eighth centuries and certainly affected East Anglia: the acceptance of Christianity by the ruling classes.

A MIND OF ONE'S OWN

That the Sutton Hoo burial parties were aware of Christianity goes without saying: Christian institutions were an integral part of the late Roman empire, and all the Germanic peoples within and beyond its borders were familiar with it (Fig.7.4). Were Christians buried at Sutton Hoo? The mound, cremation, horse-burial, ship-burial and bed-burial all have good antecedents in prehistoric northern Europe; and it is unlikely that the English (alone in Europe) would choose to express their embrace of the Christian doctrine using pagan rituals, especially rituals that cost so much in labour and the alienation of wealth. For Christians, this wealth would be put to better use building churches, carving sculpture and creating illuminated manuscripts. The amount of evidence for a Christian identity in the Sutton Hoo mounds is also slender and equivocal. Christian symbols were naturally carried on objects imported from Christian countries, such as the great silver dish stamped with the monogram of the Byzantine emperor Anastasius or the silver bowls with their cruciform pattern, also from the Eastern Mediterranean.[29] These were

7.4: Church at Bradwell-on-Sea contrived from the gatehouse of the Roman fort of Othona (author).

expensive imports: but the principal investment was in the burial rite, which involved the movement of great quantities of earth, presumably by large numbers of people. Archaeologically these rites are firmly rooted in a pagan past.

New studies of the Sutton Hoo find since 1939 have further emphasised its non-Christian character. The axe-hammer from Mound 1 has been reinterpreted as an instrument for the ritual dispatch of sacrificed animals, this being a defining function of a pagan king. Andres Dobat tells the story of the newly Christianised King Ingi of Sweden who was given the choice by his people of performing the animal sacrifice or giving up the kingdom. He chose to remain Christian and was obliged to hand over the kingdom to his brother-in-law, who carried out the sacrifice (in this case of a horse). Many other pagan Germanic rulers on the cusp of the conversion period must have faced a similar dilemma.[30] Although it lay beyond the Anglo-Saxon and probably the Scandinavian field of influence, the recently investigated site of Rhynie in Aberdeenshire has produced evidence of this deep European pre-Christian practice: a miniature axe-hammer together with pits of slaughtered and incinerated cattle contained in a palisaded enclosure with a hall. The site was enclosed and approached by an avenue of Pictish symbol stones.[31]

Recent discoveries have increased the credibility of organised pre-Christian religion in Scandinavia. Large-scale excavations of central places mainly dedicated to cult have now been recognised in the form of votive deposits, scatters of small gold plaques and temple buildings at, for example, Gudme, Helgö and Uppåkra.[32] We now have a better understanding of the roles of spiritual specialists as potent forces in society, whether for determining policy, inspiring warriors or healing mental anguish. The demonstration of the role of women as professional shamans has been particularly valuable.[33] Women were spiritual authorities in the pre-Christian period in England too, exemplified in the 'cunning woman' buried at Bidford-on-Avon in the sixth century.[34] The bishops, priests, abbots and abbesses who succeeded these experts cannot claim to have been less superstitious in their attitude to the supernatural or to have been more effective in mitigating society's chronic fears.

The material apparatus of Christianity is different but highly distinctive, and is strongly underpinned by the written record. Augustine arrived in Canterbury in AD597 as the delegate of Pope Gregory to further the development of a Christianity that had already begun to be practised here and there in Kent. At Canterbury and Reculver the remains of this expedition can still be traced in the remains of churches built in the Roman style. However, there is little sign of it elsewhere in England. Outside Kent we have no churches, no carved stone, no illuminated manuscripts, not even any casual graffiti of a Christian persuasion over the half-century that followed. The verdict of archaeology is that there was no investment in Christian institutions before AD650 and probably not before AD675. But then it comes in a rush: monasteries founded in Northumbria, illuminated gospel books such as the Book of Durrow and the Lindisfarne gospels, incised grave markers at Hartlepool - all arrive in the later seventh century. It is interesting that in Scotland, Wales and Ireland the archaeological evidence for the monastic movement also begins in the late seventh century. It seems that the whole island moves at the same moment to embrace a new institutional Christianity in a second more serious conversion.

So the archaeological picture of seventh-century England has changed. In its first decades the building of monumental mounds tells us of an upsurge of heroic warriors creating kingdoms in a pagan mode in alignment with Scandinavia. From the middle of the century it is the turn of the women, using the past to explain the present and enforce a future that protects its traditions and its alliances. All this is done with an awareness of the alternative agenda urged by Christianity, and makes occasional references to it, but most of England does not adopt the package until the late seventh century. This slow start may be because it was contested: the first 75 years of the seventh century was marked by almost continuous warfare (see below).

Christianity has its attractions: on offer was a return to the prosperity of empire and security of allegiance to a single doctrine. In our day, students of the written record naturally expect signs of Christianity from their documents, while archaeologists seem to encounter a more diverse world in the ground. This suggests that for most of the seventh century the picture was fluid, and it is doubtful if 'paganism' and 'Christianity' had the same black-and-white distinction for Sutton Hoo's mound-builders as they have for us.[35] The ideas being expressed by the seventh-century burials were varied, not predefined, demanding we discover their originality as well as their traditions and references to new beliefs and allies. The burial parties reflected not only their feelings for the dead person but the current situation and their hopes and fears at a critical moment.

IN THE HALL

If the burial ground was the theatre of the dead, the hall was the theatre of the living. For early medieval people it was the centrepiece of governance and social exchange, where kings feasted with their companions, scores were settled, decisions were made and the future was planned. The grand hall of the local leaders has yet to be found at Sutton Hoo, and examples are sparse in East Anglia. But good analogies exist: the hall is known in literature and foundations of hall buildings have been found elsewhere. That at Borg in Lofoten, Norway, was 8om long and had five rooms; the finds implied that residence, spirituality and cattle were all catered for in the same building.[36] In England the prime archaeological example remains the excavated central place at Yeavering on the River Glen in the Tweed basin, a site that has a good claim to have been frequented by Northumbria's seventh-century kings (**Fig. 7.5**). Here, built before the conversion of Edwin, was a pre-Christian seat of government: an enclosure for the management of cattle (the chief index of wealth in those parts), a temple, a burial ground, an assembly place - in this case modelled on a segment of Roman theatre - and, at its centre, the halls. Every structure was realised in great squared jointed timbers, the excellence of the carpentry being vividly demonstrated here by the excellence of the excavation.[37]

In literature, life in the hall comes across as festive, glamorous and emotional. King Hrothgar's hall *Heorot* in *Beowulf* is described as a 'great-mead hall', 'the hall of halls'. Barred with iron and decorated with gilding, it had 'a sturdy frame, braced with the blacksmith's work inside and out', 'gold-shingled and gabled'.[38] The iron chain for suspending the large cauldron found in Mound 1 was 3.75m long (with its cauldron), implying rafters and a gable that rose higher than this. Inside the hall, the pleasures of food, drink and good company were celebrated: 'the benches filled with famous men who fell to with relish, round upon round of mead was passed ... '. The giant drinking horns from Mound 1 were fashioned from the horn of the aurochs, wild cattle

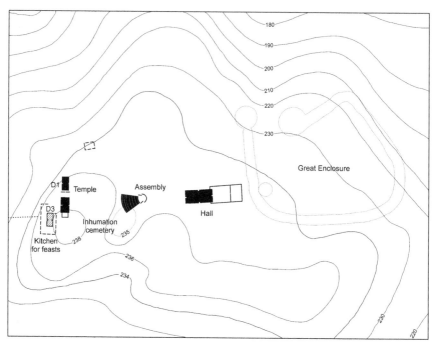

7.5: Yeavering in Northumberland, site of a central place of the Northumbrian kings, excavated by Brian Hope-Taylor. The plan is shown in his Phase IIIa, assigned to the reign of Aethelfrith, 605-616. (HMSO; HOPE-TAYLOR 1977, FIG. 77)

now extinct, and each had a capacity of six quarts (nearly seven litres). Once filled, they would have been passed round until empty.

This was not just a boys' night out: women were equally important players. 'Wealhtheow came in, Hrothgar's queen, observing the courtesies. Adorned with gold, she graciously saluted the men in the hall, then handed the cup first to Hrothgar, their homeland's guardian ... . [then] went on her rounds, queenly and dignified, decked out in rings offering the goblet to all ranks ...'[39] The hall rang with music and recitations: 'At times some hero made the timbered harp tremble with sweetness.' And after a poet had performed 'a pleasant murmur started on the benches, stewards did the rounds with wine in splendid jugs, and Wealhtheow came to sit in her gold crown between two good men, uncle and nephew ... '. It is legitimate to draw these images from Beowulf, since although the poem and the Sutton Hoo burial may not be of the same date, or describe the same thing, they were both made in praise and remembrance of the same world.[40]

The leaders of East Anglia must have had large halls and we can expect to find them, perhaps close to Sutton Hoo. In a cryptic passage, Bede mentions Rendlesham as the place where Swithelm, king of Essex, was baptised by Cedd, bishop of the East Saxons, with Aethelwold, king of East Anglia, stand-

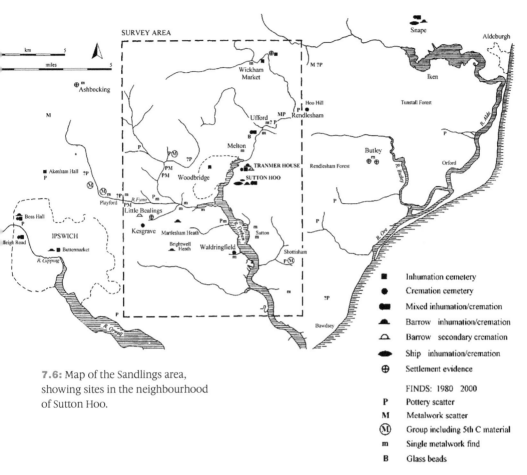

7.6: Map of the Sandlings area, showing sites in the neighbourhood of Sutton Hoo.

ing as sponsor. Rendlesham ('that is the residence of Rendil') is probably to be identified with the place of the same name a few miles up the River Deben from Sutton Hoo. It is now largely a piece of farmland with the church of St Gregory standing on a bluff overlooking the river. However, its status, potential and identity with Bede's Rendlesham have been greatly enhanced by a new archaeological campaign being run in collaboration with metal detectorists. Finds dating from the later Roman period through to the eighth century - without a break - are spread over an area of 50 hectares. An aerial photograph has located a possible hall, and surface collection has defined zones dedicated to agricultural processing and manufacture. The estate was exceptionally rich: the team has found 25 gold coins of c. AD 580-675 and 168 silver pennies (*sceattas*) dating from AD 675, the number falling away after c. AD 720. These exclude the gold coins that were fashioned into jewellery. After some years waiting in the wings, Rendlesham has been revealed as a central place growing in stature over a lengthy period between the late fourth century and the early eighth. Sutton Hoo would have counted as an event in its long history.[41]

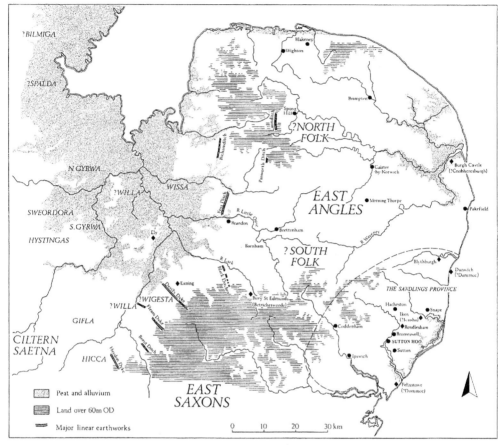

7.7: The region of Norfolk and Suffolk on the eve of the formation of the kingdom of East Anglia.

EAST ANGLIA AND ITS KINGS

Rendlesham and Sutton Hoo lie in the Sandlings, where a combination of grazing on light upland soil, arable slopes and tidal creeks thronged with wildfowl and fish offered a productive land laced by rivers and creeks (**Fig.7.6**). In the sixth and seventh centuries it was exceedingly wealthy and especially favoured: the sites of Rendlesham, Iken, Walton, Ipswich and Sutton Hoo all have documentary or archaeological indications of unusual affluence or influence.[42] The Sandlings thus has some claim to prominence within the larger East Anglian territory (**Fig.7.7**).

Tom Williamson has constructed a persuasive case for Sutton Hoo being on the East Anglian edge of the border between the ancient kingdoms of East Anglia and Essex. These regions were already defined in the Iron Age and Roman period, but reaffirmed by the Anglo-Saxons as cultural zones. Archaeologically, the whole settled area from the Deben to the Tyne has an Anglian identity.[43] As a name, East Anglia is a construct appropriate to the seventh century (by which time there are Angles to the west), and well established by the time Bede uses the term in the eighth century. Different kinds of later boundary endorse its location: the distribution of Ipswich Ware and the extent of the diocese of Norwich correspond to what is understood as East Anglia today.[44]

That such a kingdom existed is indicated by documents that survive from later Anglo-Saxon times citing the names of early kings.[45] Wehha was 'the first to rule over the East Angles', but little is known about him or his ancestors, who include the iconic figures Odin and Caesar. Wuffa (d.578) was the dynastic founder of the *Wuffingas*, whom Sam Newton sees as relating to the *Wulfingas*, known in Sweden. He argues that they came to the Deben area in the sixth century and that it was their successors in Anglian England who were responsible for writing down the Beowulf poem in the eighth century. In *Beowulf*, Hrothgar's first lady is Wealhtheow, whom we met in the hall (above). Her kin, the *Helmingas*, have been glimpsed in the place-name Helmingham in Suffolk. The Mound 1 objects feature a number of wolf images, referring to the family name. In this way, the Wuffingas, Sweden, Sutton Hoo and Beowulf can be seen as connected.[46]

Tyttla (d.599) was the son of Wuffa and himself had two sons, Eni and Raedwald (d. 624/5). Raedwald's three sons were Sigeberht (d. 636/7), Raegenhere (d.617) and Eorpwald (d.627/8?) - and there his royal line ended. Eni had four sons: Egric (d.636/7), Anna (d.654), Aethelhere (d.655) and Aethelwald (d.663/4).[47] Two of Raedwald's sons were his immediate successors as king and their cousins, Eni's sons, followed them. Raedwald was cited as a 'Bretwalda', implying some eminence in the island, and was well aware of the Christian pressure coming from Kent.[48] So we come to the famous story of Raedwald's compromise with the new religion. After his initiation in Kent he returned to East Anglia with a 'peace in our time' package that included dedicating an altar to Christ alongside the pagan gods in his temple, an appeasement that understandably annoyed both parties. Bede despised the action, pronouncing that the queen and 'certain evil counsellors' had perverted him from the faith.

Another story told by Bede is even more revealing of Raedwald's unnamed queen: she saved the life of Edwin, heir apparent of Northumbria, who had taken refuge at the East Anglian court from the murderous intents of King Aethelfrith, the current ruler, who was pursuing him. Raedwald accepted a bribe from Aethelfrith for killing Edwin, whereupon his queen took him to task, insisting it was not fitting for a great ruler to sacrifice his honour and his friend for money. The story betrays covert admiration for a woman who was both honourable and politically astute.[49] Bede was writing a century after the event, but the surviving anecdotes show what was still valued and what had lingered in the historical imagination. A king of East Anglia in Bede's day knew where Raedwald's temple was - it was still standing when he was boy.[50] This leaves us with an appealing impression that court and temple, and presumably burial ground, were close to each other and known to those that came after.

These brief passages also show us something of the flavour of Raedwald's court: abuzz with the threats of the day, where loyalty to allies and ancestors is confronted by new opportunities for enrichment, where a council is active in the decision-making process, as is the queen. To move further into the realm of conjecture, one can imagine that Raedwald's queen was the person responsible for the direction and composition of his funeral. Judging by Mound 1, this would have been an occasion when power politics, international relations, a nod to the ancestors and a confrontation of fate were combined in a material eulogy that must have been unforgettable to those that saw it. The spectacle was devised in weapons, feasting equipment and regalia, shimmering with gold and silver, ornamented with rampant animals, real and unreal. But the burial also contained fine cloaks, spare shoes, clean linen and a shaving kit. The person who devised it was concerned to maintain both the independence and dignity of the new kingdom and the intimate memory of a man (**Fig. 7.8**).[51]

WARS OF THE ANGLES

Such kings were perpetually at war and few reigned for long. In his lifetime, Raedwald lost his eldest son Raegenhere in c.616 at the battle on the River Idle.[52] When he died in c.624/5 he was succeeded by a second son, Eorpwald, who was converted by the persuasion of Edwin and assassinated, for his pains, by a heathen in c.627/8. Three years of paganism followed, until Sigeberht took the helm in c.630. This son or stepson of Raedwald had quarrelled with him and been converted while in exile in France.[53] He determined to Christianise the kingdom and installed the missionaries Felix and Fursa, but he soon abdicated in favour of his cousin Ecgric and withdrew to a monastery. His contemplative life was cut short when Ecgric dragged him out to face Penda, the ferocious pagan king of Mercia, who killed them both in c.636.[54] Some stability was achieved through Ecgric's brother Anna, who ruled a Christian kingdom until he in turn was killed by Penda in c.654, supposedly at Bulcamp near Blythburgh, where he was buried.[55] His brother Aethelhere followed him on to the throne, but a year later was killed fighting alongside Penda against the Northumbrian king Oswiu at the battle of the Winwaed, somewhere near Leeds.[56]

7.8: An evocation of the potentate buried in Mound 1, drawn by Caroline Fleming. The finds in the Mound 1 chamber included a wide range of textiles, many deriving from items of personal clothing. The dead man may have been Raedwald, a king of East Anglia named by Bede.

Before this battle, Oswiu had promised to give his daughter and 12 estates to the Church in the event of victory. John Lowden has made a case that these were primarily religious wars. The leaders were chosen by descent but their fortune in war depended on having well-chosen allies in heaven: the fact that success swung this way and that was attributed to the powers of the gods. Thus 'Christianity primarily offered victory and wise counsel, more important than any claims about the hereafter. So the changes in the rulers' religion are an index on how successful they were in battle.' At Sutton Hoo, therefore, we see an expensive attempt to secure the favour of the gods and with it victory in the struggle for England.[57] That may be so, but something that also emerges from this long war is that political alliances were not necessarily either religious or ethnic. Anglian kings of East Anglia and Northumbria may act in concert or against each other, while, in the west, pagan Mercians and Christian Welsh may act in partnership.

The Staffordshire hoard, originally buried in a wood overlooking the Roman road to Wales (now the A5) and rediscovered by a metal detectorist in 2009, may be a souvenir of this ongoing war. It consisted of more than 3,000 gold and silver pieces weighing 5kg in all and including fragments of a shield, a helmet and - at last count - 97 sword pommels. The hoard also included crumpled Christian crosses and parts of a shrine or reliquary. The objects had been ornamented with ribbon animals of Style II, showing close affiliations to Sutton Hoo and East Anglia, and to early Christian Northumbria. The links with the east and north are strong, so the hoard need not be native to Mercia. Every one of the sword pommels differed from the others, showing that the sword was personalised to its owner. Tiny scraps survive from warrior scenes that had probably decorated helmets like that at Sutton Hoo. The hoard as a whole is notable for containing predominately gold and silver: the iron blades of swords (for example) had been removed. It was thus intended to be a consignment of bullion. Its date, from the style of the artefacts, should be the middle of the seventh century.[58]

The motive and circumstances of the deposition of the hoard are unknown. Material collected from a battlefield is one possibility, a smith's collection awaiting refurbishment is another, but both are inconsistent with the degree of fragmentation and absence of iron. A more attractive idea is that the hoard represents a *weregild* - a compensation payment for the killing of a warlord or to buy peace. As already noted, the mid-seventh century was a time of much aggression against East Anglia and Northumbria, led by the Mercian king Penda. In 655 Oswiu, king of Northumbria, tried to buy him off with 'an incalculable and incredible treasure'.[59] Penda refused and was subsequently killed by Oswiu at the Battle of the Winwaed. So Oswiu decided that the treasure would be 'given to God' ... but was it? In the Anglo-Saxon value system the Staffordshire hoard's 5kg of bullion was worth roughly 1,000 head of cattle or 30,000 silver pence. This was the level of compensation appropriate to a nobleman of the highest rank.[60]

After Oswiu announced his intention of buying off Penda, payment had to be collected. One might imagine the call going out from the court to the Northumbrian nobility, requiring them to search their attics for old weapons and dismantle them to make up a suitable weight of precious metal in the vain hope that it would mollify the incorrigible Penda. The clergy (an upcoming branch of the aristocracy) were not exempt, and had to supply at least a token consignment of bent crosses and decommissioned shrines. Only gold and silver would be accepted: iron, bronze and lead would increase the weight but be easily detected - allowing Penda to keep the bullion and cancel the deal. So swords, shields, crosses and other objects had to be stripped. In the event the treasure was never delivered; but how the bag of bullion ended up buried on a slope beside Watling Street is anyone's guess.

WHO WAS IN THE MOUNDS?

Working hand in hand, archaeology, history and literature are building an increasingly detailed picture of the seventh century: its burials, its kingdoms and the players of the age. Is it possible to focus the picture still further by naming those who were buried at Sutton Hoo? The short answer to this is *no*, and it must be emphasised that the archaeological and documentary stories work well in parallel without their needing to coincide. Nevertheless, it is appreciated that the people who are drawn to this period of the past, and who visit the site, do deserve to enjoy the image that such conjecture provokes.[61]

The character of the Sutton Hoo mounds and their contrast with most other known Anglo-Saxon burials puts them in the class of leaders, and leaders at this time in England were known as kings (which is not to say that we know exactly what the powers of a king might be). Sutton Hoo has been argued (above) to lie in the kingdom of East Anglia. If this is accepted, then we can attempt to identify the burials of East Anglian kings by matching the order in which the mounds were constructed (as determined by archaeology) with the order in which the kings died (as stated in the documents). This suggests that Wuffa, who died in 578 and was founder of the dynasty, was the person that met a violent end encountered in Mound 5, and that the remains of unnamed warriors who died at much the same time are found in Mounds 6 and 7. Tyttla (who died in 599) is the right sort of age and date to have been buried with his horse in Mound 17. Raedwald's son Raegenhere, killed at the River Idle in 616, may have earned the lavish commemoration from his father that is Mound 2. Raedwald himself, dying in 624/5 and apparently famous in his own day, earns by broad consent the accolade preserved in Mound 1. His successors all died as Christians, with the exception of the quickly extinguished Aethelhere. Of the other mounds explored, Mound 14, as the only female grave, perhaps deserves a hypothetical inmate. Placing in it the only high-ranking female we know, Raedwald's nameless queen, assumes that she had died aged 60-70, still loyal to her alliances and traditions after 25 years as a widow, while her husband's successors were attempting to construct a Christian kingdom.

At least 12 more mounds at Sutton Hoo remain unassigned in this exercise, so there are plainly more mounds than eligible kings. This implies that, when all is said and done, Sutton Hoo is likely to have remained primarily a family cemetery, with the family enjoying both the privileges of power and

7.9: The regions of some early kingdoms in Britain. The black spots show the locations of the similarly decorated discs from horse harness seen in Fig. 7.10.
(CECILY SPALL)

O Location of matching horse harness

the opprobrium of its loss. It must be accepted that the association of Sutton Hoo with the East Anglian dynasty is one of similarity, not congruence: there is a glass wall between them that may never be crossed. But, while caveats are essential, they should not be allowed to stifle the imagination that keeps history alive. No scholar has demolished Chadwick's learned hypothesis, or Bruce-Mitford's comprehensive argument, that Mound 1 was the resting place of Raedwald.[62] However, it is worth repeating that, even so, the recorded names of the East Anglian kings bring very little with them in the form of biography. The archaeological discoveries at Sutton Hoo can be referred to great leaders of the early seventh century, whatever they may have been called, and report for us, in vivid detail, episodes from the early days of England.[63]

LOOKING OUTWARDS

The East Anglian kingdom was one of many that were forming at different rates, in different circumstances and with different political agendas,

7.10: Harness discs from Sutton Hoo, Dunadd and Portmahomack. (CARVER ET AL. 2016, 95)

between the sixth and eighth centuries. This was the period that gave Europe the countries it still has. In Britain the kingdoms map onto the zones of peoples distinguished by their culture and dialects: Picts, Angles, Saxons, Britons and (astride the Irish Sea) Scots (**Fig.7.9**). There was much mobility between them. The locations of the documented battles, the Staffordshire hoard and, increasingly (as the early Middle Ages are better explored), similar diagnostic artefacts found in graves and settlements all support this idea.[64] The hanging bowls in Mound 1 and in Cremation 8 at Tranmer House have their most probable place of origin among the Britons of the north-west. A gilt bronze disk from the horse bridle found in Mound 17 has fellows in the north British site of Mote of Mark (surviving as a mould), at the Scottish fort of Dunadd and at Pictish Portmahomack in the far north, in the elite farmstead that preceded the monastery there (**Fig.7.10**). These objects come from high-ranking ornamental bridles and speak to us of an island-wide equestrian class with parallel values. These values were to change with the advent of institutional Christianity in the late seventh and eighth centuries: but this in turn brought new forms of connectivity.

The East Angles, a maritime people, also reached out across the North Sea towards their ancestral homelands, where close parallels for the combs, shield and animal art are found. Their ships were sea-going (**Fig.7.11**), and their crews could navigate between Scandinavia and Britain at the time of Sutton Hoo.[65] But in quantity and quality the more exotic objects came from the continent and the eastern Mediterranean. The gold coins came from France, the sword has parallels in the Rhineland and the silverware was manufactured in the workshops of the Byzantine empire, as was the decorated Bromeswell bucket found in the Garden Field (**Fig.7.12**). The textiles seem to have come from Rome, the three yellow cloaks from Syria. Nor are these imports confined to one splendid mound. A limestone plaque carved with an angel

7.11: The late Edwin Gifford at the helm of his half-scale construction of the Mound 1 ship, *Sae Wulfing*, which is moving at about seven knots.
(PHOTOGRAPH BY CLIFF HOPPITT, COURTESY OF EDWIN GIFFORD)

or a figure of victory originating in the eastern Mediterranean (perhaps in Alexandria) was found in Mound 3. At nearby Rendlesham the finds included Frankish gold coinage, elements of hanging bowls from western or northern Britain, fragments of Byzantine copper-alloy vessels from the eastern Mediterranean and eight Byzantine copper coins of the late sixth and earlier seventh centuries (*folles* and half-*folles* of Justin II to Heraclius).[66]

Recent examination of the 'Stockholm tar' from the Mound 1 ship found it to be bitumen originating from the Middle East.[67] Whether for trade or prestigious gifts, and whether acquired directly or down-the-line, there was active movement of such artefacts from Syria through France in the late sixth and seventh century. This same track would become even more well-travelled in the next generation, when Christians from the islands of Britain exported Insular manuscripts to the scriptoria of the continent (or made them there) (Fig. 7.12). The English would now find new causes for making the journey to what was now, for them, the Holy Land. Willibald, a monk from Hampshire later to become bishop of Eichstätt, was such a pilgrim. He travelled across the Mediterranean to Syria in 720-3, stopping by the volcanic Lipari islands to collect pumice for smoothing parchment. While in Tyre he filled a calabash with balsam and succeeded in smuggling it through customs by disguising its scent with petroleum.[68]

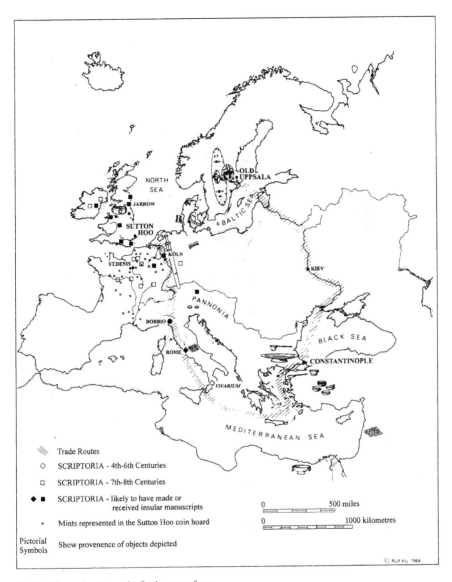

7.12: Where the Mound 1 finds came from.

THE COMPANY OF ILLUSTRIOUS MOUND BUILDERS

Christianity would bring a new monumentality, not only in manuscripts and souvenir pilgrim flasks, but in grand buildings made 'in the Roman style' and with carved stone pillars, all celebrating a religion that was itself an import. This undoubtedly expanded the range of contacts and human mobility, but that it did so very greatly is arguable. The pre-Christian age of Sutton Hoo was already an international one, and its protagonists beside the Deben did not dwell in a benighted periphery. But their legacy - mounds filled with treasure

199

7.13: The cemetery overlooking the River Fyris at Valsgärde, Sweden (author).

- is as hard to grasp as it is huge. Staying silent until reawoken by the spade, they are easily lost to history. Mound-building was an activity known all over the world from the Bronze Age, and constitutes a kind of material language on which the medieval mound-builders - among the latest - could draw. As long ago as 1950 Hilda Ellis Davidson remarked: 'if the evidence of archaeology, ancient custom and early literature is pieced together it is possible to attempt to discover something of the significance of the burial mound in the minds of those who raised it.'[69] Today we are more hopeful still of understanding its meanings.

Valsgärde in Sweden shows some of the complexity that emerges from a fully excavated cemetery. It survives today as a group of parallel mounds overlooking the River Fyris, each marked by the deep dent left by excavation trenches (**Fig.7.13**). It was intact when first investigated in 1929 and is now almost completely excavated. It began with a handful of early graves, with an Iron Age cremation at the highest point and a sprinkle of cremations of the Migration period along the ridge. The majority of the graves are from the sixth to eighth centuries, but some Viking-period burials were added in the ninth century. In all there are 62 cremations, 15 inhumations and 15 boat graves, the latter with many similarities to those at Sutton Hoo. The burials of the seventh century are attributed to two leading families, but, unlike at Sutton Hoo, all ranks are present. While the leaders are inhumed and buried in a furnished boat, the others are cremated irrespective of gender, age or status. The chron-

7.14: The great mounds at Jelling in Denmark apparently built by Harald Bluetooth to commemorate his parents. After his conversion Harald translated the remains of his father into a church built between the two mounds (author).

icle of the cemetery shows that burial is a dynamic business, the investment varying with the character and pressures of the age. Mounds and boats mark special moments in the four centuries that the cemetery was in use.[70]

Gamla Uppsala (Old Uppsala) in Sweden is known for its three giant burial mounds, measuring 50m or more in diameter, cut out of a ridge, with a fourth, 'the Thing mound', having no burials but a flat top (Fig. 3.2).[71] The cemetery also contained at least 700 or 800 other mounds and was surrounded by an extensive settlement with specialised crafts. Hard up against the mounds was a sequence of monumental halls, the latest 50m long and founded on a terrace made up of redeposited clay and midden. The finds included 550 garnets. The halls and all the excavated graves so far are dated to the fifth to eighth centuries.[72] As well as assemblies implied by the Thing, a general festival for all the provinces of Sweden, that included animal and human sacrifices, was held every nine years. These goings-on were described by the eleventh-century German historian Adam of Bremen, who also saw a temple at the site. The temple has not been found, but it may lie adjacent to the mounds under the present church that inherited its ritual functions.

A famous cult centre for Denmark was at Jelling, on Jutland; its heyday was in the Viking period. Here a church stands between two very large mounds attributed on a rune stone to Gorm and Thira, the father and mother of Harald Bluetooth, 'who conquered all Denmark and Norway and made the Danes Christians' (**Fig.7.14**). The mounds were excavated in the nineteenth century

7.15: The Oseberg ship-burial under excavation in 1904. (CREATIVE COMMONS)

and one was found to contain a ransacked wooden chamber. Recent investigations have shown that the ceremonial centre had an earlier origin as a massive ship-setting enclosed by a rhomboidal palisade.[73] The north mound stood in the centre of the ship setting, while the south mound was laid over its south end. The activities of Harald Bluetooth as revealed by archaeology have proved highly instructive for the status of ancient mounds in the years following their construction. At Jelling a skeleton, thought to be that of King Gorm, was removed from the north mound and reburied in the church: parts of the skeleton missing from the mound chamber were found in the church and grave goods in the chamber matched some in the church. So Harald seems to have effected a post-mortem 'conversion' of his father to the new religion.[74]

The body of a famous person, like a holy relic, retained its power, and where that power was detrimental to a new regime the body needed to be dug up and neutralised. The Oseberg mound on Oslo fjord was the reputed burial place of Queen Åse, who had murdered her drunken husband and put their son on the throne, acting herself as regent. Excavations in 1904 found a marvellous treasure in a ship, certainly the property of a woman, with a bed, sledges and tapestries and the ship itself, all preserved by the dense blue clay of the mound (**Fig.7.15**). The chamber had been broken into at some later date and, while the majority of the grave goods were left in place, the skeletons of two women had been removed and scattered just outside the mound. Jan Bill and Aoife Daly dated the burial by dendrochronology to AD 834, and also the wooden spades left behind by the desecrators of the tomb, which came out as AD 953-990. The same thing happened to the ship-burial at nearby Gokstad at much the same time - the time that Harald Bluetooth had 'conquered all Denmark and Norway'.[75]

Thus, after a prominent burial, the mounds themselves did not die, but remained long potent in the landscape, even if no settlement continued in use beside them. In early Norse literature dead heroes take the road to Hel by horse or by boat, leaving a scary dragon to guard their treasure.[76] A king claiming his inheritance and exercising his royal powers might do so by sitting on his father's burial mound. In preliterate lands knowledge of who was in the mounds is knowledge of history. When the poet of *Ynglingatal* recited a list of the kings of Norway, saying how each met his death and where he was buried, he acted as both historian and lawyer, in this case supporting the claim of King Ragnald to the throne of Norway.[77]

In Poland the occupants of the giant mounds near modern-day Krakow were said to be Krakus and Wanda, about whom legends were woven from at least the fifteenth century; today the dragon that lived in one of the mounds makes an annual appearance in the streets of Krakow. But recent archaeological research has shown that their origins are by no means mythical: they were built in the ninth and tenth centuries, the time when their named occupants lived. The pagan peoples living along the Visla river are thought to have created these mounds in the very centre of their state as a response to the advance of Christianity from neighbouring Moravia.[78]

Mounds are of course burial places, but they are also 'politically charged', not only when they are built but long afterwards. We can find monumental mounds with graphic political roles even further afield. In the USA a mound-city was constructed at Cahokia, near modern Saint Louis, in the mid-eleventh century AD by people of the Mississippi culture. Here were hundreds of mounds, interspersed with settlement. The largest, Monk's Mound, has a flat top on which a building once stood. It overlooks a plaza of fine packed sand measuring 300 × 500m that is likely to have been the focus for assemblies, where leaders could make decisions (**Fig. 7.16**). Activities relating to the initial years were discovered in Mound 72, half a mile south of Monk's Mound, in the form of a mass of sacrificed humans - up to 50 people at a time on repeated occasions. The city of Cahokia sprang up quite suddenly in about 1050 and at its height had 20,000 residents. But by 1400 it was deserted.[79]

Mass assembly and governance, as well as spirituality, are also themes of the Japanese *kofungen*, earth mounds shaped in plan like a giant key-hole up to 300m in length (**Fig. 7.17**). The burial is found at the circular end of the key-

7.16: Monk's Mound at Cahokia, seen from the plaza (author).

hole, often dug in from the top, implying that the mound was constructed before the death of the person commemorated. Further ancestors could then be added. The chambers may be stone-lined and the deceased contained in a tree-trunk (split-log) coffin that could be 5m in length and 1m wide.[80] The 'flange' of the keyhole was terraced and flared upwards at its tail, so that people standing on the terraces had sight of the activities on the circular platform, like the audience in a theatre or open-air concert. That they stood there is implied by numerous pottery models of houses and horses (the *haniwa*) left on the terraces. Here was an ingenious, almost architectural, design for a burial mound serving as an assembly place. The *kofungen* date from the third to the eighth centuries AD and many thousands of them have survived. It would appear that the larger mounds were constructed as Buddhism began to make its way into Japan via Korea and ceased as Buddhism became established and its temples provided a new focus. However, the previous religion, Shinto, has remained active in Japan to this day, in particular by its association with the imperial household. The largest *kofungen* in Osaka and elsewhere are revered as the resting places of named emperors and may not be trodden on by visitors.[81] So, on the other side of the world, these Japanese mounds, contemporaries of Sutton Hoo, offer intriguing echoes of analogous experience.

Governance, leaders, assembly, wealth, symbolic art, celebration of this world, apprehension of the next and inter-relationships with the ancestors and a wide variety of spirits characterise all these places. The great mounds and mound cities fulfilled a human need that in our time is expressed by town squares, town halls and cathedrals. In some cases the mounds have been later

7.17: A terraced *kofun*, surrounded by mounds of lesser status seen at Saitobaru, Kyushu, Japan (author).

demonised, peopled by dragons, robbed and ploughed flat. In others they have survived to be cherished. Maybe the time will come when the common language of mound-builders and the particular circumstances they enact are better known. Then they will be valued as gateways to a way of thinking that was widespread, yet greatly varied, giving entry to a rich colourful rambling garden of belief from which we all inherit a little.

ENVOI

Sutton Hoo seems unusual, even unique, but it belongs to a larger world. We still have much more to learn about it: about the long prehistoric prelude, about the landscape and about the other legacies of the early English. The Sutton Hoo burial grounds have together given us a dazzling sequence of life and death during the years that the English created kingdoms and became Christian. Onto this story we have mapped the little we know from documents, and used convergent evidence, parallels, analogy and imaginative conjecture to construct a three-dimensional history. We know that this is only a creative evocation, but since we are humans, not gods, we have to be content with encounter, not omniscience. Just as Mound 1 surprised the pre-war world and the Tranmer House cemetery surprised ours, a fuller, different story may still await rediscovery at Sutton Hoo, at Rendlesham or on another promontory overlooking the Deben, or the Orwell, or the Waveney. Archaeology is a dynamic enterprise, enriching the past and changing it, as new explanation follows new exploration by every inquisitive generation.

BIBLIOGRAPHY AND SOURCES

Place of publication is London unless otherwise stated.

ABBREVIATIONS

ASSAH   Anglo-Saxon Studies in Archaeology and History
BAR   British Archaeological Reports
CSH   M.O.H. Carver, *Sutton Hoo: A seventh-century princely burial ground and its context* (British Museum Press and Society of Antiquaries of London; 2005)
EAA   East Anglian Archaeology
MPG   See under Film, p. 214
SHOLA   Sutton Hoo online archive http://archaeologydataservice.ac.uk/ archives/view/suttonhoo_var_2004/
SHSB   R.L.S. Bruce-Mitford, *The Sutton Hoo Ship Burial*, vol. I (1975), vol. II (1978), vol. III (1983) (British Museum Press)

BIBLIOGRAPHY

Arnott, W.G. 1950 *Suffolk Estuary* (Ipswich: Norman Adlard)

Arrhenius, Birgit & Uaininn O'Meadhra (eds) 2011 *Excavations at Helgö XVIII Conclusions and New Aspects* (Stockholm: Kungl. Vitterhets Historie och Antikvitets Akademien)

Bakker, J.P., S. De Bie, J.H. Dallinga, P. Tjaden & Y. De Vries 1983 'Sheep-grazing as a management tool for heathland conservation and regeneration in the Netherlands', *Journal of Applied Ecology*, 20, 541–60

Barker, P.A. 1977 *Techniques of Archaeological Excavation* (Batsford)

Bassett, S. (ed.) 1989a *The Origins of Anglo-Saxon Kingdoms* (Leicester: Leicester University Press)

Bassett, S. 1989b 'In search of the origins of Anglo-Saxon kingdoms', in Bassett 1989a: 3–27

Bates, David & Robert Liddiard (eds) 2013 *East Anglia and its North Sea World in the Middle Ages* (Woodbridge: Boydell Press)

Bede (The Venerable) 1968 *A History of the English Church and People*, trans. L. Sherley-Price (Harmondsworth: Penguin Books)

Bill, Jan & Aoife Daly 2012 'The plundering of the ship graves from Oseberg and Gokstad: an example of power politics', *Antiquity*, 82, 808–82

Blinkhorn, Paul 2012 *The Ipswich Ware project. Ceramics, Trade and Society in Middle Saxon England* (Medieval Pottery Research Group Occasional Paper no. 7)

Böhme, H.W. 1993 'Adelsgräber im Frankenreich: archäologische Zeugnisse zur Herausbildung einer Herrenschicht unter den merowingischen Königen', *Jahrbuch des Römisch-Germanischen Zentralmuseums Mainz*, 40, 397–534

Bond, Julie 2005 'The cremated bone from Mounds 5, 6 and 7', in *CSH*: 275-80

Bradley, R. 1987 'Time regained: the creation of continuity', *Journal of the British Archaeological Association*, 140, 1-17

Bradley, R. 2007 *The prehistory of Britain and Ireland* (Cambridge: Cambridge University Press)

Brown, Basil 1974 'Diary', in Bruce-Mitford 1974b: 141-69

Bruce-Mitford, R.L.S. 1947-72 *The Sutton Hoo Ship Burial: A Handbook* (British Museum)

Bruce-Mitford, R.L.S. 1969 'The art of the Codex Amiatinus', *Journal of the British Archaeological Association*, Series 3, 32, 1-25

Bruce-Mitford, R.L.S. 1974a 'The Snape boat-grave', in Bruce-Mitford 1974b: 114-40

Bruce-Mitford, R.L.S. (ed.) 1974b *Aspects of Anglo-Saxon Archaeology* (Gollancz)

Bruce-Mitford, R.L.S. 1975, 1978, 1983 *The Sutton Hoo Ship Burial Vols 1-3* (British Museum) (=*SHSB*)

Bulletin of the Sutton Hoo Research Committee 1983-93 vols 1-8 (Woodbridge: Boydell Press)

Burger, P., R.J. Stacey, S.A. Bowden, M. Hacke & J. Parnell 2016 'Identification, Geochemical Characterisation and Significance of Bitumen among the Grave Goods of the Seventh-Century Mound 1 Ship-Burial at Sutton Hoo (Suffolk, UK)', *PLoS ONE 11(11)*: e0166276. doi:10.1371/journal.pone.01662

Campbell, James 1992 'The impact of the Sutton Hoo discovery on the study of Anglo-Saxon history', in Kendall & Wells 1992: 79-102

Campbell, James 2009 'Archipelagic thoughts: comparing early medieval polities in Britain and Ireland', in Stephen Baxter, Catherine Karkov, Janet L. Nelson and David Pelteret (eds) *Early Medieval Studies in Memory of Patrick Wormald* (Farnham: Ashgate): 47-61

Carver, M.O.H. 1986 'Sutton Hoo in context', *Settimane di studio del Centro italiano di studii sull'alto Medioevo*, 32, 77-123

Carver, M.O.H. 1989 'Kingship and material culture in early Anglo-Saxon East Anglia', in Bassett 1989a: 141-58

Carver, M.O.H. 1990 'Pre-Viking traffic in the North Sea', in S. McGrail (ed.) *Maritime Celts, Frisians and Saxons* (CBA Research Report 71): 117-25

Carver, M.O.H. (ed.) 1992 *The Age of Sutton Hoo* (Woodbridge: Boydell Press)

Carver, M.O.H. 1995a 'Ship burial in early Britain: ancient custom or political signal?' in Ole Crumlin-Pedersen and B. Munch Thye (eds) *The Ship as Symbol in Prehistoric and Medieval Scandinavia* (Copenhagen): 111-24.

Carver, M.O.H. 1995b 'On - and off - the Edda', in O. Olsen, J.S. Madsen and F. Riek (eds) *Ship-shape: Essays for Ole Crumlin-Pedersen* (Roskilde): 305-12

Carver, M.O.H. 2000 'Burial as poetry: the context of treasure in Anglo-Saxon graves', in E. Tyler (ed.) *Treasure in the Medieval West* (York: York Medieval Press): 25-48

Carver, M.O.H. (ed.) 2003 *The Cross goes North. Processes of Conversion in Northern Europe AD 300-1300* (York: York Medieval Press)

Carver, M.O.H. 2005 *Sutton Hoo: A seventh-century princely burial ground and its context* (Society of Antiquaries Research Report no. 69) (British Museum) (=*CSH*)

Carver, M.O.H. 2009 *Archaeological Investigation* (Routledge)

Carver, M.O.H. 2010 'Agency, intellect and the archaeological agenda', in Carver et al. 2010: 1-20

Carver, M.O.H. 2011 'Sutton Hoo - an archaeography', in John Schofield (ed.) *Great Excavations. Shaping the Archaeological Profession* (Oxford: Oxbow), 25-43

Carver, M.O.H. 2014 [1998] *Sutton Hoo: Burial Ground of Kings?* (British Museum Press)

Carver, M.O.H. and C. Fern 2005 'The seventh-century burial rites and their sequence', in *CSH*: 283-313

Carver, M.O.H. and M.R. Hummler 2014 *Sutton Hoo Research Plan* (National Trust)

Carver, M.O.H., Alex Sanmark and Sarah Semple (eds) 2010 *Signals of Belief in Early England* (Oxford: Oxbow Books)

Carver, M.O.H., Kevin Leahy, Roger Bland, Della Hooke, Alex Jones, Elizabeth Okasha, Leslie Webster, Christopher Sparey-Green, Patrick Périn & Catherine Hills 2011 'The Staffordshire (Ogle Hay) hoard', *Antiquity*, 85, 201-34

Chadwick, H.M. 1912 *The Heroic Age* (Cambridge: Cambridge University Press)

Chadwick, H.M. 1940 'Who was he?' *Antiquity*, 53, 76-87

Clark, R.M. 1975 'A calibration curve for radiocarbon dates', *Antiquity*, 49, 251-66

Coolen, Ioris 2013 'Places of justice and awe: the topography of gibbets and gallows in medieval and early modern north-western and Central Europe', *World Archaeology*, 45, 5, 762-79

Crabtree, P.J. 2013 'Animal husbandry and farming in East Anglia from the 5th to the 10th centuries CE', *Quaternary International*, http://dx.doi.org/10.1016/j.quaint.2013.09.015

Cramp, Rosemary J. 1957 'Beowulf and Archaeology', *Medieval Archaeology*, 1, 57-77

Crowfoot, E. 1983 'The textiles', in Angela Evans (ed.) *The Sutton Hoo Ship Burial*, 3, I, 409-79

Dickinson, T.M. 1993 'An Anglo-Saxon cunning woman from Bidford-on-Avon', in M. Carver (ed.) *In Search of Cult. Archaeological Investigations in Honour of Philip Rahtz* (Woodbridge: Boydell Press): 45-54

Dobat, Andres 2006 'The king and his cult: the axe-hammer at Sutton Hoo and its implications for the concept of sacral leadership in early medieval Europe', *Antiquity*, 80, 880-93

East, Katherine 1984 'The Sutton Hoo ship-burial: a case against the coffin', *Anglo-Saxon Studies in Archaeology and History,* 3, 79-84

Ellis Davidson, Hilda 1943 *The Road to Hel* (Cambridge: Cambridge University Press)

Ellis Davidson, Hilda 1950 'The Hill of the Dragon. Anglo-Saxon burial mounds in Literature and Archaeology', *Folk-Lore*, 61, 169-85

Ellis Davidson, Hilda 1992 'Human sacrifice in the late Pagan period in North-Western Europe', in Carver 1992: 331-40

Evans, A.C. 1986 *The Sutton Hoo Ship Burial* (British Museum Press)

Evans, A.C. 2005 'Seventh-century assemblages', in *CSH*: 201-82

Evison, V.I. 1979 'The body in the ship at Sutton Hoo', *ASSAH*, 1, 121-38

Evison, V.I. 1980 'The Sutton Hoo coffin', in Rahtz et al. 1980: 357-62

Farrell, R. and C. Neuman de Vegvar (eds) 1992 *Sutton Hoo: Fifty Years After* (American Early Medieval Studies 2)

Fern, Chris 2005 'The archaeological evidence for equestrianism in early Anglo-Saxon England', in Aleksander Pluskowski (ed.) *Just skin and bones? New perspectives on human-animal relations in the historical past* (Oxford: BAR Int. Ser. 1410): 43-71

Fern, Chris 2007 'Early Anglo-Saxon horse burial of the fifth to seventh centuries AD', *ASSAH*, 14, 92

Fern, Chris J. 2011 'Horses in mind', in Carver et al. 2010: 128-57

Fern, Chris J. 2015 *Before Sutton Hoo: The Prehistoric Remains and Early Anglo-Saxon Cemetery at Tranmer House, Bromeswell, Suffolk* (EAA 155)

Filmer-Sankey, W. 1996 'The "Roman Emperor" in the Sutton Hoo ship-burial', *Journal of the British Archaeological Association*, 149, 1-9

Filmer-Sankey, W. & T. Pestell 2001 *Snape Anglo-Saxon Cemetery: Excavations and Surveys 1824-1992* (EAA 95)

Frank, Roberta 1992 'Beowulf and Sutton Hoo: the odd couple', in Kendall and Wells 1992: 47-64

Fukunaga, Shin'ya 2004 'Social changes from the Yayoi to the Kofun periods', in *Proceedings of the Society of Archaeological Studies 50th Anniversary International Symposium*, 141-9

Geake, H. 1997 *The Use of Grave-Goods in Conversion-Period England, c.600-c.850* (Oxford: BAR Brit. Ser. 261)

Geake, H. 1999 'Invisible kingdoms: the use of grave-goods in seventh-century England', *ASSAH*, 10, 203-15

Geake, H. 2003 'The control of burial practice in middle Anglo-Saxon England', in Carver 2003: 259-70

Gifford, Edwin and Joyce Gifford 1995 'The sailing characteristics of Saxon ships as derived from half-scale working models with special reference to the Sutton Hoo ship', *Int. J. of Nautical Archaeology*, 24, 2, 121-31

Grainger, G. and M. Henig 1983 'A bone casket and a relief plaque from Mound 3 at Sutton Hoo', *Medieval Archaeology*, 27, 136-41

Gräslund, Anne-Sofie 2003 'The role of Scandinavian women in Christianisation: the neglected evidence', in Carver 2003: 483-96

Green, C. 1988 *Sutton Hoo: The Excavation of a Royal Ship Burial* (Merlin)

Grierson, P. 1970 'The purpose of the Sutton Hoo coins', *Antiquity*, 44, 14-18

Grimes, W.F. 1940 'The Salvaging of the Finds', *Antiquity*, 53, 69-75

Hamerow, Helena 2016 'Furnished female burial in seventh-century England: gender and sacral authority in the Conversion period', *Early Medieval Europe*, 24, 4, 423-47

Härke, H. 1990 '"Warrior graves"? The background of the Anglo-Saxon weapon burial rite', *Past & Present*, 126, 22-43

Härke, H. 2004 'The debate on migration and identity in Europe', *Antiquity*, 78, 453-56

Härke, H. 2011 'Anglo-Saxon immigration and ethnogenesis', *Medieval Archaeology*, 55, 1-28

Hawkes, C. 1964 'Sutton Hoo: twenty-five years after', *Antiquity*, 38, 252-7

Hayman, G.N. and A. Reynolds 2005 'A Saxon and Saxo-Norman execution cemetery at 42-54 London Road, Staines', *Arch. J.*, 162, 115-57

Heaney, Seamus 1999 *Beowulf: A New Translation* (Faber)

Hedeager, L. 2011 *Iron Age Myth and Materiality: An Archaeology of Scandinavia AD400-1000* (Routledge)

Hills, Catherine & Sam Lucy 2013 *Spong Hill. Part IX Chronology and Synthesis* (Cambridge: MacDonald Institute)

Hines, J. 1984 *The Scandinavian Character of Anglian England in the pre-Viking Period* (Oxford: BAR Brit. Ser. 124)

Hines, John 2013 'The Origins of East Anglia in a North Sea zone', in Bates & Liddiard 2013: 16-43

Hines, John & Alex Bayliss (eds) 2013 *Anglo-Saxon Graves and Grave Goods of the 6th and 7th Centuries AD: A Chronological Framework* (Society for Medieval Archaeology Monograph 33)

Hinton, D. 2005 *Gold and Gilt, Pots and Pins* (Oxford: Oxford University Press)

Hirst, S.M. 1985 *An Anglo-Saxon Inhumation Cemetery at Sewerby East Yorkshire* (York: York Univ. Arch. Publ. 4)

Hodder, I. 1986 *Reading the Past* (Cambridge: Cambridge University Press)

Hope-Taylor, B. 1977 *Yeavering: An Anglo-British Centre of Early Northumbria* (HMSO)

Hoppitt, R. 1985 'Sutton Hoo 1860', *Proc. Suffolk Inst. of Archaeology*, 36, 1, 41-2

Hummler, Madeleine 2005 'Before Sutton Hoo: The prehistoric settlement (c. 3000 BC to c. AD 550)', in *CSH*: 391-458

Hutton, Ronald 1991 *The Pagan Religions of the Ancient British Isles. Their Nature and Legacy* (Oxford: Blackwell)

Huxley, Aldous 1956 *Heaven and Hell* (New York: Harper)

Hvass, S. 2011 *Jelling-monumenterne: deres historie og bevaring* (Copenhagen: Kulturarvsstyrelsen)

Jenkins, Claude 1968 'Christian pilgrimages', in A.P. Newton (ed.) *Travel and Travellers of the Middle Ages* (Routledge): 39-69

Kendall, C.B. and P.S. Wells (eds) 1992 *Voyage to the Other World: The Legacy of Sutton Hoo* (Minneapolis: University of Minnesota Press)

Kendrick, T.D. (ed.) 1960 *Evangeliorum Quattuor Codex Lindisfarnensis* (Lausanne: Urs Graf)

Krogh, K.J. 1982 'The royal Viking Age monuments at Jelling in the light of recent archaeological excavations', *Acta Archeologica*, 53, 182-216

Lamm, J.P. and H.-A. Nordstrom (eds) 1983 *Vendel Period Studies* (Stockholm: National Museum of Antiquities)

Larsson, Lars 2007 'The Iron Age ritual building at Uppåkra, southern Sweden', *Antiquity*, 81: 11-25

Leahy, K. & Roger Bland 2009 *The Staffordshire Hoard* (British Museum)

Ljungkvist, John 2008 'The development and chronology of the Valsgärde cemetery', in *Valsgärde Studies: the Place and its People, Past and Present* (Uppsala University, Faculty of Arts, Department of Archaeology and Ancient History): 13-55

Ljungkvist, John, Per Frölund, Hans Göthberg & Daniel Löwenborg 2011 'Gamla Uppsala - structural development of a centre in middle Sweden', *Archäologisches Korrespondenzblatt*, 41, 4, 571-85

Longworth, I. and I. Kinnes 1980 *Sutton Hoo Excavations 1966, 1968-70* (British Museum Occasional Paper no. 23)

Lowden, J. 1999 'On the purpose of the Sutton Hoo ship-burials', in D. Buckton and T.A. Heslop (eds) *Studies in Medieval Art and Architecture Presented to Peter Lasko* (Stroud: Sutton): 91-101

Lucy, Sam, Jess Tipper & Alison Dickens 2009 *The Anglo-Saxon Settlement and Cemetery at Bloodmoor Hill, Carlton Colville, Suffolk* (EAA 131)

McClure, J. and R. Collins (eds) 2008 *Bede The Ecclesiastical History of the English People*, trans. Bertram Colgrave (Oxford: Oxford University Press)

Mango, Marlia Mundell, Cyril Mango, Angela Care Evans & Michael Hughes 1989 'A 6th-century Mediterranean bucket from Bromeswell Parish, Suffolk', *Antiquity*, 63, 295-311

Marsden, B. 1974 *The Early Barrow Diggers* (Stroud: Tempus)

Müller-Wille, M. 1976 *Das Bootkammergrab von Haithabu* (Berichte über die Ausgrabungen in Haithabu, 8) (Neumünster: Wachholtz)

Müller-Wille, M. 1995 'Boat-graves, old and new views', in O. Crumlin-Pedersen & B.M. Thye (eds) *The Ship as Symbol in Prehistoric and Medieval Scandinavia* (Studies in Archaeology and History 1) (Stockholm: National Museum): 101-10

Müller-Wille, M. 1998 'Zwei religiöse Welten: Bestattungen der fränkischen Könige Childerich und Chlodwig', in *Abhandlung der Wissenschaften und Literatur* (Mainz-Stuttgart: Steiner: Geistes- und Sozialwissenschaftliche Klasse I): 3-45

Munch, G.S., O.S. Johansen and E. Roesdahl 2003 *Borg in Lofoten. A Chieftain's Farm in North Norway* (Trondheim: Tapir)

Murphy, P. 1983 'Iron Age to Late Saxon land use in the Breckland', in M. Jones (ed.) *Integrating the Subsistence Economy* (Oxford: BAR Int. Ser. 181): 177-209

Myhre, Bjorn 1987 'Chieftains' graves and chiefdom territories in South Norway in the Migration period', *Studien zur Sachsenforschung*, 6, 169-97

Myrhe, B. 1992 'The royal cemetery at Borre, Vestfold: a Norwegian centre in a European periphery', in Carver 1992: 301-14

Newman, John 2005 'Survey in the Deben Valley', in *CSH*: 477-87

Newton, Sam 1993 *The Origins of Beowulf* (Woodbridge: Boydell Press)

Nielsen P.O., K. Randsborg & H. Thrane (eds) 1993 *The Archaeology of Gudme and Lundeborg* (Copenhagen: Akademisk Forlag, Universitetsforlaget i København)

Noble, Gordon, Meggen Gondek, Ewan Campbell & Murray Cook 2013 'Between prehistory and history: the archaeological detection of social change among the Picts', *Antiquity*, 87, 1136-50

Nordeide, Saebjørg Walaker & Stefan Brink (eds) 2013 *Sacred Sites and Holy Places* (Turnhout: Brepols)

Nylen, E. 1983 I *Österled: Vikingaskepp mot Miklagård* (Visby: Riksantikvarieämbetet)

O'Connor, Terry 2005 'The horse from Mound 17', in *CSH*: 281-2

Olsen, O. & O. Crumlin-Pedersen 1985 *Five Viking Ships from Roskilde Fjord* (Copenhagen: National Museum)

Pantos, Aliki & Sarah Semple (eds) 2004 *Assembly Places and Practices in Medieval Europe* (Dublin: Four Courts Press)

Parker-Pearson, M., R. van de Noort & A. Woolf 1993 'Three men and a boat: Sutton Hoo and the East Anglian kingdom', *Anglo-Saxon England*, 22, 27-50

Pauketat, Tim 2004 *Ancient Cahokia and the Mississippians* (Cambridge: Cambridge University Press)

Pauketat, Tim 2009 *Cahokia. Ancient America's Great City on the Mississippi* (New York: Penguin)

Penn, K. 2011 *An Anglo-Saxon Cemetery at Shrubland Hall Quarry, Coddenham, Suffolk* (EAA 139)

Persson, K. & B. Olofsson 2004 'Inside a mound: applied geophysics in archaeological prospecting at the Kings' Mounds, Gamla Uppsala, Sweden', *Journal of Archaeological Science*, 31, 551-62

Pestell, T. & K. Ulmschneider (eds) 2003 *Markets in Medieval Europe: Trading and 'Productive' Sites, 650-850* (Macclesfield: Windgather Press)

Phillips, C.W. 1987 *My Life in Archaeology* (Stroud: Sutton)

Phillips, C.W. 2004 Sutton Hoo en pantoufles, at SHOLA 2/3.3

Price, Neil S. 2007 *The Viking Way: Religion and War in the Late Iron Age of Scandinavia* (Oxford: Oxbow Books)

Rahtz, Philip 1980 'Sutton Hoo opinions - forty years after', in Rahtz et al. 1980: 313-26

Rahtz, P.A., T.M. Dickinson & L. Watts (eds) 1980 *Anglo-Saxon Cemeteries 1979* (Oxford: BAR Brit. Ser. 82)

Rainbird Clarke, R. and H. Apling 1935 'An Iron Age tumulus on Warborough Hill, Stiffkey, Norfolk', *Norfolk Archaeology*, 25, 408-28

Ramqvist, P.H. 1992 *Högom: The Excavations 1949-1984* (Neumünster: Wachholz)

Reynolds, Andrew 2009 *Anglo-Saxon Deviant Burial Customs* (Oxford: Oxford University Press)

Reynolds, Andrew 2013 'Judicial culture and social complexity: a general model from Anglo-Saxon England', *World Archaeology*, 45, 5, 699-713

Scarfe, Norman 1986 *Suffolk in the Middle Ages* (Woodbridge: Boydell Press)

Scull, C. 1992 'Before Sutton Hoo: structures of power and society in early East Anglia', in Carver 1992: 3-24

Scull, C. 2002 'Ipswich: development and contexts of an urban precursor in the seventh century', in B. Hårdh & L. Larsson (eds) *Central Places in the Migration and the Merovingian Periods* (Stockholm: Almqvist & Wiksell International): 303-16

Scull, C. 2009 *Early Medieval (Late 5th-Early 8th Centuries AD) Cemeteries at Boss Hall and Buttermarket Ipswich, Suffolk* (Society of Medieval Archaeology Monograph 27)

Scull, Christopher 2013 'Ipswich: contexts of funerary evidence form an urban precursor of the seventh century AD', in Bates & Liddiard 2013: 218-29

Scull, Christopher, Faye Minter & Judith Plouviez 2016 'Social and economic complexity in early medieval England: a central place complex of the East Anglian kingdom at Rendlesham, Suffolk', *Antiquity*, 90, 1594-612

Semple, Sarah 2013 *Perceptions of the Prehistoric in Anglo-Saxon England* (Oxford: Oxford University Press)

Shephard, J. 1979 'The social identity of the individual in isolated barrows and barrow-cemeteries in Anglo-Saxon England', in B.C. Burnham and J. Kingsbury (eds) *Space, Hierarchy and Society* (Oxford: BAR Int. Ser. 59): 47-79

Słupecki, Leszek Paweł 1999 'The Krakus' and Wanda's Burial Mounds', *Studia Mythologica Slavica*, II, 77-98

Speake, G. 1989 *A Saxon Bed Burial on Swallowcliffe Down. Excavations by F de M Vatcher* (English Heritage)

Stahl, A.M. 1992 'The nature of the Sutton Hoo coin parcel', in Kendall and Wells 1992: 3-14

Stahl, A.M. & W.A. Oddy 1992 'The date of the Sutton Hoo coins', in Farrell and Neuman de Vegvar 1992: 129-48

Stenton, F. 1971 *Anglo-Saxon England*, 3rd edn (Oxford: Oxford University Press)

Tarlow, Sarah & Zoe Dyndor 2015 'The landscape of the gibbet', *Landscape History*, 36, 1, 71-88

Tester, Andrew, Sue Anderson, Ian Riddler & Robert Carr 2014 *Staunch Meadow, Brandon, Suffolk: A High Status Middle Saxon Settlement on the Fen Edge* (EAA 151)

Tsude, Hiroshi 1996 'Significance of the Yukinoyama excavations: summary and conclusions', in S. Fukunaga and T. Sugh (eds) *Studies of the Yukinoyama Tumulus*, vol. I (Osaka): 239-54

Tyler, Elizabeth M. (ed.) 2000 *Treasure in the Medieval West* (York: York Medieval Press)

Vierck, H. 1980 'The cremation in the ship at Sutton Hoo: a postscript', in Rahtz et al. 1980: 343-56

Wade, K. 1980 'A settlement site at Wicken Bonhunt, Essex', in D.G. Buckley (ed.) *Archaeology in Essex to AD1500* (CBA Res. Rep. 34): 96-102

Wade, K. 1983 'The early Anglo-Saxon period', in A.J. Lawson, *The Archaeology of Witton near North Walsham* (EAA 18): 50-69

Walton Rogers, P. 2005 'The textiles from Mounds 5, 7, 14 and 17', in *CSH*: 262-8

Walton Rogers, P. 2007 *Cloth and Clothing in Early Anglo-Saxon England, AD450-700* (York: CBA Research Report 145)

Warner, P. 1996 *The Origins of Suffolk* (Manchester: Manchester University Press)

Webster, L. 1992 'Death's diplomacy: Sutton Hoo in the light of other male princely burials', in Farrell and Neuman de Vegvar 1992: 75-82

Werner, J. 1982 'Das Schiffgrab von Sutton Hoo: Forschungsgeschichte und Informationsstand zwischen 1939 und 1980', *Germania*, 60, 193-209

West, S. 1985 *West Stow: the Anglo-Saxon village* (EAA 24)

West, S. 1998 *A Corpus of Anglo-Saxon Material from Suffolk* (EAA 84)

Wheeler, R.E. Mortimer 1955 *Still Digging: Interleaves from an Antiquary's Notebook* (Michael Joseph)

Whitelock, D. 1954 *The Beginnings of English Society* (Harmondsworth: Penguin)

Williams, Howard 1997 'Ancient landscapes and the dead: the reuse of prehistoric and Roman monuments as early Anglo-Saxon burial sites', *Medieval Archaeology*, 41, 1-32

Williams, Howard 2006 *Death and Memory in Early Medieval Britain* (Cambridge: Cambridge University Press)

Williams, Howard 2011 'The sense of being seen: ocular effects at Sutton Hoo', *Journal of Social Archaeology*, 11, 1, 99-121

Williamson, Tom 2008 *Sutton Hoo and its Landscape. The Context of Monuments* (Oxford: Oxbow)

Wright, David 1957 *Beowulf* (Penguin)

Yates, D.T. 2007 *Land, Power and Prestige: Bronze Age Field Systems in Southern England* (Oxford: Oxbow)

Young, Arthur 1804 *General View of the Agriculture of the County of Suffolk*, 3rd edn (London: G. & W. Nicol)

ONLINE RESOURCES

Sutton Hoo online archive (SHOLA): http://archaeologydataservice.ac.uk/
archives/view/suttonhoo_var_2004/ (see SHOLA 1/3.1 for landmark publications
on Sutton Hoo by year)
Sutton Hoo Society: www.suttonhoo.org
National Trust Centre: https://www.nationaltrust.org.uk/sutton-hoo

FILM

The BBC commissioned a series of television films that were produced by Ray
Sutcliffe, whose knowledge of archaeology and history proved as valuable as
his skills as a filmmaker.
The Million Pound Grave (*MPG*) was an updated version of a film first made about
the excavation of the Mound 1 ship-burial in the 1960s; it contained invaluable
interviews with many of the principals who took part, which have been
liberally drawn on here.
Of the three later films, *New Beginnings* was on the rather severe topic of the site
evaluation, which nevertheless attracted a summer audience of over 3 million.
The Last of the Pagans and *Sea Peoples* described the discoveries made up to
1989.

BACKGROUND READING ON ANGLO-SAXON ENGLAND

Dickinson, T. & D. Griffiths (ed.) 1999 *The Making of Kingdoms* (*ASSAH* 10) (Oxford:
Oxford University Committee for Archaeology)
Fleming, Robin 2010 *Britain after Rome. The Fall and Rise 400-1070* (Allen Lane)
Hamerow, Helena, David A. Hinton & Sally Crawford (eds) 2011 *The Oxford
Handbook of Anglo-Saxon Archaeology* (Oxford: Oxford University Press)
Hills, Catherine 2003 *Origins of the English* (Duckworth)
Lucy, Sam 2000 *The Anglo-Saxon Way of Death. Burial Rites in Early England* (Stroud:
Sutton)
Webster, L. 2012 *Anglo-Saxon Art. A New History* (British Museum)
Whitelock, D. 1954 *The Beginnings of English Society* (Harmondsworth: Penguin)

ARCHAEOLOGICAL RECORDS

The British Museum holds all the finds and field records from the 1938-9, 1965-71 and 1983-92 campaigns. The 1983-92 campaign recovered 100,000 objects, of which about 300 were early medieval. *The Finds Index* will be found in SHOLA downloads.

LIST OF INTERVENTIONS AT SUTTON HOO

Int 1 1844, 1860: Survey of mounds and later and separate excavation of a mound on land occupied by Mr Barritt. Reported in *Ipswich Journal* for 24 Nov 1860

Int 2 1938: Excavation of Mound 3 by Basil Brown for Mrs Pretty (landowner). *SHSB* 1, 100

Int 3 1938: Excavation of Mound 2 by Basil Brown for Mrs Pretty (landowner). *SHSB* 1, 100

Int 4 1938: Excavation of Mound 4 by Basil Brown, instigated by Mrs Pretty (landowner). *SHSB* I, 100

Int 5 1939: Excavation of Mound 1 by (1) Basil Brown (2) Charles Phillips (3) Cdr. Hutchinson, instigated by Mrs Pretty (landowner). *SHSB* I, II, III

Int 6 1965-7: Re-excavation of Mound 1 by R.L.S. Bruce-Mitford for British Museum. *SHSB* I

Int 7 1967-70: Excavations beneath Mound 1 by P. Ashbee for British Museum. *SHSB* I

Int 8 1971: Excavation of a trench in the vicinity of Mound 1 by T. Carney for British Museum. Unpub

Int 9 1971: Excavation of a trench in the vicinity of Mound 1 by T. Carney for British Museum. Unpub

Int 10 1971: Excavation of a trench in the vicinity of Mound 1 by T. Carney for British Museum. Unpub

Int 11 1966: Excavation of an area ('Area A') near Mound 17 by I. Longworth and I. Kinnes for British Museum. Longworth & Kinnes 1980

Int 12 1970: Excavation of an area ('Area C') over Mound 5 by I. Longworth and I. Kinnes for the British Museum. Longworth & Kinnes 1980

Int 13 1968-9: Excavation of a trench ('Area B') east of Int 12 by I. Longworth and I. Kinnes for the British Museum. Longworth & Kinnes 1980

Int 14 1968-9: Excavation of a trench ('Area B') east of Int 13 by I. Longworth and I. Kinnes for British Museum. Longworth & Kinnes 1980

Int 15 1968-9: Excavation of a trench ('Area B') east of Int 14 by I. Longworth and I. Kinnes for British Museum. Longworth & Kinnes 1980

Int 16 1968-9: Excavation of a trench ('Area B') east of Int 15 by I. Longworth and I. Kinnes for British Museum. Longworth & Kinnes 1980

Int 17 1982: Recording by S. West for Suffolk Archaeological Unit of a robber pit made in centre of Mound 2

Int 18 1983-4: Surface mapping of plants over Zone A by A.J. Copp and J. Rothera for Sutton Hoo Research Trust

Int 19 1983-4: Surface collection of artefacts over Zones D, E and F by A.J. Copp and C. Royle for Sutton Hoo Research Trust

Int 20 1984: Excavation of 100m-long trench to the east of the burial mounds in Zone F by M.O.H. Carver for Sutton Hoo Research Trust

Int 21 1984: Excavation of a trench across a buried anti-glider ditch in Zone F by M.O.H. Carver for Sutton Hoo Research Trust

Int 22 1984: Excavation of a 100m-long trench to the south of the burial mounds in Zone D by M.O.H. Carver for Sutton Hoo Research Trust

Int 23 1984: Re-excavation of a length of anti-glider ditch in Zone A by M.O.H. Carver for Sutton Hoo Research Trust

Int 24 1984: Excavation of a trench in Top Hat Wood, Zone B, by M.O.H. Carver for Sutton Hoo Research Trust

Int 25 1984: An attempt to smother vegetation over the area of Mound 5 preparatory to total excavation, by M.O.H. Carver for Sutton Hoo Research Trust

Int 26 1984-5: Re-excavation of the central point of Basil Brown's trench across Mound 2 by M.O.H. Carver, A.C. Evans and G. Hutchinson for Sutton Hoo Research Trust

Int 27 1983-4: Metal detector survey of Zone A by C.L. Royle for Sutton Hoo Research Trust

Int 28 1984: Magnetometer survey on pilot area in Zone F by M. Gorman for Sutton Hoo Research Trust

Int 29 1984: Soil-sounding radar test on pilot area in Zone F and over Mound 2 and Mound 12 by M. Gorman for Sutton Hoo Research Trust

Int 30 1983-4: Topographic survey of the burial mound (Zone A) by J. Bruce, E. Ingrams and M. Cooper for Sutton Hoo Research Trust

Int 31 1984: Re-excavation of east edge of silage pit, Zone C, by M.O.H. Carver for Sutton Hoo Research Trust

Int 32 1985: Excavation of an area in Zone F by M.O.H. Carver and P. Leach for Sutton Hoo Research Trust

Int 33 1966: Topographic survey of the burial mounds by Hipkin for British Museum

Int 34 1980: Topographical survey of the burial mounds by Hipkin for British Museum

Int 35 1984: Fluxgate gradiometer survey over a pilot area in Zone F by A. Bartlett for Sutton Hoo Research Trust

Int 36 1985: Resistivity survey over a pilot area in Zone F by R. Walker for Sutton Hoo Research Trust

Int 37 1985: Phosphate survey over Zones D and F by P.A. Gurney for Sutton Hoo Research Trust

Int 38 1986: Stripping and recording of Horizon 1 of an area in Zone F, north of Int 32, by M.O.H. Carver for Sutton Hoo Research Trust

Int 39 1986: Excavation of an area in Zone F east of Int 32 by M.O.H. Carver for Sutton Hoo Research Trust

Int 40 1986: A sieving experiment on the ploughsoil in Zone F by M.O.H. Carver for Sutton Hoo Research Trust

Int 41 1986-8: Excavation of an area in Zone A containing Mounds 2 and 5 by M.O.H. Carver and A.J. Copp, with A.C. Evans (Mound 5) for Sutton Hoo Research Trust

Int 42 1986: Establishment of a permanent loom grid over Zone A by C.L. Royle for Sutton Hoo Research Trust

Int 43 1986: An experiment to determine the inorganic chemical signatures of deteriorated human remains by P. Bethell for Sutton Hoo Research Trust/Leverhulme Trust

Int 44 1988-9: Excavation of an area in Zone A containing Mounds 6 and 7 by M.O.H. Carver and A.J. Copp, with A.C. Evans (Mound 7) for Sutton Hoo Research Trust

Int 45 1988: Magnetic susceptibility survey; pilot studies in Zones A, D and F by C.L. Royle and A. Clark for Sutton Hoo Research Trust

Int 46 1988: Soil-sounding radar survey over Mounds 6 and 7 (Zone A) by Oceanfix Ltd for Sutton Hoo Research Trust

Int 47 1988: Resistivity survey in Zones D and F for Sutton Hoo Research Trust

Int 48 1989-92: Excavation of an area on the west side of Zone A containing Mounds 17 and 18 by M.O.H. Carver and M.R. Hummler, with A. Roe (Mound 17) and A.C. Evans (Mound 18) for Sutton Hoo Research Trust

Int 49 1989: Resistivity survey in Zones D and F by K. Clark for Sutton Hoo Research Trust

Int 50 1990-1: Excavation of an area between Int 32 and 41 containing Mound 14 by M.O.H. Carver and J. Garner-Lahire, with G. Bruce (Mound 14) for Sutton Hoo Research Trust

Int 51 1991: Resistivity survey of northern half of Int 50 prior to excavation by J. Dunk and I. Lawton for Sutton Hoo Research Trust

Int 52 1991: Excavation of the trench between Int 50 and Int 32 by M.O.H. Carver and A.J. Copp for Sutton Hoo Research Trust

Int 53 1991: Excavation of a trench in the valley below Top Hat Wood (Zone G) to obtain environmental samples by M.O.H. Carver for Sutton Hoo Research Trust

Int 54 1991: Excavation of organic materials buried experimentally in Int 43 to investigate their rate of decay by P. Bethell for Sutton Hoo Research Trust

Int 55 1991-2: Excavation of an area to the south of Mound 7, containing parts of Mound 13, Mound 3 and Mound 4, by M.O.H. Carver and M.R. Hummler for Sutton Hoo Research Trust

Int 56 1993: Reconstitution of the areas excavated and reconstruction of the original form of Mound 2 by M.O.H. Carver, A.J. Copp and P. Berry for Sutton Hoo Research Trust

LIST OF BURIALS BROUGHT TO LIGHT SO FAR

BURIAL MOUNDS

Mounds unexplored in modern times
Mounds 8, 9, 10 (possibly robbed), 11 (attempted robbing 1982, Int 17), 12, 13 (robbed nineteenth century, sectioned 1980-91, Int 44/55), 15, 16 (not securely located)

Investigated mound burials
Burial 1, Mound 1: The Mound 1 ship-burial. Richly furnished inhumation W-E in a coffin in a chamber in a ship in a trench beneath a mound. Attempted robbing sixteenth century. Discovered intact and excavated in 1939 (Int 2). Re-excavated 1966-71 (Int 5-10; *SHSB* I, II, III). Dated: after AD 613 (coins). C14: 520-610; 685-765

Burial 2, Mound 2: The Mound 2 ship-burial. Inhumation W-E in a chamber beneath a ship. Robbed in sixteenth century and in 1860 (Int I). Re-excavated 1938 (Int 3, *SHSB* I) and 1986-8 (Int 41)

Burial 3, Mound 3: Cremation on a wooden tray or dug-out boat in a pit. Robbed sixteenth/ nineteenth centuries. Re-excavated 1938 (Int 2, *SHSB* I)

Burial 4, Mound 4: Cremation under cloth in a bronze bowl in a pit. Robbed sixteenth/ nineteenth centuries. Re-excavated 1938 (Int 4, *SHSB* I)

Burial 5, Mound 5: Cremation under cloth in a bronze bowl in a pit of a young person with blade injuries to head. Robbed sixteenth/nineteenth centuries. Re-excavated 1970 (Int 12) and 1988 (Int 41). Surrounded by satellite burials of Group 2

Burial 6, Mound 6: Cremation under cloth in a bronze bowl. Robbed sixteenth/nineteenth centuries. Re-excavated 1988-9 (Int 44)

Burial 7, Mound 7: Cremation under cloth in a bronze bowl. Robbed sixteenth/nineteenth century. Re-excavated 1988-9 (Int 44)

Burial 8, Mound 14: Inhumation in chamber, possibly in coffin, possibly of female. Robbed sixteenth/nineteenth centuries. Re-excavated 1991 (Int 50)

Burial 9, Mound 17: Intact inhumation W-E of young male in coffin; beneath mound with:
Burial 10, Mound 17: Horse in pit without furnishing. Excavated 1991 (Int 48)

Burial 11, Mound 18: Cremation in bronze bowl under cloth. Robbed sixteenth/nineteenth centuries. Re-excavated 1989 (Int 48)

Other possible mound burials or furnished graves
Burial 12: Inhumation of a child NW-SE, in a coffin. Originally beneath a mound. Excavated 1987 (Int 41)

Burial 13: Cremation without urn, undated. Excavated 1966 (Int 11, Aiii; Longworth & Kinnes 1980). Perhaps a secondary burial in a mound over Burial 56

Burial 14: Cremation in pottery urn. Excavated 1966 (Int 11 Aiv; Longworth & Kinnes 1980). Perhaps a secondary burial in a mound over Burial 56

Burial 15: Inhumation W-E, extended on back, in coffin. Probably young male (Int 50)

Burial 16: Inhumation W-E, extended on back, in coffin. Probably young female (Int 50)

Burial 56: Pit containing displaced skull. Excavated 1966 (Int 11, pit I; Longworth & Kinnes 1980). Represents a disturbed inhumation originally under a mound or an execution victim associated with Mound 5. C14: AD 680-840

EXECUTION BURIALS

Group 1: Inhumations on the eastern periphery
Excavated 1984-91, Int 32, 52. Dates calibrated at 95%

Burial 17: N-S, flexed on back. C14: AD 570-890

Burial 18: W-E, extended, on back, in coffin

Burial 19: E-W, extended, prone, with hands tied behind back

Burial 20: NW-SE, extended, on back, in coffin

Burial 21: W-E, extended, on back, without head

Burial 22: W-E, extended, on back, with head of Burial 21 on lap. C14: AD 640-990

Burial 23: E-W, extended, on back, with broken neck. Probably male

Burial 24: Crouched, in pit beneath Burial 23. Probably male

Burial 25: SE-NW, extended, prone, with wrists and ankles 'tied'. Probable male

Burial 26: W-E, extended, on back, above Burial 25

Burial 27: W-E, on side in 'hurdling' position. With timber pieces. Probably male

Burial 28: W-E, kneeling, top of head missing

Burial 29: W-E, extended, on back, hands 'tied' and stretched above the head

Burial 30: W-E, extended, on back, wrist laid over wrist. C14: AD 980-1220

Burial 31: N-S, extended

Burial 32: W-E, extended, prone

Burial 33: W-E, extended, prone, lying with Burial 32

Burial 34: W-E, flexed, in square coffin, chest or barrel

Burial 35: W-E, extended, on back, head detached and placed over right arm looking north. C14: AD 640-980

Burial 36: NW-SE, tightly crouched, lying on right side, head facing north

Burial 37: NW-SE, flexed at knees, lying on back

Burial 38: NW-SE, lying on back, knees bent back to shoulders

Burial 39: NW-SE, kneeling, face to ground, left arm behind back. C14 AD 880-1030

Group 2: Inhumations around Mound 5
Int 41, 44, 48, 50

Burial 40: W-E, flexed, on side, with head detached and rotated. Probably male. C14: AD 890-1160

Burial 41: S-N, flexed, on side, with additional limbs. Cut into Mound 5 quarry pit

Burial 42A: N-S, prone. Probably young female. On body of Burial 42B

Burial 42B: N-S, extended, on back, with head detached and lying with neck uppermost. Probably mature male. C14: AD 640-780

Burial 43: N-S, prone. Probably young female. On body of Burial 42B

Burial 44: NW-SE, extended, on back

Burial 45: W-E, posture uncertain. C14: AD880-1040

Burial 46: NW-SE, flexed, on side. Cut into Mound 5 quarry pit

Burial 47: Suspected body piece, in Mound 5 quarry pit. Probably not a grave

Burial 48: S-N, slightly flexed, on side, head detached and placed over left knee

Burial 49: NW-SE, extended, on back, head wrenched out of alignment, with organic 'rope' around neck. Cut in Mound 5 quarry pit containing bones of large mammal

Burial 50: S-N, flexed, on side

Burial 51: W-E, extended, on back

Burial 52: NW-SE, extended, on back, right arm beneath body. Head detached and replaced at neck end

Burial 53: N-S, extended, prone, right arm beside head. In or cut into Mound 5 quarry pit

Burial 54: S-N, flexed on side, without head. Cut into Mound 6 quarry pit

Burial 55: Dismembered body

LIST OF EARLY MEDIEVAL FINDS

FINDS FROM THE SHIP-BURIALS

Mound 1
Assemblage summary for Mound 1 (for descriptions see *SHSB* I, II, III)

No.	Object	Provenance	Date	BM inventory numbers
	WEST WALL			
1	Iron standard			161
2	Support for no. 1?			210
3	Shield	Sweden?	7th c.	94, 206 (ring), 197 (tape), 29 (board)
4	Sceptre			160, 205 (stag)
5	Bucket no. 3			119
6	Hanging bowl no. 1	N. Britain	7th c.	110
7	Nail supporting no. 6			222
8	Lyre in beaver-skin bag			203-4, 208, 215(bag)
9	Coptic bowl	E. Mediterranean		109
10	3 angons			99–100
11	5 spears and 3 ferrules			101-5, 106-8 (ferrules)
	ON THE COFFIN LID			
12	Helmet	Sweden?		93; 188, 199 (cloth)
13	Gaming pieces			172
14	Bell			212
15	2 silver spoons	Byzantine		88-9
16	10 silver bowls	Byzantine		78-87
17	Spear 6 (south of keel)			97
18	Spear 7 (north of keel)			211
19	Great gold buckle	E. Anglia	late 6th/ early 7th c.	1
20	Purse, with gold frame and gold and garnet plaques			2, 3
21	Two shoulder clasps, of gold and garnet	E. Anglia	late 6th/ early 7th c.	4, 5
22	Baldric, with gold and garnet connectors and buckles	E. Anglia	late 6th/ early 7th c.	6-18

No.	Object	Provenance	Date	BM inventory numbers
23	37 gold coins, 3 blank flans, and 2 small ingots (in purse)	France	early 7th c.	34-75
24	Sword, with gold and garnet pommel and scabbard studs			19-31, 95, wrapped in cloth 191
25	3 fine yellow cloaks	Syria?		SH10
26	6 maple-wood bottles		7th c.	122-7, 213
27	Two drinking horns	Sweden?	7th c.	120-1, 218 wrapped in cloth pads A-C
28	[Animal] bone			201, cloth SH26
29	Silver dish [Anastasius]	Byzantine	491-518 AD	76

INSIDE THE COFFIN, HEAP C

30	Leather bag with studs			209a-f
31	Fluted silver bowl		6th c.	77, containing cowhair, 217
32	Otter-fur cap			196, 216
33	Silver ladle and cup	Byzantine	6/7th c.	90-91
34	7 burrwood bottles	local		128-34
35	4 knives with horn handles			162-5
36	3 combs			169-71
37	Leather garment with buckles			175, 153 (double buckle), buckles 137-59 [or shoes]

HEAP B

38	Pillow, filled with goose down			207, in pillow-case 186-7
39	Two pairs of shoes (size 7/40)			173-4, 181, 198
40	Wooden bowl			136
41	Hanging bowls 2 and 3	N. Britain		111, 112
42	Horn cup			135
43	Leather garment			
44	Iron axe-hammer			96

HEAP A

45	Coils of tape			188
46	Mailcoat			92 with flower (?) 229
47	Folded twill			

BY EAST WALL

48	wooden pegs			230a-c
49	Cauldron 1			113
50	Cauldron 2			114
51	Cauldron 3			115
52	Nail supporting 49			223
53	Chain for cauldron 1			167
54	Nail supporting 51			225
55	Iron-bound tub (yew)			116
56	Bucket 1			117
57	Nail			221

ON THE FLOOR

58	Iron lamp	wax gave early 7th c. C14		166, with beeswax 305
59	Pottery bottle	? N. France		168

No.	Object	Provenance	Date	BM inventory numbers
60	Bucket 2			118
61	Bitumen (Stockholm tar)			250/1
62	Floor covers			193-4
63	20 cleats for coffin			219
64	c.1560 ship rivets			202

Mound 2 (CSH, 260-262)

From the 1938 excavation

1. Gilt-bronze roundel
2. Blue glass squat jar
3. Gilt-bronze hemispherical stud
4. Fragments of silver gilt drinking horn mount
5. Fragment of cast gilt-bronze strip
6. Small silver buckle
7. Bronze ring
8. Tip of sword blade with mineral replaced textile
9. Iron knife
10. Iron knife
11. Iron blade
12. Double sheath containing two iron knives
13. Objects of wood and iron
14. Iron nail
15. Ship rivets
16. Iron ring and attached rod
17. Lengths of iron bands
18. Segmented bead of blue faience (Bronze Age)

From the 1984-1991 excavations

19. Silver fittings and wood from a box(?)
20. Joining fragments from a silver bowl
21. Silver and gilt bronze fittings probably from a small cup
22. Gilded copper-alloy roundel from a shield or saddle
23. Silver gilt terminal from a drinking horn
24. Gilded copper-alloy foil
25. Gilding from a foil
26. Gilt bronze fitting
27. Copper-alloy sheet or foil
28. Silver-gilt foil
29. Fragments of a copper-alloy cauldron
30. Fragments of a copper-alloy cauldron
31. Fragments of a copper-alloy bowl
32. Copper-alloy pin
33. Copper-alloy stud
34. Lump of amber
35. Iron nails and wood from box(?)
36. Three iron rivet heads
37. Leather strip
38. Fragments of decayed textile (?)
39. 496 rivets, rib-bolts and gunnel spikes from the ship, 192 complete

Finds from cremation burials

Mound 3 (SHSB I, 100-36)

1. Fragment of a limestone plaque. From East Mediterranean. Now lost (*SHSB* I, 101, 112)
2. Bronze lid of ewer. Possibly from Nubia (*SHSB* I, 101, 113)
3. Iron axe-head with wooden haft, from a throwing axe (francisca)
4. Pottery sherd with incised decoration. Thought to be early medieval in date. Said to be very similar in fabric, and possibly the same shape, as the pot found holding a cremation in Area A (Burial 14)
5. Pottery sherd, undecorated
6. Textile fragment and replaced textiles on iron concretion
7. Six fragments of thin bone sheeting (from a casket, with chi-rho)
8. Fragment of decorated facing of a bone comb
9. Unidentified iron concretion carrying textile
10. Fragments of cremated bone, from an adult male human and a horse (*SHSB* I, 135-6)

Mound 4 (SHSB I, 100-36)

1. Sheet bronze from a bowl
1a. Textiles
2. Bone or ivory gaming counter
3. Scrap of iron slag
4. Cremated bone from an adult male, an adult female, a horse and possibly a dog (*SHSB* I, 135-6)

Mound 5 (CSH, 205-6)

1. Fragment of fused glass
2. Fragments of copper-alloy bowl
3. Fragments of silver rim-binding for a wooden vessel
4a. Iron shears
4b. Textiles associated by shears
5. Iron knife in leather sheath
6. Fragments of textiles associated with artefacts

7. Fragments of bone gaming pieces (burnt)

8. Fragments of composite bone comb

9. Copper-alloy rivet, perhaps from a casket

10. Ivory, perhaps part of the lid of a box for a stylus

11. Silver collar

Cremated bone of human with a skull cleft by nine blade cuts

Cremated animal bone, possibly of horse and sheep

Mound 6 (CSH, 207-80)

1. Copper-alloy pin

2. Fragments of thin-walled copper-alloy bowl, with flat out-turned rim

3. Pyramidal strap-mount of copper alloy with garnet and glass inlay (found on the side of the mound)

4. Fragments of organic material possibly textile

5. Bone facings from combs and a box

6. Fragments of bone gaming pieces

7. Bone or ivory rod

Cremated human bone

Cremated animal bone, possibly horse, cattle, sheep and pig

Mound 7 (CSH, 209-10)

1. Fragments of a copper-alloy bowl

2. Fragment of fused silver and gold

3. Fragment of copper-alloy cauldron

4. Iron strip

5. Fragments of textile

6. Biconical reticella glass bead

7. Bone gaming counters

8. Fragments of a bone box(?)

9. Copper-alloy pin

10. Iron knife

Cremated human bone

Cremated animal bone, from horse, red deer, cattle, sheep/goat and pig

Mound 18

1. Fragments of a copper-alloy bowl

2. Fragment of a bone comb

3. Fragments of mineralised textiles

Cremated human bone

Finds from inhumation burials

Mound 14 (CSH 214-5)

1. Fragment of a silver bowl

2. Fragments of silver fittings, possibly from a drinking cup

3. Fragments of silver fittings, possibly from a leather purse

4. Silver hinges, possibly from a box

5. Tiny fragments of silver wire, probably from a fox-tail chain

6. Fragments of silver buckle loops

7. Silver dress fastener

8. Two copper-alloy pins

9. Parts of a copper-alloy and iron châtelaine, including links, rods, rings, a knife and layers of preserved textiles

10. Iron nails from coffin or couch

11. Iron nails possibly from a wooden box

Mound 17 (summarised from CSH 243-249)

1. Coffin with four iron clamps, with oak coffin wood (1a-f)

Within the coffin

2, 3. Frame of a leather pouch, with a small copper-alloy buckle containing a beak-shaped garnet, seven other rough-cut garnets, a millefiori fragment and a fragment of glass inlay

4, 5. Sword, with horn pommel, in wooden scabbard, with associated leather, textile, iron buckle, scabbard slide with garnet settings, two pyramidal strap-mounts and silver buckle

6. Copper-alloy belt buckle, with garnet, blue glass, ivory and gold foil inlay

7. Iron knife with horn handle in leather sheath

8. Fragment of mineralised leather with copper-alloy rivet

Outside the coffin

9. Soil mark from tub

10. Iron spear head

11. Iron spear head

12. Shield, with central iron boss, two rivets and buckle and fragment of leather strap

13. Iron-bound wooden tub or bucket

14. Copper-alloy cauldron

15. Chaff-tempered pot

16. Soil mark from bag

17. Animal bone, ribs of a young sheep or goat

18. Copper-alloy bowl

19. Copper-alloy rim repair, implying wooden bowl

20. Bone comb, composite, double-sided

Harness at west end, F358

21. Snaffle bit, with ornamental cheekpieces and two strap connectors attached to each side

22. Four strap fittings from the reins, made ensuite with the bit, with 21mm-wide straps

23. Three buckles from the harness with 20-22mm-wide strap

24. Three gilded copper-alloy rivets
25. Set of five gilded copper-alloy roundels with axe-shaped pendants from the bridle
26. Set of five gilded copper-alloy strap ends or pendants
27. Three-way strap distributor, gilded and copper alloy
28. Four iron and copper-alloy buckles
29. Two identical silver, copper-alloy and iron strap links
30. Pair of matching silver and copper-alloy axe-shaped mounts or pendants
31a. Iron buckle
31b. Large iron buckle, probably for the girth
32. Iron fragments associated with wood and probably from the saddle
33. Copper-alloy nails, probably from the saddle
34. Copper-alloy pins/tacks and leather from the saddle
35. Fragments of decayed leather strap
36. Fragments of replaced textile
Human bone from a young male
Animal bone from a male horse, about 5-6 years old, standing 14 hands high

Finds from other furnished burials

Mound 13
1, 2. Fragments of an iron cauldron

Near Mound 13
Stray find of gold and garnet cylinder, perhaps from a purse

Burial 56
1. Glass bead
2. Fragments of a decorated copper-alloy mount
3. Skull. C14: AD 670–990 @95%

Burial 12 (CSH, 252)
1. Miniature iron spear-head
2. Copper-alloy buckle
3. Fragments of a copper-alloy pin

Burial 15 (CSH, 252)
1. Copper-alloy buckle and plate
2. Knife with horn handle in leather sheath
3. Copper-alloy buckle and plate, with garnet in gold cell
4. Iron nail

Burial 16 (CSH, 253)
1. Glass bead
2. Copper-alloy cylinder
3. Iron châtelaine, links, rod and ring
4. Iron knife, probably part of the châtelaine
5. Copper-alloy pin, with ring head (associated with the annular white glass bead)
6. Fragments of leather bag

NOTES

Chapter 1

1. Biographical sketch of Mrs Edith May Pretty by Mary Hopkirk in *SHSB* 1, xxxvi-xxxviii, supplemented by information from relatives David Pretty, Ann Carver (née Perkins), Andora Carver, Russell Carver and others. Basil Brown maintained that it was Mrs Pretty's spiritualist interests that had prompted her to open the mounds (information from Stanley West, a Suffolk archaeologist who knew Brown well). Another major source used for this chapter was a memoir by Charles Phillips that was given to the author on the condition that it would not be published until after his death. It is termed here by the provisional title he gave it: Sutton Hoo en Pantoufles. The full text will be found in the Sutton Hoo Online Archive (SHOLA), 2/3.3. Some of this material appeared in Phillips 1987, ch.7.

2. Source material used for Basil Brown includes his diary of the excavation 1938-1939 (Brown 1974). Basil Brown's own notebook with his watercolour paintings was also used (Ipswich Museum). Brown referred to Mound 1 as 'Tumulus 1', Mound 3 as 'Tumulus A', Mound 2 as 'Tumulus D', and Mound 4 as 'Tumulus E'. Another source, acknowledged with gratitude, was the memoir by R. Dumbreck (SHOLA 2/3.4).

3. SHOLA 2/3.4

4. Quote from the BBC film *The Million Pound Grave* (henceforward *MPG*).

5. Brown's method, according to his own citation, was enshrined in Rainbird Clarke and Apling 1935. This also recommended the use of a cross trench.

6. Brown 1974, 19 July 1938. Bruce-Mitford in *SHSB* I, 108 describes the shape of the Mound 3 wood lining as 'like a butcher's carrying tray'.

7. We found this during our 1987 season.

8. At that date, the only early medieval ship to have been recognised in England was that at nearby Snape, unearthed from a mound in 1862. Some rivets from the excavation were still kept in a little museum in Aldeburgh, the adjacent town. The following Wednesday, Brown went to see them and was able to confirm his diagnosis.

9. Found during the 1987 season: *CSH*, 177.

10. Phillips 2004. Maynard's role in the Mound 1 strategy remains unclear. In his letter to Miss Allen (SHOLA 2/3.2) he takes the credit for guiding Brown to a definition of the ship. Phillips, on the other hand, says that Maynard was away on holiday in Cornwall during the early part of the Mound 1 excavation.

11. Phillips 1987, 72. Other sources report J. Reid Moir and B. Reynolds as being present.

12. *MPG*.

13. *MPG*.

14. *MPG*.

15. Phillips 2004.

16. *MPG*.

17. *SHSB* 1, 725.

18. Chadwick 1940; *SHSB* I, ch. 10; BL MS Cotton Vespasian B VI, f. 109v.

written down in the ninth century; *SHSB* I, 693; Bede, II, 5.

19. Wright 1957, 27-8.

Chapter 2

1. The excavators of the 1965 and 1983 campaigns discovered slit-trenches and recovered large quantities of expended shell cases and ammunition clips, as well as live mortar bombs and grenades. A cap-badge of the South Wales Borderers was also found. *SHSB* I, 239 and *CSH* ch. 12.

2. Quoted in a memoir by Rupert Bruce-Mitford entitled *40 Years with Sutton Hoo*, deposited in SHOLA 2/3.5.

3. Bede, II, 16. *SHSB* II, 428-9.

4. *SHSB* II, 340.

5. Evans 1986, 98.

6. *SHSB* II, 146.

7. Williams 2011, 106.

8. Wright 1957, 15.

9. *SHSB* III, 611 ff.

10. *SHSB* III, ch. 4.

11. See Lamm and Nordstrom 1983 for an introduction to the cemeteries at Vendel and Valsgärde.

12. Kendrick 1960. Equally important was Bruce-Mitford's work on the Codex Amiatinus, a huge seventh-century bible shown to have been made in Northumbria and abandoned on the way to Rome in the early eighth century. Bruce-Mitford 1969.

13. Chadwick 1940.

14. Bede II, 5.

15. Bede II, 15; II, 12.

16. Grierson 1970.

17. Bede III, 22.

18. Bruce-Mitford 1974a. See Chapter 3, below, for the recent researches.

19. Identified in 2016 as bitumen - see Chapter 7.

20. Prenumbering by excavators has caused some confusion. The current tally is 17 mounds numbered 1-18, of which Mound 16 still remains uncertain (see *CSH*, p. 3, Figure 2).

21. These dents, whether at Sutton Hoo or Valsgärde, are actually caused by earlier trenches.

22. E.g. Hawkes 1964; Werner 1982.

23. *SHSB* I, II, III; Bruce-Mitford 1947-72; Green 1988; Evans 1986. The British Museum's Sutton Hoo team included Katherine East, Angela Evans, Valerie Fenwick, Marilyn Luscombe and Susan Youngs.

24. *MPG*. Here Bruce-Mitford showed an engaging familiarity with Bob Dylan.

25. Hodder 1986. Rahtz et al. 1980: see particularly in this volume Rahtz 1980, which caught the mood and proposed a plan, with responses from the audience.

26. 'We have experienced the thrill of opening a new history book, only to have it slammed shut again ... . The discoveries of 1939 ... have turned upside down our interpretation of seventh-century history, of its cultural and economic history, the status of kings and of East Anglia, their relations to the Continent and to the Baltic, and numerous other topics. But it is also an incomplete document, torn out of the context from which it has been taken.' Christopher Brooke's address to the meeting at University College London on 15 April 1983. SHOLA 1/4.

27. For 'total excavation' and its rationale see Barker 1977, challenged in e.g. Carver 2009. In essence, the new ethic returned to Sir Mortimer Wheeler's exhortation: 'have a plan' (Wheeler 1955, 231).

Chapter 3

1. Carver 2000. See also Shephard 1979, a summary of his Cambridge PhD.
2. Later published as Böhme 1993.
3. Hope-Taylor 1977.
4. Bradley 1987.
5. Carver 1989.
6. Myhre 1987.
7. See Lamm and Nordstrom 1983. For Jelling: Krogh 1982. For Borre: Myrhe 1992.
8. *MPG*. The BBC films produced by Ray Sutcliffe in the Sutton Hoo series for BBC 2 were *New Beginnings, The Last of the Pagans and Sea Peoples*. (see www. bbc.co.uk/archive/chronicle/8622. shtml) For maritime experience, see Carver 1990 and Carver 1995b.
9. The 1989 conferences were published as follows: Kalamazoo: Farrell and Neuman de Vegvar 1992; Minnesota: Kendall and Wells 1992; York: Carver 1992. The work in progress was published (more or less) annually from 1983 to 1993 in the *Bulletin of the Sutton Hoo Research Committee* (Boydell Press), numbers 1-8.
10. Wade 1980.
11. The dates lay between the eighth and tenth century.
12. *Bulletin of the Sutton Hoo Research Committee*, 1986, 4. The proposed budget was £1.35 million to the end of fieldwork. In the event expenditure was less than £1 million for the complete programme, including post-excavation costs and site management from 1983 up to 1997.
13. Horizon mapping was a development of the 'horizontal section' pioneered by Hope-Taylor at Yeavering. Hope-Taylor was a valued and often inspirational visitor to the site during the latest campaign at Sutton Hoo.
14. The full report is given in Hummler 2005. Details of all features, contexts and finds will be found in the Sutton Hoo Online Archive (SHOLA).
15. Angela Evans' reconstruction of the bridle and her verdicts on the other objects are incorporated in Chapter 5. The full report will be found in Evans 2005.
16. Just after the removal of the Anastasius dish and the objects beneath it down to the axe-hammer, W.F. Grimes noted 'the underlying wood of the trough in which all these objects had been deposited': Grimes 1940, 71 and pl. XXIV.
17. A floor of some kind has been accepted or assumed by most commentators (*SHSB* I, 179, 274; East 1984, 81; Evans 1986, 33). The presence of a coffin is more controversial. Evison (1980) proposed a large coffin (327 × 121cm) in which the body was placed on its side. Vierck (1980) saw the burial rite as a cremation placed on the Anastasius dish, and explained the clamps as belonging to a podium. East argued that the position of the clamps and the traces of wood and textiles they carried precluded their use in a coffin. Evans preferred a slightly raised dais or bier, and Speake (1989) a wagon-body. The coffin, proposed here, developed from Evison's, is argued in *CSH*, 191-4.
18. For the historic legal status of burial mounds in England, see Carver 2000.
19. The central area containing the mounds was scheduled in 1949 and extended to the north in 1975. See *Bulletin*, Fig. 8.

20. Updated in 2015 as 'The Sir Paul and Lady Ruddock Gallery of Sutton Hoo and Europe, AD 300-1100'.

21. It should be gratefully acknowledged that, whatever the official policy, English Heritage officers were consistently vigilant and supportive, and were instrumental in providing financial assistance to the Sutton Hoo Research Trust for the maintenance of the site through a management agreement.

22. The announcement of 12 August 1997 stated: 'The National Trust has been offered the 96 hectare (232 acre) Sutton Hoo Estate, which includes the Anglo-Saxon burial site and Sutton Hoo House and stables, as a gift by the owners, the Trustees of the Annie Tranmer Charitable Trust. The grant from the Heritage Lottery Fund means that the National Trust can now accept the gift of the Estate, increase public access and adapt existing buildings to provide visitor reception and explanatory exhibitions. The exhibitions will tell the story of the Sutton Hoo burials, and the programme of excavations from the original discovery of the Sutton Hoo treasure in 1939 to more recent work carried out by Professor Martin Carver of the University of York and the Sutton Hoo Research Trust'. The Trust's multi-million pound visitor centre was opened by Seamus Heaney on 13 March 2002 and has been continually updated and upgraded at intervals since then.

23. Fern 2015. All the campaigns to date are compared and contrasted in Carver 2011. For a day-by-day history of archaeological work on the site see the Sutton Hoo online archive at: http://archaeologydataservice. ac.uk/archives/view/suttonhoo_ var_2004/1.4.

Chapter 4

1. This section on the prehistory of Sutton Hoo is owed to the researches of Dr Madeleine Hummler, who will hopefully forgive my reckless paraphrase. Her detailed analytical account will be found in Hummler 2005 and Carver and Hummler 2014, sections 1.3, 1.4, 2.1 and 2.2. Information on the settlement pattern comes from John Newman, much of whose work on the Deben Valley survey first appeared in the *Bulletin* (passim), and then in his account published in the research report (Newman 2005).

2. Interpretation of the role of the function of the pits is contested. For some, the burial of nearly complete pots is a ritual act; for others the pits represent a tidying up of the site before its occupants moved on (Hummler 2005).

3. Yates 2007; Bradley 2007, 187-90. This first wave dates to the Bronze Age.

4. It was estimated that a depth of sandy soil of at least half a metre had been lost between the Bronze Age and the Anglo-Saxon period; see *CSH*, 376.

5. Hummler 2005, 447-8.

6. See discussion in Hummler 2005, 455.

7. Fern 2015, 182.

8. Newman 2005, 483.

9. Newman 2005, 481-3.

10. Recent experiments in Holland found that sheep preferred grass pasture in the summer and

heathland in the winter. Heathland vegetation became increasingly grassy where greater amounts of dung were found, so grazing sheep help to make more grassland. It might be fairer to regard the local farming model in the Sandlings as pasture on the heights and arable on the slope, 'heath' being what happens to pasture when it is not grazed over lengthy periods: Bakker et al. 1983.

11. Bede, *passim*. I, 16 describes the Britons in the late fifth century as trying to avoid complete extermination; at the time Bede was writing in the early eighth century, the Britons were noted as having 'a national hatred for the English', V, 23.

12. Härke 2004; Härke 2011; Hills and Lucy 2013.

13. Bassett 1989a, especially Carver's chapter 'Kingship and material culture' (Carver 1989). The clearest new account of the Anglo-Saxon settlement is in the account of the Spong Hill cemetery by Hills and Lucy (2013). See also Chapter 7.

14. Referred to here as The Tranmer House cemetery; it has been referred to elsewhere as 'The Car Park cemetery'.

15. The Tranmer House cemetery has been fully published in East Anglian Archaeology (Fern 2015). I am grateful to Chris Fern and Jenny Glazebrook for permission to use images from his report.

16. Fern 2015, 189.

17. Fern 2015, Fig. 7.5; p. 217.

18. Fragments from annular, cast saucer, small long and cruciform brooches have been found; Fern 2015, 178.

19. Mango et al. 1989. The authors comment: 'The discovery of a bucket of East Mediterranean origin near Sutton Hoo should cause no great surprise as the contents of the four mounds excavated in 1938 and 1939 together provide the largest concentration of silver and copper-alloy objects from eastern Mediterranean workshops yet excavated in Europe.' We now know that Byzantine coins and objects were in circulation at the neighbouring and contemporary site at Rendlesham, further up the River Deben (see Chapter 7).

20. Fern 2015, 220, comments that 'the artefacts and burials indicate a community receptive to both Saxon and Anglian cultural influences. The dominant custom of placing a shield over the head ... could argue for an Anglian male majority.'

Chapter 5

1. Newman 2005; West 1998, and see Chapter 7. The observation about the stretch of open water at Sutton Hoo was made from a boat. The water meadows would be well-covered at high tide if it were not for the present flood barrier.

2. Published (uncalibrated) in 1975: *SHSB*, I, 682.

3. See Chapter 3 pp. 71-2, where the strategy was argued.

4. All the finds from the excavated mounds are listed in *Archaeological Records*.

5. Evans 2005, 202-6.

6. Bond 2005, 276.

7. The surviving part of the plaque is only 29 × 26mm and shows the wing (*SHSB* I, 112). Grainger and Henig, who spotted the chi-ro on the casket facing, suggested it came from Italy or France, while

the plaque was more likely to have come from the Byzantium area and may come from a diptych. They place the manufacture of both in the fifth century (1983).

8. Evans 2005, 210, 273. For a handlist of all the finds from the Anglo-Saxon burials at Sutton Hoo see *Archaeological Records*, pp.215-23.

9. *CSH*, 128. A post socket was found in the wall of the grave as if from a hoist or sloping pole. This might have been a pole-ladder like one leg of an Anglo-Saxon scaffold (see Fig. 6.7). This suggestion is owed to Rosemary Hoppitt.

10. O'Connor 2005, 282.

11. Reconstruction of the bridle, saddle and body harness by Angela Evans: Evans 2005, 221-41.

12. *CSH*, p. 161.

13. Some of these details were deduced by chemical mapping; see Chapter 3, p.87.

14. See Chapter 3, pp.86-8, Fig. 3.20, 3.24 for the basis of these deductions. Only one other example is known of a ship placed over the top of a chamber, and that is a later Viking burial at Hedeby: Müller-Wille 1976.

15. *CSH*, 57; 170-1; 390.

16. See, for example, the portage experiments, including the use of a wheeled axle, described in Nylen 1983.

17. Longer than Sutton Hoo 1, at 29m, is the Skudelev longship, radiocarbon-dated to AD 810-1010. Olsen and Crumlin-Pedersen 1985.

18. *SHSB*, I, 180.

19. The arguments are detailed in *CSH*, 183-7 and 192-4.

20. Carver and Fern 2005, *CSH*, 292-8.

21. Alternatives mainly require the body to be lying directly on a floor or bier with objects heaped on top of the dead man (*CSH*, 192-4).

22. See *CSH*, 187. The textiles and their roles were identified in Elizabeth Crowfoot's classic report: Crowfoot 1983.

23. Evans 1986, 77, 78.

24. It has been suggested that the gold pieces in the purses represented the pay of the ghostly crew of 40 oarsmen: Grierson 1970. *CSH*, 181 finds that the evidence for the number of oars is strongest at 14 pairs (seven each side of the chamber). Since the purse lay upside down with respect to the gold buckle, it may have been worn at the back (*contra SHSB* II, 579), or even across the back, a position echoed by the ceremonial 'dispatch case' carried on parade by a stick-orderly in the British Army.

25. When the 'Honours of Scotland' (the regalia of the Scottish kings) were rediscovered by Sir Walter Scott in a chest in Edinburgh Castle, they were likewise wrapped in cloth to inhibit corrosion (Edinburgh Castle exhibition). The textiles discovered in the Mound 1 burial, and their use, are discussed by Crowfoot 1983.

26. Evans 2005, 249-53.

27. Argued in *CSH*, 107-15.

28. Evans 2005, 211-15.

29. Walton Rogers 2005, 262-8. See also her synthesis on Anglo-Saxon dress: Walton Rogers 2007.

30. The tablet-woven cuffs recall brocades found with clerics such as St Cuthbert who died in 687 and was disinterred at Durham: 'The design of the Mound 14 [tablet-woven] band presages the gold brocaded bands of later church vestments' (Walton Rogers 2005, 'The textiles', 266).

31. Carver and Fern 2005, 310-12.

32. Stahl and Oddy 1992; Alan Stahl also argues that the Sutton Hoo coins could be a typical commercial assemblage of the early seventh century, rather than a symbolic selection: Stahl 1992. The named rulers are a Frankish monarch, Theodebert II (595-612) and two Byzantine emperors, Justin II (565-78) and Maurice Tiberius (582-602). In 1975 J.P.C. Kent concluded 'I have no hesitation in concluding that c. 620-5 is the date when the latest coin to enter the Sutton Hoo purse was minted' (*SHSB*, I, 607).

33. These dates were published in 1975 (*SHSB*, I, 682). These dates calibrate to 520-610 and 685-765 with 68% certainty, using Clark 1975.

34. Filmer-Sankey 1996.

35. We do not know who was buried at Sutton Hoo; it may have been the named kings of East Anglia, although this would not of itself provide an explanation for the cemetery; see Chapter 7.

Chapter 6

1. The understanding of these burials owes a great deal to the researches of Andrew Reynolds (2009; 2013).

2. *CSH*, 322; Reynolds 2009, 160.

3. *CSH*, 324-5.

4. BL MS Cotton Claudius BIV, f.59v. Reynolds' researches found groups of two and four posts at execution cemeteries at Ashtead, Stockbridge Down and South Acre, all interpreted as gallows (Reynolds 2009, 133, 135, 158-9).

5. Located on Fig. 3.31. The 'skull-pit' (Burial 56) was excavated by the British Museum team in 1966 and its skull radiocarbon-dated to the eighth century (Longworth and Kinnes 1980,11). The skull was later seen as lying in a pit at the centre of a vanished early medieval mound, with two disturbed cremations, Burials 13 and 14 (*CSH*, 105, 144-6; fig. 5). It is possible that a mound originally covered a cremation displaced when the mound was levelled and the skull was thrown into the central pit. One of Sutton Hoo's untold stories.

6. Decomposed heads of cattle and horse were found in the primary fill of quarry pit (F129) on the east side of Mound 5, leaving traces of jaws and teeth (*CSH*, 83, 347). These can perhaps be associated with feasting just after the mound was built.

7. Reynolds 2009, 165.

8. For an inventory of the burials see *CSH*, 332-46 and 55 for the original radiocarbon dates. The dates given here have been adopted from more recent recalibrations by Jane Sidell with verdicts by Andrew Reynolds; Reynolds 2009, 153-5.

9. Reynolds 2009, 179, for seven examples from Bran Ditch.

10. For human sacrifice see Ellis Davidson 1992, and Reynolds 2009, 51-2.

11. Reynolds 2009, 170, 175; Hayman and Reynolds 2005, 238.

12. Reynolds 2009, 24-5. Whitelock 1954, 149: 'The Church had to enforce its rules forbidding divorce and marriage within the prohibited degrees, and this was not done without a long struggle'; and p. 150: 'One thing that caused grave scandal to the Church was the Germanic practice which allowed a man to marry his stepmother.'

13. 'Pagan religious rituals and public assemblies may have been conducted at such sites, and the

burials of wrong doers could argued to emphasize their importance as central or focal places ...' (Reynolds 2009, 237-8).

14. Coolen 2013, 773. Tarlow and Dyndor (2015) show that to hang on a gallows can confer a certain notorious immortality.
15. Reynolds 2013, 702-3.
16. Reynolds 2013, 704-9.
17. Heaney 1999, ll. 2460-2.
18. *CSH*, 462.
19. As at Dunningworth Hearth, where the 'cocked hats' are labelled 'warren' (*CSH*, 467).
20. See Marsden 1974.
21. Young 1804.
22. Arnott 1950, 169.
23. For an assessment of the scope and purpose of the five campaigns at Sutton Hoo, see Carver 2011.
24. Carver 2000.
25. The survey had been carried out 16 years previously, in 1844. This reference was rediscovered by Hugh Moffat and published in Hoppitt 1985. Also R. Serjeant in Saxon 23 (1995), 4 for Mr Barritt.
26. *Gentleman's Magazine*, 130, 2 (1860), 634; *Proceedings of the Suffolk Institute for Archaeology and Natural History*, 3 (1863), 410; *Journal of the British Archaeological Association*, 21 (1865) 343; *Archaeological Journal*, 9 (1852), 115.

Chapter 7

1. *Henry V*, Act IV. His *chorus* introduces every act by urging the audience to an effort of group imagination, beginning famously with Act I: 'Think, when we speak of horses that you see them printing their proud hooves in the receiving earth; for 't is your thoughts that now must deck our kings ...'.
2. For the Scandinavian elements see Hines 1984 and 2013.
3. The picture is nicely described in Bassett 1989b.
4. Hills & Lucy 2013.
5. West 1995.
6. Crabtree 2013: 'the continued cultivation of spelt and the use of larger cattle and sheep point to some degree of continuity between Late Roman and Early Anglo-Saxon agricultural practices'. See also Murphy 1983 and Williamson 2008, 29-37.
7. Wicken Bonhunt is not fully published (Wade 1980); Brandon is comprehensively published in Tester et al. 2014.
8. Wade 1983.
9. Lucy et al. 2009.
10. Filmer-Sankey and Pestell 2001.
11. Penn 2011, Coddenham.
12. Sometimes referred to as 'productive' sites (i.e. productive for treasure hunters). Pestell and Ulmschneider 2003.
13. Scull 2009; and see also Scull 1992.
14. Scull 2009, 304 and Scull 2002. This is a new model; the previous model had Ipswich ware begin a century earlier and the settlement expansion a century later.
15. Heinrich Härke shows that many spear carriers were unlikely to have been fighting men; weapons show rather a trophy of rank and family (Härke 1990).
16. Howard Williams has studied the relationships between Anglo-Saxon burial practice and the prehistoric landscape in several publications. See Williams 1997 and 2006, 179-85.
17. Carver and Fern 2005, 285-7; for the Bromeswell bucket see Chapter 4.
18. Chadwick 1912, 75, 462.
19. Müller-Wille 1998.
20. Reviewed in Fern 2005.

21. Heaney 1999, ll. 1018-51.
22. Fern 2011, 150-1.
23. See Müller-Wille 1995; Carver 1995.
24. Ellis Davidson 1943, 49, 170.
25. Ramqvist 1992.
26. Speake 1989.
27. Geake 1997, 128; Geake 1999; Geake 2003; Hines and Bayliss 2013, 490-1; Hamerow 2016.
28. Hamerow states: 'the archaeological evidence, when considered together with written sources, points to an undocumented tradition of females embodying the spiritual power of landowning families, a tradition upon which the royal abbesses of the later seventh and eighth centuries were able to build' (2016, 443).
29. Hinton 2005, 60 suggests that 'The attraction of exotica from the Byzantine world may not have been their religious meaning, but their association with its surviving imperial tradition. This would include the inscribed spoons, which may have transmuted into tableware for secular feasting like other things in the grave.' But he believes that the cruciform pattern on the sword bosses may have been intended as an explicit Christian symbol. However, 'if Christianity mattered much to the occupant of the mound, surely he would have ordered his own smiths to be a lot more explicit about it. The scabbard-bosses may mean nothing more than awareness that the cross was some sort of protective symbol.' This seems a fair assessment.
30. Dobat 2006, 889.
31. Noble et al. 2013.
32. See Nielsen et al. 1993; Arrhenius and O'Meadhra 2011; Larsson 2007; important new general works are

Hedeager 2011; Nordeide and Brink 2013.
33. Price 2007; Carver et al. 2010.
34. Gräslund 2003; Dickinson 1993.
35. The varied nature of both paganism and Christianity in this transitional phase are discussed in Carver 2010.
36. Munch et al. 2003.
37. Hope-Taylor 1977. Where there are no structures, open-air assembly places tend to be elusive, but convergent evidence is helping to identify many other candidates; see Semple 2013; Pantos and Semple 2004.
38. Heaney 1999, ll. 65-98, 1784-815.
39. Heaney 1999, ll. 607-40, 1150-75.
40. For views on the relations between Sutton Hoo and Beowulf, positive and negative, see Cramp 1957; Carver 2000; Frank 1992.
41. Scull et al. 2016. The authors paint a picture of the place at the time of Sutton Hoo: 'Our preliminary interpretation of the sixth- to eighth-century complex is that it was a farm, a residence and a tribute centre where the land's wealth was collected and redirected, major administrative payments made, and important social and political events transacted' (1605).
42. Williamson 2008, 119.
43. Williamson 2008, 132, 136. He sees the Wuffa hegemony expanding north from the Sandlings, rather than south into Essex to 'gain supremacy over their own kind'. Williamson effectively answers the argument of Parker Pearson et al. (1993) that the Sutton Hoo Mound 1 ship contained a king of Essex.
44. Blinkhorn 2012, fig. 36, 70. The distribution is concentrated in the counties of Norfolk and Suffolk. Carver 1989, 145, fig. 10.1. shows

the boundaries of the thirteenth-century diocese of Norwich, thought to mirror those of the Anglo-Saxon kingdom of East Anglia. From the Wash it follows the line of the Nene, the Ouse and the Stour.

45. *SHSB* I, 693-6.

46. Newton 1993, 106-7, 126-7, 133, 135. The Wuffa name may also be remembered in the local crossing point of the Deben at Ufford.

47. Bede II.15.

48. Stenton 1971, 33-5, felt that the term indicated a poetic title of Germanic origin professing primacy among kings, but the etymology and meaning are still disputed.

49. Bede II.12. Norman Scarfe commented: 'The nature, survival and strength of the queen's influence are highly relevant to anyone considering the circumstances of Raedwald's burial' (1986, 31).

50. Bede II.15.

51. '...what we know of the personnel of the period suggests that his wife was the person responsible' (Chadwick 1940, 87).

52. 'Near the point where the River Idle is crossed by the Roman road from Lincoln to Doncaster': Stenton 1971, 79.

53. McClure and Collins 2008, 392.

54. '... probably on the western frontier of East Anglia, perhaps in Cambridgeshire' (Chadwick 1940, 82).

55. According to Warner 1996, 113; Newton 1993, 135n.

56. Stenton 1971, 84.

57. Lowden 1999, 98-9: 'Then as now it was the living that buried the dead, so it is largely irrelevant whether the rulers buried in Mound 1 or 2 were pagan or Christian in their lifetimes: what matters is that their successors were resolutely pagan and deemed it necessary to draw this to the gods' attention.'

58. Leahy and Bland 2009; Carver et al. 2011.

59. Bede III.24.

60. Whitelock 1954, 9, 50. An ox was worth 30 pence, or one mancus, a weight of gold equivalent to 70 grains. The great gold buckle from Mound 1 weighs 412.7g, equivalent to 90 mancus/head of cattle.

61. Williamson 2008, 115.

62. Chadwick 1940, 87; *SHSB* I, 717.

63. The modern editors of Colgrave's translation of Bede's History find the evidence for Raedwald as the person buried in Mound 1 to be 'almost non-existent' (McClure and Collins 2008, 381, n98). This is certainly true of the historical evidence since Sutton Hoo is not mentioned in documents. But at this moment the archaeological evidence for a paramount leader being buried in East Anglia at Sutton Hoo at the same time as Raedwald's recorded death is pretty convergent. Of course, other Sutton Hoos may await discovery, but this occupational hazard is no reason for throwing in the t(r)owel.

64. For other comparisons between British and English kingdoms, see Campbell 2009.

65. For navigation and winds see Carver 1990. The Mound 1 ship was a working vessel because it had been repaired with a patch (for a full description see Angela Evans in *SHSB* I, Ch.V). Edwin and Joyce Gifford built a half-sized replica of the Mound 1 ship and found that it could sail and make 1 knot to windward, and was easily beached on shingle (Gifford and Gifford 1995).

66. See Grainger and Henig 1983 for the plaque; Scull et al. 2016, 1603.

67. Burger et al. 2016.

68. Jenkins 1968, 68.

69. Ellis Davidson 1950.

70. Ljundqvist 2008.

71. Persson & Olofsson 'Inside a mound'.

72. Ljundqvist et al. 2011.

73. Hvass 2011.

74. Krogh 1982.

75. Bill and Daly 2012.

76. Ellis Davidson 1950, 179. Dragons are aerial, as on the Sutton Hoo shield (Fig. 2.11), and had a powerful bite. Beowulf's dragon was 50 feet long, 'the size of a large sperm whale'. Combining the murderous talents of every malign creature, the descriptions recall the hallucinations brought on by anxiety, starvation and extreme deprivation discussed by Aldous Huxley in *Heaven and Hell* (1956).

77. Ellis Davidson 1950, 174. The archaeological evidence for pagan practice in England was recently reviewed in Carver et al. 2010. See also Hutton 1991.

78. Słupecki 1999.

79. Pauketat 2004; Pauketat 2009.

80. The Yukinoyama *kofun* dating to the fourth century CE was 70m long and contained a coffin 5m long in a stone chamber furnished with five bronze mirrors, iron tools, fish spears, an iron helmet, 66 bronze arrowheads and a quiver. Tsude 1996.

81. Japanese archaeologists regard the context of the *kofun* tombs as that of state formation: see Fukunaga 2004. I was fortunate to be able to spend time discussing these mounds when acting as a consultant for the Osaka world heritage bid in 2012.

INDEX

Page numbers in bold indicate illustrations.
The provenance of all early medieval finds will be found on pp 217-221.